The True

Benjamin Franklin

THIRD EDITION - WITH AN APPENDIX

SYDNEY GEORGE FISHER

Benjamin Franklin FRS, FRSE
(January 17, 1706 – April 17, 1790)

A PORTRAIT BY: JOSEPH DUPLESSIS

" If rigid moral analysis be not the purpose of historical writing, there is no more value in it than in the fictions of mythological antiquity. "

- CHARLES FRANCIS ADAMS, SR.

GIFT *Certificate*

TO:

_____

_____

FROM:

_____

_____

DATE: _____

Would you like to buy a copy of
THE TRUE BENJAMIN FRANKLIN ?

Please visit:
http://www.diamondbooks.ca/books

The True

Benjamin Franklin

THIRD EDITION - WITH AN APPENDIX

BY

SYDNEY GEORGE FISHER

(March 2, 1809 – July 25, 1871)

Author of " Men, Women, and Manners in Colonial Times," " The Making
of Pennsylvania," " The Evolution of the Constitution," etc.
Sidney George Fisher was a Philadelphia gentleman, lawyer, farmer,
plantation owner, political essayist and occasional poet.

DIAMOND
BOOKS
www.diamondbooks.ca

TORONTO, CANADA – 2016

DIAMOND **BOOKS** - CANADA

Toronto, ON, CANADA

http://www.**diamond**books.ca

BIBLIOGRAPHIC INFORMATION

' THE TRUE BENJAMIN FRANKLIN ', was first published in 1903 by J.B. LIPPINCOTT COMPANY, Philadelphia, USA.

PUBLISHED IN CANADA

Published in Canada by DIAMOND BOOKS - CANADA, an imprint of DIAMOND PUBLISHERS - http://www.diamondpublishers.com

First Edition: August, 2016.

PAPERBACK EDITION : ISBN: 978-1-988942-38-4
E-BOOK EDITION : ISBN: 978-1-988942-39-1

PRINTED IN CANADA

Preface to the Third Edition

SINCE the appearance of the first edition there has been some discussion of the question whether Mrs. Foxcroft was really Franklin's daughter. In the present edition I have added an appendix going fully into this question.

Franklin's plain language about love and marriage and his very frank descriptions of his own short-comings in these matters seem to have surprised many people. I might have explained this more fully in the first edition, but to any one who knows the age in which Franklin lived there is nothing that need cause surprise.

It was an age of frank autobiographies and plain, detailed, introspective statements about love affairs. Rousseau flourished in those days, also Gozzi and Madame Roland; and Casanova began writing his most extraordinary memoirs just about the time of Franklin's death. Anyone who is at all familiar with these authors will readily understand why Franklin wrote his " Advice on the Choice of a Mistress." His "Speech of Polly Baker " was of the same sort. It had a most extraordinary circulation because people were then looking at these matters from that point of view. The philosophic thought of that age was somewhat inclining to the opinion, since then much developed by German theorists like Nietzche, that religion had made love impure. Franklin, as at page 106, was also inclining that way.

Such things must be mentioned and given their proper position and importance in a book calling itself " The True Benjamin Franklin." There are many books describing the false Franklin, the impossible Franklin, the Franklin that never existed, and could not in the nature of things exist, and to these books those who do not like the truth are referred.

Preface

THIS analysis of the life and character of Franklin has in view a similar object to that of the volume entitled "The True George Washington," which was prepared for the publishers by Mr. Paul Leicester Ford and issued a year or two ago.

Washington sadly needed to be humanized to be rescued from the myth-making process which had been destroying all that was lovable in his character and turning him into a mere bundle of abstract qualities which it was piously supposed would be wholesome examples for the American people. This assumption that our people are children who must not be told the eternal truths of human nature, but deceived into goodness by wooden heroes and lay figures, seems, fortunately, to be passing away, and in a few years it will be a strange phase to look back upon.

So thorough and systematic has been the expurgating during the last century that some of its details are very curious. It is astonishing how easily an otherwise respectable editor or biographer can get himself into a state of complete intellectual dishonesty. It is interesting to follow one of these literary criminals and see the minute care with which he manufactures an entirely new and imaginary being out of the real man who has been placed in his hands. He will not allow his victim to say even a single word which he considers unbecoming. The story is told that Washington wrote in one of his letters that a certain movement of the enemy would not amount to a flea-bite; but one of his editors struck out the passage as unfit to be printed. He thought, I suppose, that Washington could not take care of his own dignity.

Franklin in his Autobiography tells us that when working as a journeyman printer in London he drank nothing but water, and his fellow-workmen, in consequence, called him the "Water-American;" but Weems in his version of the Autobiography makes him say that they called him the "American Aquatic," an expression which the vile taste of that time was pleased to consider elegant diction. In the same way Temple Franklin made alterations in his grandfather's writings, changing their vigorous Anglo-Saxon into stilted Latin phrases.

It is curious that American myth-making is so unlike the ancient myth-making which as time went on made its gods and goddesses more and more human with mortal loves and passions. Our process is just the reverse. Out of a man who actually lived among us and of whose life we have many truthful details we make an impossible abstraction of idealized virtues. It may be said that this could never happen among a people of strong artistic instincts, and we have certainly in our conceptions of art been the-atrical and imitative rather than dramatic and real. Possibly the check which is being given to our peculiar myth-making is a favorable sign for our art.

The myth-makers could not work with Franklin

in quite the same way that they worked with Washington. With Washington they ignored his personal traits and habits, building him up into a cold military and political wonder. But Franklin's human side would not down so easily. The human in him was so interlaced with the divine that the one dragged the other into light. His dramatic and artistic sense was very strong, far stronger than in most distinguished Americans; and he made so many plain statements about his own shortcomings, and followed pleasure and natural instincts so sympathetically, broadly, and openly, that the efforts to prepare him for exhibition are usually ludicrous failures.

But the eulogists soon found an effective way to handle him. Although they could ignore certain phases of his character only so far as the genial old fellow would let them, they could exaggerate the other phases to an almost unlimited extent; for his career was in many ways peculiarly open to exaggeration. It was longer, more varied, and more full of controversy than Washington's. Washington was twenty-six years younger than Franklin and died at the age of sixty-seven, while Franklin lived to be eighty-four. Washington's important public life was all covered by the twenty-two years from 1775 to 1797, and during more than three of those years he was in retirement at Mount Vernon. But Franklin was an active politician, philosopher, man of science, author, philanthropist, reformer, and diplomat for the forty-odd years from 1745 to 1788.

Almost every event of his life has been distorted until, from the great and accomplished man he really was, he has been magnified into an impossible prodigy. Almost everything he wrote about in science has been put down as a discovery. His wonderful ability in expressing himself has assisted in this ; for if ten men wrote on a subject and Franklin was one of them, his statement is the one most likely to be preserved, because the others, being inferior in language, are soon forgotten and lost.

Every scrap of paper he wrote upon is now considered a precious relic and a great deal of it is printed, so that statements which were but memoranda or merely his way of formulating other men's knowledge for his own convenience or for the sake of writing a pleasant letter to a friend, are given undue importance. Indeed, when we read one of these letters or memoranda it is so clearly and beautifully expressed and put in such a captivating form that, as the editor craftily forbears to comment on it, we instinctively conclude that it must have been a gift of new knowledge to mankind.

The persistency with which people have tried to magnify Franklin is curiously shown in the peculiar way in which James Logan's translation of Cicero's essay on old age was attributed to him. This translation with notes and a preface was made by Logan and printed in 1744 by Franklin in his Philadelphia printing-office, and at the foot of the title-page Franklin's name appeared as the printer. In 1778 the book was reprinted in London, with Franklin's name on the title-page as the translator. In 1809 one of his editors, William Duane, actually had this translation printed in his edition of Franklin's works. The editor was afterwards accused of having done this with full knowledge that the translation had not been made by Franklin; but, under the code of literary morals which has so long prevailed, I suppose he would be held excusable.

One of Franklin's claims to renown is that he was a self-made man, the first distinguished American who was created in that way; and it would seem, therefore, all the more necessary that he should be allowed to remain as he made himself. I have endeavored to act upon this principle and so far as possible to let Franklin speak for himself. The analytical method of writing a man's life is well suited to this purpose. There are already chronological biographies of Franklin in two volumes or more giving the events in order with very full details from his birth to his death. The present single volume is more in the way of an estimate of his position, worth, and work, and yet gives, I believe, every essential fact of his career with enough detail to enable the reader to appreciate it. At the same time the chapters have been arranged with such regard to chronological order as to show the development of character and achievement from youth to age.

Contents

List of Illustrations with Notes

LIST OF ILLUSTRATIONS WITH NOTES

LIST OF ILLUSTRATIONS WITH NOTES

LIST OF ILLUSTRATIONS WITH NOTES

The True
Benjamin Franklin

I

PHYSICAL CHARACTERISTICS

FRANKLIN was a rather large man, and is supposed to have been about five feet ten inches in height. In his youth he was stout, and in old age corpulent and heavy, with rounded shoulders. The portraits of him reveal a very vigorous-looking man, with a thick upper arm and a figure which, even in old age, was full and rounded. In fact, this rounded contour is his most striking characteristic, as the angular outline is the characteristic of Lincoln. Franklin's figure was a series of harmonious curves, which make pictures of him always pleasing. These curves extended over his head and even to the lines of his face, softening the expression, slightly veiling the iron resolution, and entirely consistent with the wide sympathies, varied powers, infinite shrewdness, and vast experience which we know he possessed.

In his earliest portrait as a youth of twenty he looks as if his bones were large ; but in later portraits this largeness of bone which he might have had from his Massachusetts origin is not so evident.

He was, however, very muscular, and prided himself on it. When he was a young printer, as he tells us in his Autobiography, he could carry with ease a large form of letters in each hand up and down stairs. In his old age, when past eighty, he is described as insisting on lifting unaided heavy books and dictionaries to show the strength he still retained.

He was not brought up on fox-hunting and other sports, like Washington, and there are no amusements of this sort to record of him, except his swimming, in which he took great delight and continued until long after he had ceased to be a youth. He appears, when a boy, to have been fond of sailing in Boston Harbor, but has told us little about it. In swimming he excelled. He could perform all the ordinary feats in the water which were described in the swimming-books of his day, and on one occasion tied himself to the string of his kite and was towed by it across a pond a mile wide. In after-years he believed that he could in this way cross the English Channel from Dover to Calais, but he admitted that the packet-boat was preferable.

His natural fondness for experiment led him to try the effect of fastening oval paddles to his hands, which gave him greater speed in swimming, but were too fatiguing to his wrists. Paddles or large sandals fastened to his feet he soon found altered the stroke, which the observant boy had discovered was made with the inside of the feet and ankles as well as with the flat part of the foot.

While in London, as a wandering young journeyman printer, he taught an acquaintance, Wygate, to

FRANKLIN TOWED BY HIS KITE

swim in two lessons. Returning from Chelsea with a party of Wygate's friends, he gave them an exhibition of his skill, going through all the usual tricks in the water, to their great amazement and admiration, and swimming from near Chelsea to Blackfriars, a distance of four miles. Wygate proposed that they should travel through Europe, maintaining themselves by giving swimming-lessons, and Franklin was at first inclined to adopt the suggestion.

Just as he was on the eve of returning to Pennsylvania, Sir William Wyndham, at one time Chancellor of the Exchequer, having heard of his swimming feats, wanted to engage him to teach his sons ; but his ship being about to sail, Franklin was obliged to decline. If he had remained in England, he tells us, he would probably have started a swimming-school.

When forty-three years old, retired from active business, and deep in scientific researches, he lived in a house at Second and Race Streets, Philadelphia. His garden is supposed to have extended to the river, where every warm summer evening he used to spend an hour or two swimming and sporting in the water.

This skill in swimming and the agility and grace which Franklin displayed in performing feats in the water are good tests of general strength of muscles, lungs, and heart. So far as can be discovered, only one instance is recorded of his using his physical power to do violence to his fellow-man.

He had a friend named Collins, rather inclined to drink, who, being in a boat with Franklin and some other youths, on the Delaware, refused to take his turn at rowing. He announced that the others should row him home. Franklin, already much provoked at him for not returning money which he had lent him, and for other misconduct, insisted that he row his share. Collins replied that Franklin should row or he would throw him overboard, and, as he was approaching him for that purpose, Franklin seized him by the collar and breeches and threw him into the river, where they kept him till his strength was exhausted and his temper cooled.

Until he was forty years old Franklin worked on his own account or for others as a printer, which included hard manual labor; for, even when in business for himself, he did everything,—made his own ink, engraved wooden cuts and ornaments, set the type, and worked the heavy hand-presses. His pleasures were books, the theatre, and love-affairs. Except swimming, he had no taste for out-door amusements. Sport, either with rod, gun, horse, or hound, was altogether out of his line. As he became prosperous and retired from the active business of money-getting, he led an entirely sedentary life to the end of his long career.

Although he did a vast amount of work in his time, was fond of early rising, and had the greatest endurance and capacity for labor, there was, nevertheless, a touch of indolence about him. He did the things which he loved and which came easy to him, cultivated his tastes and followed their bent in a way rather unusual in self-made men. It has been said of him that he never had the patience to write a book. His writings have exerted great influence, are now considered of inestimable value, and fill ten large volumes, but they are all occasional pieces, letters, and pamphlets written to satisfy some need of the hour.

His indolence was more in his manner than in his character. It was the confident indolence of genius. He was never in a hurry, and this was perhaps one of the secrets of his success. His portraits all show this trait. In nearly every one of them the whole attitude, the droop of the shoulders and arms, and the quietude of the face are reposeful.

He seems to have been totally without either irritability or excitability. In this he was the reverse of Washington, who was subject to violent outbursts of anger, could swear "like an angel of God," as one of his officers said, and had a fiery temper to control. Perhaps Franklin's strong sense of humor saved him from oaths; there are no swearing stories recorded of him; instead of them we have innumerable jokes and witticisms. His anger when aroused was most deliberate, calculating, and judicious. His enemies and opponents he always ridiculed, often, however, with so little malice or sting that I have no doubt they were sometimes compelled to join in the laugh. He never attacked or abused.

Contentment was a natural consequence of these qualities, and contributed largely to maintain his vigor through eighty-four years of a very stormy life. It was a family trait. Many of his relations possessed it; and he describes some of them whom he looked up in England as living in happiness and enjoyment, in spite of the greatest poverty. Some able men struggle with violence, bitterness, and heartache for the great prizes of life, but all these prizes tumbled in on Franklin, who seems to have had a fairy that brought them to him in obedience to his slightest wish.

His easy-going sedentary life, of course, told on him in time. After middle life he had both the gout and the stone, but his natural vitality fortified him against them. He was as temperate as it was possible to be in that age, and he studied his constitution and its requirements very closely. He was so much interested in science that he not infrequently observed, reasoned, and to some extent experimented in the domain which properly belongs to physicians.

When only fifteen years old, and apprenticed in the printing-office of his brother in Boston, in the year 1721, he became a vegetarian. A book written by one of the people who have for many centuries been advocating that plan of living fell in his way and converted him. It appealed to his natural economy and to his desire for spare money with which to buy books. He learned from the book the various ways of cooking vegetables, and told his brother that if he would give him half the money paid for his board he would board himself. He found very soon that he could pay for his vegetable diet and still save half the money allowed him, and that he could also very quickly eat his rice, potatoes, and pudding at the printing-office and have most of the dinner-hour for reading the books his spare money procured.

This was calculating very closely for a boy of fifteen, and shows unusual ability as well as willingness to observe and master small details. Such ability usually comes later in life with strengthened intellect, but Franklin seems to have had this sort of mature strength very early.

He did not remain an entire convert to the vegetarians, but he often practised their methods and apparently found no inconvenience in it. He could eat almost anything, and change from one diet to another without difficulty. Two years after his first experiment with vegetarianism he ran away from his brother at Boston, and found work at Philadelphia with a rough, ignorant old printer named Keimer, who wanted, among other projects, to form a religous sect, and to have Franklin help him. Franklin played with his ideas for a while, and finally said that he would agree to wear a long beard and observe Saturday instead of Sunday, like Keimer, if Keimer would join him in a vegetable diet.

He found a woman in the neighborhood to cook for them, and taught her how to prepare forty kinds of vegetable food, which reduced their cost of living to eighteen pence a week for each. But Keimer, who was a heavy meat-eater, could stand it only three months, and then ordered a roast-pig dinner, to be enjoyed by the two vegetarians and a couple of women. Keimer, however, arrived first at the feast, and before any of his guests appeared had eaten the whole pig.

While working in the printing-office in London, Franklin drank water, to the great astonishment and disgust of the beer-guzzling Englishmen who were his fellow-laborers. They could not understand how the water-American, as they called him, could go without strength-giving beer and yet be able to carry a large form of letters in each hand up and down stairs, while they could carry only one with both hands.

The man who worked one of the presses with Franklin drank a pint before breakfast, a pint with bread and cheese for breakfast, one between breakfast and dinner, one at dinner, another at six o'clock, and another after he had finished his day's work. The American boy, with his early mastery of details, reasoned with him that the strength furnished by the beer could come only from the barley dissolved in the water of which the beer was composed ; that there was a larger portion of flour in a penny loaf, and if he ate a loaf and drank a pint of water with it he would derive more strength than from a pint of beer. But the man would not be convinced, and continued to spend a large part of his weekly wages for what Franklin calls the cursed beverage which kept him in poverty and wretchedness.

Franklin was, however, never a teetotaler. He loved, as he tells us, a glass and a song. Like other people of that time, he could drink without inconvenience a quantity which nowadays, especially in America, seems surprising. Some of the chief-justices of England are described by their biographer, Campbell, as two- or four-bottle men, according to the quantity they could consume at a sitting. Washington, Mr. Ford tells us, drank habitually from half a pint to a pint of Madeira, besides punch and beer, which would now be thought a great deal.

But Franklin considered himself a very temperate man. When writing his Autobiography, in his old age, he reminds his descendants that to temperance their ancestor "ascribes his long-continued health and what is still left to him of a good constitution."

Like most of those who live to a great age, he was the child of long-lived parents. "My mother," he says, "had likewise an excellent constitution; she suckled all her ten children. I never knew either my father or mother to have any sickness but that of which they died,—he at eighty-nine and she at eighty-five years of age."

He was fond of air-baths, which he seems to have thought hardened his skin and helped it to perform its functions, and when in London in 1768 he wrote one of his pretty letters about them to Dr. Dubourg in Paris.

"You know the cold bath has long been in vogue here as a tonic; but the shock of the cold water has always appeared to me, generally speaking, as too violent, and I have found it much more agreeable to my constitution to bathe in another element, I mean cold air. With this view I rise almost every morning and sit in my chamber, without any clothes whatever, half an hour or an hour, according to the season, either reading or writing. This practice is not in the least painful, but, on the contrary, agreeable; and if I return to bed afterwards, before I dress myself, as sometimes happens, I make a supplement to my night's rest of one or two hours of the most pleasing sleep that can be imagined. I find no ill consequences whatever resulting from it, and that at least it does not injure my health, if it does not in fact contribute much to its preservation. I shall therefore call it for the future a *bracing* or *tonic* bath." (Bigelow's Works of Franklin, vol. iv. p. 193.)

Some years afterwards, while in Paris and suffering severely from gout in his foot, he used to expose the foot naked out of bed, which he found relieved the pain, because, as he supposed, the skin was given more freedom to act in a natural way. His remarks on air-baths were published in the early editions of his works and induced many people to try them. Davis, in his "Travels in America," says that they must have been suggested to him by a passage in Aubrey's "Miscellanies;" but, after searching all through that old volume, I cannot find it. Franklin, however, made no claim to a discovery. Such baths have been used by physicians to strengthen delicate persons, but in a more guarded and careful manner than that in which Franklin applied them.

It was characteristic of his genial temperament that he loved to dream in his sleep and to recollect his dreams. "I am often," he says, "as agreeably entertained by them as by the scenery of an opera." He wrote a pleasant little essay, addressed to an unknown young lady, on "The Art of Procuring Pleasant Dreams," which may be said to belong among his medical writings. Fresh air and ventilation are the important dream-persuaders, and bad dreams and restlessness in bed are caused by excess of perspirable matter which is not allowed to get away from the skin. Eat less, have thinner and more porous bedclothes, and if you are restless, get up, beat and turn your pillows, shake all the sheets twenty times, and walk about naked for a while. Then, when you return, the lovely dreams will come.

Closely connected with his faith in air-baths was his opinion that people seldom caught cold from exposure to air or even to dampness. He wrote letters on the subject and prepared notes of his observations. These notes are particularly interesting and full of curious suggestions. The diseases usually classed as colds, he said, are not known by that name in any other language, and the name is misleading, for very few of them arise from cold or dampness. Indians and sailors, who are continually wet, do not catch cold ; nor is cold taken by swimming. And he went on enumerating the instances of people who lived in the woods, in barns, or with open windows, and, instead of catching cold, found their health improved. Cold, he thought, was caused in most cases by impure air, want of exercise, or over-eating.

"I have long been satisfied from observation, that besides the general colds now termed influenzas (which may possibly spread by contagion, as well as by a particular quality of the air), people often catch cold from one another when shut up together in close rooms and coaches, and when sitting near and conversing so as to breathe in each other's transpiration ; the disorder being in a certain state. I think, too, that it is the frouzy, corrupt air from animal substances, and the perspired matter from our bodies, which being long confined in beds not lately used, and clothes not lately worn, and books long shut up in close rooms, obtains that kind of putridity which occasions the colds observed upon sleeping in, wearing, and turning over such bedclothes or books, and not their coldness or dampness. From these causes, but more from too full living, with too little exercise, proceed, in my opinion, most of the disorders which, for about one hundred and fifty years past, the English have called *colds*."

Much of this is true in a general way, for medical practitioners have long held that all colds do not arise from exposure or draughts ; but they do not admit that colds can be taken from turning over old books and clothes, although the dust from these might make one sneeze.

John Adams and Franklin while travelling together through New Jersey to meet Lord Howe, in 1776, discussed the question of colds, and the former has left an amusing account of it. The taverns were so full at Brunswick that they had to sleep in the same bed. Franklin insisted on leaving the window wide open, and discoursed on the causes of colds until they both fell asleep.

"I have often asked him whether a person heated with exercise going suddenly into cold air, or standing still in a current of it, might not have his pores suddenly contracted, his perspiration stopped, and that matter thrown into the circulation, or cast upon the lungs, which he acknowledged was the cause of colds. To this he never could give me a satisfactory answer, and I have heard that in the opinion of his own able physician, Dr. Jones, he fell a sacrifice at last, not to the stone, but to his own theory, having caught the violent cold which finally choked him, by sitting for some hours at a window, with the cool air blowing upon him." (Adams's Works, vol. iii. p. 75.)

In some of his letters Franklin denied positively that colds could be taken by exposure. He got a young physician to experiment on the effect of nakedness in increasing perspiration, and when he found, or thought he had found, that the perspiration was greater than when the body was clothed, he jumped to the conclusion that exposure could not check perspiration. In a passage in his notes, however, he seems to admit that a sudden cold air or a draught might check it.

He wrote so well and so prettily on colds that people began to think he was the discoverer of their causes,

THE SUMNER PORTRAIT OF FRANKLIN

and his biographer, Parton, goes so far as to say so. But upon inquiry among learned physicians I cannot find that they recognize him as a discoverer, or that he has any standing on this question in medical history. It would seem that he merely collected and expressed the observations of others as well as his own ; none of them were entirely new, and many of them are now considered unsound.

Nearer to the truth is Parton's statement that "he was the first effective preacher of the blessed gospel of ventilation." He certainly studied that subject very carefully, and was an authority on it, being appointed while in England to prepare a plan for ventilating the Houses of Parliament. It would, however, be better to say that he was one of the most prominent advocates of ventilation rather than the first effective preacher of it; for in Bigelow's edition of his works* will be found an excellent essay on the subject in which the other advocates are mentioned. But Parton goes on to say, "He spoke, and the windows of hospitals were lowered ; consumption ceased to gasp and fever to inhale poison ;" which is an extravagant statement that he would find difficulty, I think, in supporting.

In Franklin's published works there is a short essay called "A Conjecture as to the Cause of the Heat of the Blood in Health and of the Cold and Hot Fits of Some Fevers." The blood is heated, he says, by friction in the action of the heart, by the

* Vol. iv. p. 271.

distention and contraction of the arteries, and by being forced through minute vessels. This essay is very ingenious and well written, and the position given to it in his works might lead one to suppose that it was of importance ; but I am informed by physicians that it was merely the revamping of an ancient theory held long before his time, and quite without foundation.

Franklin's excursions into the domain of medicine are not, therefore, to be considered among his valuable contributions to the welfare of man, except so far as they encouraged him to advocate fresh air and ventilation, though they may have assisted him to take better care of his own health.

Of the numerous portraits of him of varying merit, nearly all of which have been reproduced over and over again, only a few deserve consideration for the light they throw on his appearance and character. The Sumner portrait, as it used to be called, is supposed to have been painted in London in 1726, when he was there as a young journeyman printer, twenty years old, and was brought by him to America and given to his brother John, of Rhode Island. He evidently dressed himself for this picture in clothes he was not in the habit of wearing at his work ; for he appears in a large wig, a long, decorated coat and waistcoat, with a mass of white ruffles on his bosom and conspicuous wrist-bands. The rotund and strongly developed figure is well displayed. Great firmness and determination are shown in the mouth and lower part of the face. The animal forces are evidently strong. The face is somewhat frank, and at the same time very shrewd. The eyes are larger than in the later portraits, which is not surprising, for eyes are apt to grow smaller in appearance with age.

This portrait, which is now in Memorial Hall at Harvard University, has been supposed by some critics not to be a portrait of Franklin at all. How, they ask, could Franklin, who was barely able to earn his living at that time, and whose companions were borrowing a large part of his spare money, afford to have an oil-painting made of himself in such expensive costume? and why is there no mention of this portrait in any of his writings? But, on the other hand, the portrait has the peculiar set expression of the mouth and the long chin which were so characteristic of Franklin; and it would have been entirely possible for him to have borrowed the clothes and had the picture painted cheaply or as a kindness. It is not well painted, need not have been expensive, and, as there were no photographs then, paintings were the only way by which people could give their likenesses to relatives.

The Martin portrait, painted when he was about sixty years old, represents him seated, his elbows resting on a table, and holding a document, which he is reading with deep but composed and serene attention. It was no doubt intended to represent him in a characteristic attitude. As showing the calm philosopher and diplomat reading and thinking, somewhat idealized and yet a more or less true likeness, it is in many respects the best picture we have of him. But we cannot see the eyes, and it does not reveal as much character as we could wish.

The Grundmann portrait, an excellent photograph of which hangs in the Philadelphia Library, was painted by a German artist, after a careful study of Franklin's career and of all the portraits of him which had been painted from life. As an attempt to reproduce his characteristics and idealize them it is a distinct success and very interesting. He is seated in a chair, in his court-dress, with long stockings and knee-breeches, leaning back, his head and shoulders bent forward, while his gaze is downward. He is musing over something, and there is that characteristic shrewd smile on the lower part of the rugged face. It is the smile of a most masterful and cunning intellect ; but no one fears it : it seems as harmless as your mother's. You try to imagine which one of his thousand clever strokes and sayings was passing through his mind that day ; and the strong, intensely individualized figure, which resembles that of an old athlete, is wonderfully suggestive of life, experience, and contest.

But the Duplessis portrait, which was painted from life in Paris in 1778, when he was seventy-two, reveals more than any of them. The Sumner portrait is Franklin the youth ; the Martin and the Grundmann portraits are Franklin the philosopher and statesman ; the Duplessis portrait is Franklin the man.

Unfortunately, it is impossible to get a good reproduction of the Duplessis portrait, because there is so much detail in it and the coloring and lights and shadows cannot be successfully copied. But any one who will examine the original or any good replicas

THE MARTIN PORTRAIT OF FRANKLIN

of it in oil will, I am convinced, see Franklin as he really was. The care in details, the wrinkles, and the color of the skin give us confidence in it as a likeness. The round, strong, but crude form of the boy of twenty has been beaten and changed by time into a hundred qualities and accomplishments, yet the original form is still discernible, and the face looks straight at us : we see the eyes and every line close at hand.

In this, the best portrait for studying Franklin's eye, we see at once that it is the eye of a very sensuous man, and we also see many details which mark the self-made man, the man who never had been and never pretended to be an aristocrat. This is in strong contrast to Washington's portraits, which all disclose a man distinctly of the upper class and conscious of it.

But, in spite of this homeliness in the Duplessis portrait and the easy, careless manner in which the clothes are worn, there are no signs of what might be called vulgarity. The wonderful and many-sided accomplishments of the man carried him well above this. Brought up as a boy at candle- and soap-making, he nevertheless, when prosperous, turned instinctively to higher things and refined accomplishments and was comparatively indifferent to material wealth. Nor do we find in him any of that bitter hostility and jealousy of the established and successful which more modern experience might lead us to expect.

The Duplessis portrait conforms to what we read of Franklin in representing him as hale and vigorous at seventy-two. The face is full of lines, but they are the lines of thought, and of thought that has come easily and cheerfully ; there are no traces of anxiety, gnawing care, or bitterness. In Paris, at the time the Duplessis portrait was painted, Franklin was regarded as a rather unusual example of vigor and good health in old age. John Adams in his Diary uses him as a standard, and speaks of other old men in France as being equal or almost equal to him in health.

Although not so free from disease as were his parents, he was not much troubled with it until late in life. When a young man of about twenty-one he had a bad attack of pleurisy, of which he nearly died. It terminated in an abscess of the left lung, and when this broke, he was almost suffocated by the quantity and suddenness of the discharge. A few years afterwards he had a similar attack of pleurisy, ending in the same way ; and it was an abscess in his lung which finally caused his death. The two abscesses which he had when a young man seem to have left no ill effects ; and after his two attacks of pleurisy he was free from serious sickness for many years, until at the age of fifty-one he went to England to represent the Province of Pennsylvania. Soon after landing he was attacked by an obscure fever, of which he does not give the name, and which disabled him for eight weeks. He was delirious, and they cupped him and gave him enormous quantities of bark.

After he had passed middle life he found that he could not remain entirely well unless he took a

THE GRUNDMANN IDEAL PORTRAIT OF FRANKLIN

journey every year. During the nine years of his residence in Paris as minister to France he was unable to take these journeys, and as a consequence his health rapidly deteriorated. He had violent attacks which incapacitated him for weeks, sometimes for months, and at the close of the nine years he could scarcely walk and could not bear the jolting of a carriage.

In France his diseases were first the gout and afterwards the stone. He was one of those stout, full-blooded men who the doctors say are peculiarly liable to gout, and his tendency to it was evidently increased by his very sedentary habits. He confesses this in part of that clever dialogue which he wrote to amuse the Parisians :

"Midnight, October 22, 1780.

"*Franklin.*—Eh ! Oh ! Eh ! What have I done to merit these cruel sufferings?

"*Gout.*—Many things ; you have ate and drank too freeely, and too much indulged those legs of yours in their indolence.

"*Franklin.*—Who is it that accuses me?

"*Gout.*—It is I, even I, the Gout.

"*Franklin.*—What ! my enemy in person?

"*Gout.*—No, not your enemy.

"*Franklin.*—I repeat it ; my enemy ; for you would not only torment my body to death, but ruin my good name ; you reproach me as a glutton and a tippler ; now all the world, that knows me, will allow that I am neither the one nor the other.

"*Gout.*—The world may think as it pleases ; it is always very complaisant to itself, and sometimes to its friends ; but I very well know that the quantity of meat and drink proper for a man, who takes a reasonable degree of exercise, would be too much for another, who never takes any.

"*Franklin.*—I take—Eh ! Oh !—as much exercise—Eh !—as I can, Madam Gout. You know my sedentary state, and on that account, it would seem, Madam Gout, as if you might spare me a little, seeing it is not altogether my own fault.

" *Gout.*—Not a jot ; your rhetoric and your politeness are thrown away ; your apology avails nothing. If your situation in life is a sedentary one, your amusements, your recreations, at least, should be active. You ought to walk or ride ; or, if the weather prevents that, play at billiards. But let us examine your course of life. While the mornings are long, and you have leisure to go abroad, what do you do ? Why, instead of gaining an appetite for breakfast, by salutary exercise, you amuse yourself with books, pamphlets, or newspapers, which commonly are not worth the reading. Yet you eat an inordinate breakfast, four dishes of tea, with cream, and one or two buttered toasts, with slices of hung beef, which I fancy are not things the most easily digested. Immediately afterward you sit down to write at your desk, or converse with persons who apply to you on business. Thus the time passes till one, without any kind of bodily exercise. But all this I could pardon, in regard, as you say, to your sedentary condition. But what is your practice after dinner ? Walking in the beautiful garden of those friends, with whom you have dined, would be the choice of men of sense ; yours is to be fixed down to chess, where you are found engaged for two or three hours ! . . . Wrapt in the speculations of this wretched game, you destroy your constitution. What can be expected from such a course of living, but a body replete with stagnant humors, ready to fall a prey to all kinds of dangerous maladies, if I, the Gout, did not occasionally bring you relief by agitating those humors, and so purifying or dissipating them ? . . . But amidst my instructions, I had almost forgot to administer my wholesome corrections ; so take that twinge,—and that. . . ."

He tried to give himself exercise by walking up and down his room. In that humorous essay, "The Craven Street Gazette," in which he describes the doings of Mrs. Stevenson's household, where he lived in London, there is a passage evidently referring to himself : "Dr. Fatsides made four hundred and sixty turns in his dining-room as the exact distance of a visit to the lovely Lady Barwell, whom he did not find at home ; so there was no struggle for and against a kiss, and he sat down to dream in the easy-chair that he had it without any trouble."

Some years afterwards, when he was in Paris, John Adams upbraided him for not taking more exercise ; but he replied, "Yes, I walk a league every day in my chamber. I walk quick, and for an hour, so that I go a league ; I make a point of religion of it." This was not a very good substitute for out-of-door exertion. In fact, Franklin's opinions on the subject of exercise were not wise. The test of exercise was, he thought, the amount of warmth it added to the body, and he inferred, therefore, that walking must be better than riding on horseback, and he even recommended walking up and down stairs. Walking, being monotonous and having very little effect on the trunk and upper portions of the body, is generally admitted to be insufficient for those who require much exercise ; while running up and down stairs would now be considered positively injurious. But it is, perhaps, hardly in order to criticise the methods of a man who succeeded in living to be eighty-four and who served the public until the last year of his life.

Even when he was at his worst in Paris and unable to walk, his mind was as vigorous as ever, and he looked well. Adams, who was determined to comment on his neglect of exercise, says of him when in his crippled condition, in 1785, "but he is strong and eats freely, so that he will soon have other complaints besides the stone if he continues to live as entirely without exercise as he does at present." Adams also said that his only chance for life was a sea-voyage.

Soon afterwards Franklin was carried in a litter

by easy journeys from Paris to the sea-coast, and crossed to Southampton, England, to wait for the vessel that was to take him to Philadelphia. While at Southampton he says,—

"I went at noon to bathe in the Martin salt water hot bath, and floating on my back, fell asleep, and slept near an hour by my watch without sinking or turning! a thing I never did before and should hardly have thought possible. Water is the easiest bed that can be."

It was certainly odd that in his seventy-ninth year and enfeebled by disease he should renew his youthful skill as a swimmer and justify to himself his favorite theory that nakedness and water are not the causes of colds.

His opinion that occasional journeys were essential to his health and Adams's opinion of the necessity of a sea-voyage were both justified; for when he reached Philadelphia, September 14, 1785, he could walk the streets and bear the motion of an easy car-- riage. He was almost immediately elected Governor of Pennsylvania, and held the office by successive annual elections for three years. The public, he said, have "engrossed the prime of my life. They have eaten my flesh, and seem resolved now to pick my bones." During the summer of 1787 he served as a member of the convention which framed the national Constitution, although unable to stand up long enough to make a speech, all his speeches being read by his colleague, James Wilson; and yet it was in that convention, as we shall see, that he performed the most important act of his political career.

In December, 1787, he had a fall down the stone steps of his garden, spraining his right wrist and bringing on another attack of the stone. But he recovered in the spring ; and at this period, and indeed to the end of his life, his wonderful vitality bore up so well against severe disease that his mental faculties were unimpaired, his spirits buoyant, and his face fresh and serene.

But towards the end he had to take to his bed, and the last two or three years of his life were passed in terrible pain, with occasional respites of a few weeks, during which he would return to some of his old avocations, writing letters or essays of extraordinary brightness and gayety. He wrote a long letter on his religious belief to President Stiles about five weeks before his death, his humorous protest against slavery two weeks later, and an important letter to Thomas Jefferson on the Northeast Boundary question nine days before his death.

His grandchildren played around his bedside ; friends and distinguished men called to see him, and went away to write notes of what they recollected of his remarkable conversation and cheerfulness. One of his grandchildren, afterwards Mrs. William J. Duane, was eight years old during the last year of his life, and she has related that every evening after tea he insisted that she should bring her Webster's spelling-book and say her lesson to him.

"A few days before he died, he rose from his bed and begged that it might be made up for him so that he might die in a decent manner. His daughter told him that she hoped he would recover and live many years longer. He calmly replied, 'I hope not.'

Upon being advised to change his position in bed, that he **might** breathe easy, he said, ' A dying man can do nothing **easy.**' " (Bigelow's Franklin from his own Writings, vol. iii. p. 464.)

His physician, Dr. Jones, has described his last illness,—

" About sixteen days before his death he was seized with a feverish indisposition, without any particular symptoms attending it, till the third or fourth day, when he complained of a pain in the left breast, which increased till it became extremely acute, attended with a cough and laborious breathing. During this state when the severity of his pains drew forth a groan of complaint, he would observe—that he was afraid he did not bear them as he ought—acknowledged his grateful sense of the many blessings he had received from that Supreme Being, who had raised him from small and low beginnings to such high rank and consideration among men—and made no doubt but his present afflictions were kindly intended to wean him from a world, in which he was no longer fit to act the part assigned him. In this frame of body and mind he continued till five days before his death, when his pain and difficulty of breathing entirely left him, and his family were flattering themselves with the hopes of his recovery, when an imposthumation, [abscess] which had formed itself in his lungs suddenly burst, and discharged a great quantity of matter, which he continued to throw up while he had sufficient strength to do it ; but, as that failed, the organs of respiration became gradually oppressed—a calm lethargic state succeeded—and, on the 17th of April, 1790, about eleven o'clock at night, he quietly expired, closing a long and useful life of eighty-four years and three months."

II

SELF-MADE men of eminence have been quite numerous in America for a hundred years. Franklin was our first hero of this kind, and I am inclined to think our greatest. The others have achieved wealth or political importance ; sometimes both. But Franklin achieved not only wealth and the reputation of a diplomatist and a statesman, but made himself a most accomplished scholar, a man of letters of world-wide fame, a philosopher of no small importance, and as an investigator and discoverer in science he certainly enlarged the domain of human knowledge.

His father, Josiah Franklin, an industrious candle-maker in Boston, intended that his youngest son, Benjamin, should enter the ministry of the Puritan Church. With this end in view he sent him, when eight years old, to the Boston Grammar-School; but before a year had expired he found that the cost of even this slight schooling was too much for the slender means with which he had to provide for a large family of children. So Franklin went to another school, kept by one George Brownell, where he stayed for about a year, and then his school-days were ended forever. He entered his father's shop to cut wicks and melt tallow. During his two years of schooling he had learned to read and write, but was not very good at arithmetic.

His associations were all humble, but they cannot be said to have been those of either extreme poverty or ignorance. At Ecton, Northamptonshire, England, whence his father came, the family had lived for at least three hundred years, and how much longer is not known. Several of those in the lineal line of Benjamin had been blacksmiths. They were plain people who, having been always respectable and lived long in one neighborhood, could trace their ancestry back for several centuries.

They were unambitious, contented with their condition, and none of them except Benjamin ever rose much above it, or even seriously tried to rise. This may not have been from any lack of mental ability. Franklin's father was a strong, active man, as was to be expected of the descendant of a line of blacksmiths. He was intelligent and inquiring, conversed well on general subjects, could draw well, played the violin and sang in his home when the day's work was done, and was respected by his neighbors as a prudent, sensible citizen whose advice was worth obtaining. It does not appear that he was studious. But his brother Benjamin, after whom our Franklin was named, was interested in politics, collected pamphlets, made short-hand notes of the sermons he heard, and was continually writing verses.

This Uncle Benjamin, while in England, took a great interest in the nephew in America who was named after him, and he sent verses to him on all sorts of subjects. He was unsuccessful in business,

HOUSE IN WHICH FRANKLIN WAS BORN

lost his wife and all his children, save one, and finally came out to America to join the family at Boston.

Franklin's mother was Abiah Folger, the second wife of his father. She was the daughter of Peter Folger, of Nantucket, a surveyor, who is described by Cotton Mather as a somewhat learned man. He made himself familiar with some of the Indian languages, and taught the Indians to read and write. He wrote verses of about the same quality as those of Uncle Benjamin. One of these, called "A Looking Glass for the Times," while it is mere doggerel, shows that its author was interested in literature. He was a man of liberal views and opposed to the persecution of the Quakers and Baptists in Massachusetts.

From this grandfather on his mother's side Franklin no doubt inherited his fondness for books, a fondness that was reinforced by a similar tendency which, though not very strong in his father, evidently existed in his father's family, as Uncle Benjamin's verses show. These verses sent to the boy Franklin and his efforts at times to answer them were an encouragement towards reading and knowledge. Franklin's extremely liberal views may possibly have had their origin in his maternal grandfather, Peter Folger.

But independently of these suppositions as regards heredity, we find Franklin at twelve years of age reading everything he could lay his hands on. His first book was Bunyan's "Pilgrim's Progress," which would not interest boys nowadays, and scarcely interests mature people any more ; but there were no novels then and no story-books for boys. "Pilgrim's Progress" is a prose story with dialogues between the characters, the first instance of this sort of writing in English, and sufficient to fascinate a boy when there was nothing better in the world.

He liked it so well that he bought the rest of Bunyan's works, but soon sold them to procure Burton's Historical Collections, which were forty small chapmen's books, full of travels, adventures, history, and descriptions of animals, well calculated to stimulate the interest of a bright lad. Among his father's theological books was Plutarch's "Lives," which young Franklin read eagerly, also De Foe's "Essay upon Projects," and Cotton Mather's "Essays to do Good," which he said had an important influence on his character.

He so hated cutting wicks and melting tallow that, like many other boys of his time, he wanted to run away to sea ; and his father, to check this inclination and settle him, compelled him to sign articles of apprenticeship with his brother James, who was a printer. The child's taste for books, the father thought, fitted him to be a printer, which would be a more profitable occupation than the ministry, for which he was at first intended.

So Franklin was bound by law to serve his brother until he was twenty-one. He learned the business quickly, stealing time to read books, which he sometimes persuaded booksellers' apprentices to take from their masters' shops in the evening. He would sit up nearly all night to read them, so that they might be returned early in the morning before they were missed.

PRINTING-PRESS AT WHICH FRANKLIN WORKED WHEN A BOY IN BOSTON

He wrote ballads, like his uncle Benjamin and his grandfather Peter Folger, on popular events,—the drowning of a Captain Worthilake, and the pirate Blackbeard,—and, after his brother had printed them, sold them in the streets. His biographer, Weems, quotes one of these verses, which he declares he had seen and remembered, and I give it with the qualification that it comes from Weems :

> "Come all you jolly sailors,
>   You all, so stout and brave ;
> Come hearken and I'll tell you
>   What happened on the wave.
>
> "Oh ! 'tis of that bloody Blackbeard
>   I'm going now for to tell ;
> And as how by gallant Maynard
>   He soon was sent to hell—
>   With a down, down, down, derry down."

His father ridiculed these verses, in spite of their successful sale, and dissuaded him from any more attempts ; but Franklin remained more or less of a verse-writer to the end of his life. Verse-writing trained him to write good prose, and this accomplishment contributed, he thought, more than anything else to his advancement.

He had an intimate friend, John Collins, likewise inclined to books, and the two argued and disputed with each other. Franklin was fond of wordy contention at that time, and it was possibly a good mental training for him. He had caught it, he says, from reading his father's books of religious controversy. But in after-years he became convinced that this disputatious turn was a very bad habit, which made one extremely disagreeable and alienated friends; he therefore adopted during most of his life a method of cautious modesty.

He once disputed with Collins on the propriety of educating women and on their ability for study. He took the side of the women, and, feeling himself worsted by Collins, who had a more fluent tongue, he reduced his arguments to writing and sent them to him. A correspondence followed, and Franklin's father, happening to find the papers, pointed out to his son the great advantage Collins had in clearness and elegance of expression. A hint is all that genius requires, and Franklin went resolutely to work to improve himself.

"About this time I met with an odd volume of the Spectator. It was the third. I had never before seen any of them. I bought it, read it over and over, and was much delighted with it. I thought the writing excellent, and wished, if possible, to imitate it. With this view I took some of the papers, and, making short hints of the sentiment in each sentence, laid them by a few days, and then, without looking at the book, try'd to compleat the papers again, by expressing each hinted sentiment at length, and as fully as it had been expressed before, in any suitable words that should come to hand. Then I compared my Spectator with the original, discovered some of my faults, and corrected them. But I found I wanted a stock of words, or a readiness in recollecting and using them, which I thought I should have acquired before that time if I had gone on making verses; since the continual occasion for words of the same import, but of different length, to suit the measure, or of different sound for the rhyme, would have laid me under a constant necessity of searching for variety, and also have tended to fix that variety in my mind, and make me master of it. Therefore I took some of the tales and turned them into verse; and, after a time, when I had pretty well forgotten the prose, turned them back again. I also sometimes jumbled my collections of hints into confusion, and after some weeks endeavored to reduce them into the best order, before I began to form the full sentences and compleat the paper. This was to teach me method in the arrangement of thoughts. By comparing my work afterwards with the original, I discovered many faults and amended them ; but I sometimes had the pleasure of fancying that, in certain particulars of small import, I had been lucky enough to improve the method or the language, and this encouraged me to think I might possibly in time come to be a tolerable English writer, of which I was extremely ambitious."

In some respects this is the most interesting passage in all of Franklin's writings. It was this severe training of himself which gave him that wonderful facility in the use of English that made him a great man. Without it he would have been second-rate or ordinary. His method of improving his style served also as a discipline in thought and logic such as is seldom, if ever, given nowadays in any school or college.

Many of those who have reflected deeply on the subject of college education have declared that its ultimate object should be to give in the highest degree the power of expression. Some have said that a sense of honor and the power of expression should be its objects. But there are few who will dispute the proposition that a collegian who receives his diploma without receiving with it more of the art of expression than most men possess has spent his time and his money in vain.

During the last thirty years we have been trying every conceivable experiment in college education, many of them mere imitations from abroad and many of them mere suggestions, suppositions, or utopian theories. When we began these experiments it was taken for granted that the old methods, which had produced in this country such scholars, writers, and thinkers as Lowell, Longfellow, Holmes, Hawthorne, Webster, Prescott, Motley, Bancroft, Everett, Phillips, Channing, Parker, and Parkman, and in England a host too numerous to name, must necessarily be wrong. We began to imitate Germany. It was assumed that if we transplanted the German system we should begin to grind out Mommsens and Bunsens by the yard, like a cotton-mill; and that if we added to the German system every plausible suggestion of our own for making things easy, the result would be a stupendous success.

But how many men have we produced who can be compared with the men of the old system? Not one. The experiment, except so far as it has given a large number of people a great deal of pretty information about history and the fine arts, is a vast failure. After thirty years of effort we have just discovered that the boys whose nerves and eyesight are being worn out under our wonderful system cannot write a decent letter in the English language; and a committee of Harvard University have spent months of labor and issued a voluminous report of hundreds of pages on this mortifying discovery, leaving it as perplexing and humiliating as they found it.

Remedies are proposed. We have made a mistake, say some, and they suggest that for a change we adopt the English University system. After partially abolishing Latin and Greek we were to have in place of them a great deal of history and mathematics, which were more practical, it was said; but now we are informed that this also was a mistake, and a movement is on foot to abolish history and algebra.

EDUCATION

Others suggest the French system, and one individual writes a long article for the newspapers proving beyond the possibility of a doubt that French education is just the thing we need. Always imitating something; always trying to bring in the foreign and distant. And until we stop this vulgar provincial snobbery and believe in ourselves and learn to do our own work with our own people in our own way, we shall continue to flounder and fail.

Let us distinguish clearly between information and education. If it is necessary, especially in these times, to give people information on various subjects, —on science, history, art, bric-a-brac, or mud pies,— very good; let it be done by all means, for it seems to have a refining influence on the masses. But do not call it education. Education is teaching a person to do something with his mind or his muscles or with both. It involves training, discipline, drill; things which, as a rule, are very unpleasant to young people, and which, unless they are geniuses, like Franklin, they will not take up of their own accord.

You can never teach a boy to write good English by having him read elegant extracts from distinguished authors, or by making him wade through endless text-books of anatomy, physics, botany, history, and philosophy, or by giving him a glib knowledge of French or German, or by perfunctory translations of Latin and Greek prepared in the new-fashioned, easy way, without a grammar.

The old English method, by which boys were compelled to write Latin verses, was simply another form of Franklin's method, but rather more severe in some respects, because the boy was compelled to discipline his versifying power and hunt for and use words in two languages at once. The result was some of the greatest masters of language that the world has ever known, and the ordinary boy, though perhaps not a wonder in all the sciences, did not have a learned committee of a university investigating his disgraceful failure to use his native tongue. His mind, moreover, had been so disciplined by the severe training in the use of language—which is only another name for thought—that he was capable of taking up and mastering with ease any subject in science or philosophy, and could make as good mud pies and judge as well of bric-a-brac as those who had never done anything else.

In this country people object to compelling boys to write verse, because, as they say, it is an endeavor to force them to become poets whether they have talent for it or not. Any one who reflects, however, knows that there is no question of poetry in the matter. It is merely a question of technical versifying and use of language. Franklin never wrote a line of poetry in his life, but he wrote hundreds of lines of verse, to the great improvement of the faculty which made him the man he was.

When he voluntarily subjected himself to a mental discipline which modern parents would consider cruel he was only fifteen years old ; certainly a rather unusual precocity, from which some people would prophesy a dwarfed career or an early death. But he did some of his best work after he was eighty, and died at the age of eighty-four.

EDUCATION

He lived in the little village of Boston nearly two hundred years ago, the wholesome wilderness on one side of him and the wholesome ocean on the other. He worked with his strong arms and hands all day, and the mental discipline and reading were stolen sweets at the dinner-hour, at night, and on Sunday,—for he neglected church-going for the sake of his studies. Could he have budded and grown amid our distraction, dust, and disquietude? and have we any more of the elements of happiness than he?

Ashamed of his failure to learn arithmetic during his two short years at school, he procured a book on the subject and studied it by himself. In the same way he studied navigation and a little geometry. When scarcely seventeen he read Locke's "Essay on the Human Understanding" and "The Art of Thinking," by Messieurs du Port-Royal.

"While I was intent on improving my language I met with an English grammar (I think it was Greenwood's) at the end of which there were two little sketches of the arts of rhetoric and logic, the latter finishing with a specimen of a dispute in the Socratic method; and soon after I procured Xenophon's memorable things of Socrates, wherein there are many instances of the same method. I was charmed with it, adopted it, dropt my abrupt contradiction and positive argumentation, and put on the humble inquirer and doubter."

It was very shrewd of the boy to see so quickly the strategic advantage of the humbler method. It was also significant of genius that he should of his own accord not only train and discipline himself, but feed his mind on the great masters of literature instead of on trash. He could hardly have done any better at school, for he was gifted with unusual power of self-education. Boys are occasionally met with who have by their own efforts acquired a sufficient education to obtain a good livelihood or even to become rich; but it would be difficult to find another instance of a boy with only two years' schooling self-educating himself up to the ability not only of making a fortune, but of becoming a man of letters, a man of science, a philosopher, a diplomat, and a statesman of such very distinguished rank.

There was no danger of his inclination for the higher departments of learning making him visionary or impractical, as is so often the case with the modern collegian. He was of necessity always in close contact with actual life. His brother, in whose printing-office he worked as an apprentice, was continually beating him; perhaps not without reason, for Franklin himself admits that he was rather saucy and provoking. He was, it seems, at this period not a little vain of his learning and his skill as a workman. He had been writing important articles for his brother's newspaper, and he thought that his brother failed to appreciate his importance. They soon quarrelled, and Franklin ran away to New York.

He went secretly on board a sloop at Boston, having sold some of his books to raise the passage-money; and after a three days' voyage, which completely cured his desire for the sea, he found himself in a strange town, several hundred miles from home. He applied for work to old Mr. William Bradford, the famous printer of the colonies, who had recently removed from Philadelphia. But he had no position to give the boy, and recommended him to go to

Philadelphia, where his son kept a printing-office and needed a hand.

Franklin started for Amboy, New Jersey, in a sloop; but in crossing the bay they were struck by a squall, which tore their rotten sails to pieces and drove them on Long Island. They saved themselves from wreck on the beach by anchoring just in time, and lay thus the rest of the day and the following night, soaked to the skin and without food or sleep. They reached Amboy the next day, having had nothing to eat for thirty hours, and in the evening Franklin found himself in a fever.

He had heard that drinking plentifully of cold water was a good remedy; so he tried it, went to bed, and woke up well the next morning. But it was probably his boyish elasticity that cured him, and not the cold water, as he would have us believe.

He started on foot for Burlington, a distance of fifty miles, and tramped till noon through a hard rain, when he halted at an inn, and wished that he had never left home. He was a sorry figure, and people began to suspect him to be a runaway servant, which in truth he was. But the next day he got within eight miles of Burlington, and stopped at a tavern kept by a Dr. Brown, an eccentric man, who, finding that the boy had read serious books, was very friendly with him, and the two continued their acquaintance as long as the tavern-keeper lived.

Reaching Burlington on Saturday, he lodged with an old woman, who sold him some gingerbread and gave him a dinner of ox-cheek, to which he added a pot of ale. His intention had been to stay until the following Tuesday, but he found a boat going down the river that evening, which brought him to Philadelphia on Sunday morning.

He walked up Market Street from the wharf, dirty, his pockets stuffed with shirts and stockings, and carrying three great puffy rolls, one under each arm and eating the third. Passing by the house of a Mrs. Read, her daughter, standing at the door, saw the ridiculous, awkward-looking boy, and was much amused. But he continued strolling along the streets, eating his roll and calmly surveying the town where he was to become so eminent. One roll was enough for his appetite, and the other two, with a boy's sincere generosity, he gave to a woman and her child. He had insisted on paying for his passage, although the boatman was willing to let him off because he had assisted to row. A man, Franklin sagely remarks, is sometimes more generous when he has but little money through fear of being thought to have but little.

He wandered into a Quaker meeting-house and, as it was a silent meeting, fell fast asleep. Aroused by some one when the meeting broke up, he sought the river again, and was shown the Crooked Billet Inn, where he spent the afternoon sleeping, and immediately after supper went sound asleep again, and never woke till morning.

The next day he succeeded in obtaining work with a printer named Keimer, a man who had been a religious fanatic and was a good deal of a knave ; and this Keimer obtained lodging for him at the house of Mrs. Read, whose daughter had seen him walking up Market Street eating his roll. Well lodged, at work, and with a little money to spend, he lived agreeably, he tells us, in Philadelphia, made the acquaintance of young men who were fond of reading, and very soon his brother-in-law, Robert Holmes, master of a sloop that traded between Boston and the Delaware River, heard that the runaway was in Philadelphia.

Holmes wrote from New Castle, Delaware, to the boy, assuring him of the regret of his family at his absconding, of their continued good will, and urging him to return. Franklin replied, giving his side of the story, and Holmes showed the letter to Sir William Keith, Governor of Pennsylvania and Delaware, who happened to be at New Castle.

Keith was one of the most popular colonial governors that Pennsylvania ever had, and enjoyed a successful administration of ten years, which might have lasted much longer but for his reckless ambition. He had allowed himself to fall into habits of extravagance and debt, and had a way of building up his popularity by making profuse promises, most of which he could not keep. Chicanery finally became an habitual vice which he was totally unable to restrain, and he would indulge in it without the slightest reason or excuse.

He was surprised at the ability shown in Franklin's letter, declared that he must be set up in the printing business in Philadelphia, where a good printer was sadly needed, and promised to procure for him the public printing. A few days afterwards Franklin and Keimer, working near the window, were very much surprised to see the governor and Colonel French, of New Castle, dressed in all the finery of the time, walking across the street to their shop. Keimer thought that the visit was to him, and "stared like a poisoned pig," Franklin tells us, when he saw the governor addressing his workman with all the blandishments of courtly flattery. "Why," exclaimed the unscrupulous Keith, "did you not come to me immediately on your arrival in the town? It was unkind not to do so." He insisted that the boy should accompany him to the tavern, where he and Colonel French were going to try some excellent Madeira.

At the tavern the boy's future life was laid out for him. The governor and Colonel French would give him the public printing of both Pennsylvania and Delaware. Meantime he was to go back to Boston, see his father, and procure his assistance in starting in business. The father would not refuse, for Sir William would write him a letter which would put everything right. So Franklin, completely deceived, agreed, and, until a ship could be found that was going to Boston, he dined occasionally with the governor, and became very much inflated with a sense of his own importance.

Arrived at Boston, he strolled into his brother's printing-office, dressed in beautiful clothes, with a watch, and jingling five pounds sterling in silver in his pockets. He drew out a handful of the silver and spread it before the workmen, to their great surprise, for at that time Massachusetts was afflicted with a paper currency. Then, with consummate impudence and in his brother's presence, he gave the men a piece of eight to buy drink, and, after telling them what a good place Philadelphia was, swaggered out of the shop. It is not surprising that his brother turned away from him and refused to forgive or forget his conduct.

His father, being a man of sense, flatly refused to furnish money to start a boy of eighteen in an expensive business, and was curious to know what sort of man Governor Keith was, to recommend such a thing. So Franklin, with his conceit only slightly reduced, returned to Philadelphia, but this time with the blessing and consent of his parents.

He stopped in Rhode Island on his way, to visit his brother John, who had quite an affection for him, and while there was asked by a Mr. Vernon to collect thirty-five pounds due him in Pennsylvania, and was given an order for the money. On the vessel from Newport to New York were two women of the town, with whom Franklin, in his ignorance of the world, talked familiarly, until warned by a matronly Quaker lady. When the vessel reached New York, the women robbed the captain and were arrested.

His education in worldly matters was now to begin in earnest. His friend Collins accompanied him to Philadelphia ; but Collins had taken to drink and gambling, and from this time on was continually borrowing money of Franklin. The Governor of New York, son of the famous Bishop Burnet, hearing from the captain that a plain young man who was fond of books had arrived, sent for him, flattered him, and added to his increasing conceit. The boy who within a year had been made so much of by two governors was on the brink of ruin.

On his journey to Philadelphia he collected the money due Mr. Vernon, and used part of it to pay the expenses of Collins and himself. Collins kept borrowing Mr. Vernon's money from him, and Franklin was soon in the position of an embezzler.

Governor Keith laughed at the prudence of his father in refusing to set up in business such a promising young man. "I will do it myself," he said. "Give me an inventory of the things necessary to be had from England, and I will send for them. You shall repay me when you are able."

Thinking him the best man that had ever lived, Franklin brought him the inventory.

"But now," said Keith, "if you were on the spot in England to choose the types and see that everything was good, might not that be of some advantage? And then you may make acquaintances there and establish correspondences in the bookselling and stationery way."

Of course that was delightful.

"Then," said Keith, "get yourself ready to go with Annis," who was captain of a vessel that traded annually between Philadelphia and London.

Meantime, Franklin made love to Miss Read, who had seen him parading up Market Street with his rolls, and, if we may trust a man's account of such matters, he succeeded in winning her affections. He had lost all faith in religion, and his example unsettled those friends who associated and read books with him. He was at times invited to dine with the governor, who promised to give him letters of credit for money and also letters recommending him to his friends in England.

He called at different times for these letters, but they were not ready. The day of the ship's sailing came, and he called to take leave of his great and good friend and to get the letters. The governor's secretary said that his master was extremely busy, but would meet the ship at New Castle, and the letters would be delivered.

The ship sailed from Philadelphia with Franklin and one of his friends, Ralph, who was going to England, ostensibly on business, but really to desert his wife and child, whom he left in Philadelphia. While the vessel was anchored off New Castle, Franklin went ashore to see Keith, and was again informed that he was very busy, but that the letters would be sent on board.

The despatches of the governor were brought on board in due form by Colonel French, and Franklin asked for those which were to be under his care. But the captain said that they were all in the bag together, and before he reached England he would have an opportunity to pick them out. Arrived in London after a long, tempestuous voyage, Franklin found that there were no letters for him and no money. On consulting with a Quaker merchant, Mr. Denham, who had been friendly to him on the ship, he was told that there was not the slightest probability of Keith's having written such letters; and Denham laughed at Keith's giving a letter of credit, having, as he said, no credit to give.

Franklin was stranded, alone and almost penniless, in London. When seven years old he had been given pennies on a holiday and foolishly gave them all to another boy in exchange for a whistle which pleased his fancy. Mortified by the ridicule of his brothers and sisters, he afterwards made a motto for himself, "Don't give too much for the whistle." More than fifty years afterwards, when minister to France, he turned the whistle story into a little essay which delighted all Paris, and "Don't give too much for the whistle" became a cant saying in both Europe and America. He seldom forgot a lesson of experience ; and, though he says but little about it, the Keith episode, like the expensive whistle, must have made a deep impression on him and sharpened his wits.

His life in London may be said to have been a rather evil one. He forgot Miss Read ; his companion, Ralph, forgot the wife and child he had left in Philadelphia, and kept borrowing money from him, as Collins had done. Franklin wrote a small pamphlet about this time, which he printed for himself and called "A Dissertation on Liberty and Necessity, Pleasure and Pain." It was an argument in favor of fatalism, and while acknowledging the existence of God, it denied the immortality of the soul; suggesting, however, as a possibility, that there might be a transmigration of souls. It was a clever performance in its way, with much of the power of expression and brightness which were afterwards so characteristic of him ; but in later years he regretted having published such notions.

He sums up his argument on Liberty and Necessity as follows :

"When the Creator first designed the universe, either it was his will and intention that all things should exist and be in the manner they are at this time ; or it was his will they should be otherwise, i.e. in a different manner : To say it was his will things should be otherwise than they are is to say somewhat hath contracted his will and broken his measures, which is impossible because inconsistent with his power ; therefore we must allow that all things exist now in a manner agreeable to his will, and in consequence of that are all equally good, and therefore equally esteemed by him."

His argument, though shorter, is almost precisely the same as that with which Jonathan Edwards afterwards began his famous essay against the freedom of the will, and it is strange that Franklin's biographers have not claimed that he anticipated Edwards. But, so far as Franklin is concerned, it is probable that he was only using ideas that were afloat in the philosophy of the time ; the two men were merely elaborating an argument and dealing with a metaphysical problem as old as the human mind. But Edwards carried the train of thought far beyond Franklin, and added the doctrine of election, while Franklin contented himself with establishing to his own satisfaction the very ancient proposition that there can be no freedom of the will, and that God must be the author of evil as well as of good.

In the second part of his pamphlet, "Pleasure and Pain," he argues that pleasure and pain are exactly equal, because pain or uneasiness produces a desire to be freed from it, and the accomplishment of this desire produces a corresponding pleasure. His argument on this, as well as on the first half of his subject, when we consider that he was a mere boy, is very interesting. He had picked up by reading and conversation a large part of the philosophy that permeated the mental atmosphere of the time, and his keen observation of life and of his own consciousness supplied the rest.

" It will possibly be objected here, that even common Experience shows us, there is not in Fact this Equality : Some we see hearty, brisk and cheerful perpetually, while others are constantly burden'd with a heavy ' Load of Maladies and Misfortunes, remaining for Years perhaps in Poverty, Disgrace, or Pain, and die at last without any Appearance of Recompence.' . . . And here let it be observed, that we cannot be proper Judges of the good or bad Fortune of Others ; we are apt to imagine, that what would give us a great Uneasiness or a great Satisfaction, has the same Effect upon others ; we think, for instance, those unhappy, who must depend upon Charity for a mean Subsistence, who go in Rags, fare hardly, and are despis'd and scorn'd by all ; not considering that Custom renders all these Things easy, familiar, and even pleasant. When we see Riches, Grandeur and a chearful Countenance, we easily imagine Happiness accompanies them, when often times 'tis quite otherwise : Nor is a constantly sorrowful Look, attended with continual Complaints, an infallible Indication of Unhappiness. . . . Besides some take a Satisfaction in being thought unhappy, (as others take a Pride in being thought humble,) these will paint their Misfortunes to others in the strongest Colours, and leave no Means unus'd to make you think them thoroughly miserable ; so great a Pleasure it is to them to be pitied ; Others retain the form and outside Shew or Sorrow, long after the thing itself, with its Cause, is remov'd from the Mind ; it is a Habit they have acquired and cannot leave."

A very sharp insight into human nature is shown in this passage, and it is not surprising that the boy who wrote it afterwards became a mover of men. His mind was led to the subject by being employed to print a book which was very famous in its day, called "The Religion of Nature Delineated." He disliked its arguments, and must needs refute them by his pamphlet "Liberty and Necessity," which was certainly a most vigorous mental discipline for him, although he was afterwards dissatisfied with its negative conclusions.

Obscure and poor as he was, he instinctively seized on everything that would contribute to his education and enlargement of mind. He made the acquaintance of a bookseller, who agreed for a small compensation to lend him books. His pamphlet on Liberty and Necessity brought him to the notice of Dr. Lyons, author of "The Infallibility of Human Judgment," who took him to an ale-house called The Horns, where a sort of club of free-thinkers assembled. There he met Dr. Mandeville, who wrote "The Fable of the Bees." Lyons also introduced him to Dr. Pemberton, who promised to give him an opportunity of seeing Sir Isaac Newton ; but this was never fulfilled.

The conversation of these men, if not edifying in a religious way, was no doubt stimulating to his intelligence. He had brought over with him a purse made of asbestos, and this he succeeded in selling to Sir Hans Sloane, who invited him to his house and showed him his museum of curiosities.

He says of the asbestos purse in his Autobiography that Sir Hans "persuaded me to let him add it to his collection, for which he paid me handsomely." But the persuasion was the other way, for the letter which he wrote to Sir Hans, offering to sell him the purse, has been discovered and printed.

Even the woman he lodged with contributed to his education. She was a clergyman's daughter, had lived much among people of distinction, and knew a thousand anecdotes of them as far back as the time of Charles II. She was lame with the gout, and, seldom going out of her room, liked to have company. Her conversation was so amusing and instructive that he often spent an evening with her; and she, on her part, found the young man so agreeable that after he had engaged a lodging near by for two shillings a week she would not let him go, and agreed to keep him for one and sixpence. So the future economist of two continents enlarged his knowledge and at the same time reduced his board to thirty-seven cents a week.

He certainly needed all the money he could get, for he was helping to support Ralph, who was trying to become a literary man and gradually degenerating into a political hack. Ralph made the acquaintance of a young milliner who lodged in the same house with them. She had known better days and was genteelly bred, but before long she became Ralph's mistress.

Ralph went into the country to look for employment at school-teaching, and left his mistress in Franklin's care. As she had lost friends and employment by her association with Ralph, she was soon in need of money, and borrowed from Franklin. Presuming on her dependent position, he attempted liberties with her, and was repulsed with indignation.

Ralph hearing of it on his return, informed him that their friendship was at an end and all obligations cancelled. This precluded Franklin's hope of being repaid the money he had lent, but it had the advantage of putting a stop to further lending.

For a year and a half he lived in London, still keeping up his reading, but also going to the theatres and meeting many odd characters and a few distinguished ones. It was an experience which at least enlarged his mind if it did not improve his morals. He eventually became very tired of London, longing for the simple pleasures and happy days he had enjoyed in Pennsylvania, and he seized the first opportunity to return. Mr. Denham, the Quaker merchant who had come over in the same ship with him, was about to return, and offered to employ him as clerk. He eagerly accepted the offer, helped his benefactor to buy and pack his supply of goods, and landed again in Philadelphia in the autumn of 1726.

Keith was no longer governor. Miss Read, despairing of Franklin's return, had yielded to the persuasions of her family and married a potter named Rogers, and Keimer seemed to be prospering. But the young printer was in a business that he liked. He was devoted to Mr. Denham, with whom his prospects were excellent, and he thought himself settled at last. In a few months, however, both he and Mr. Denham were taken with the pleurisy. Mr. Denham died, and Franklin, fully expecting to die, made up his mind to it like a philosopher who believed that there was nothing beyond the grave. He was rather disappointed, he tells us, when he got well, for all the troublesome business of resignation would some day have to be done over again.

Finding himself on his recovery without employment, he went back again to work at his old trade with Keimer, and before long was in business for himself with a partner. He had never paid Mr. Vernon the money he had collected for him; but, fortunately, Mr. Vernon was easy with him, and, except for worrying over this very serious debt and the loss of Miss Read, Franklin began to do fairly well, and his self-education was continued in earnest.

It was about this time that he founded the club called the Junto, which he has described as " the best school of philosophy, morality, and politics that then existed in the province."

This description was true enough, but was not very high praise, for at that time Pennsylvania had no college, and the schools for children were mostly of an elementary kind. Franklin, in making this very sweeping assertion, may have intended one of his deep, sly jokes. It was the only school of philosophy in the province, and in that sense undoubtedly the best.

It was a sort of small debating club, in which the members educated one another by discussion; and Franklin's biographer, Parton, supposes that it was in part suggested by Cotton Mather's benefit societies, which were well known in Boston when Franklin was a boy.

The first members of the Junto were eleven in number, young workmen like Franklin, four of them being printers. The others were Joseph Brient-nal, a copier of deeds; Thomas Godfrey, a self-taught mathematician, inventor of the quadrant now known as Hadley's; Nicholas Scull; William Parsons, a shoe-maker; William Maugridge, a carpenter; William Coleman, a merchant's clerk; and Robert Grace, a witty, generous young gentleman of some fortune. The Junto was popularly known as the Leather-Apron Club, and Franklin has told us in his Auto-biography of its methods and rules:

"We met on Friday evenings. The rules that I drew up required that every member, in his turn, should produce one or more queries on any point of Morals, Politics, or Natural Philosophy, to be dis-cuss'd by the company; and once in three months produce and read an essay of his own writing, on any subject he pleased. Our debates were to be under the direction of a president, and to be conducted in the sincere spirit of inquiry after truth, without fondness for dis-pute, or desire of victory; and, to prevent warmth, all expressions of positiveness in opinions, or direct contradiction, were after some time made contraband, and prohibited under small pecuniary penal-ties."

From other sources we learn that when a new member was initiated he stood up and, with his hand on his breast, was asked the following questions:

"1. Have you any particular disrespect to any present member? Answer: I have not.

"2. Do you sincerely declare that you love mankind in general of what profession or religion soever? Answer: I do.

"3. Do you think any person ought to be harmed in his body, name, or goods for mere speculative opinions or his external way of worship? Answer: No.

"4. Do you love truth for truth's sake, and will you endeavor impartially to find and receive it yourself and communicate it to others? Answer: Yes."

At every meeting certain questions were read, with a pause after each one ; and these questions might very well have been suggested by those of the Mather benefit societies. The first six are sufficient to give an idea of them all :

"1. Have you met with anything in the author you last read, remarkable or suitable to be communicated to the Junto, particularly in history, morality, poetry, physic, travels, mechanic arts, or other parts of knowledge?

"2. What new story have you lately heard, agreeable for telling in conversation?

"3. Hath any citizen in your knowledge failed in his business lately, and what have you heard of the cause?

"4. Have you lately heard of any citizen's thriving well, and by what means?

"5. Have you lately heard how any present rich man, here or elsewhere, got his estate?

"6. Do you know of a fellow-citizen, who has lately done a worthy action, deserving praise and imitation ; or who has lately committed an error, proper for us to be warned against and avoid?"

The number of members was limited to twelve, and Franklin always opposed an increase. Instead of adding to the membership, he suggested that each member form a similar club, and five or six were thus organized, with such names as The Vine, The Union, The Band. The original club is said to have continued for forty years. But it did not keep up its old character. Its original purpose had been to educate its members, to supply the place of the modern academy or college ; but when the members became older and their education more complete, they cared no longer for self-imposed tasks of essay-writing and formal debate on set questions. They turned it into a social club, or, rather, they dropped its educational and continued its social side, —for it had always been social, and even convivial, which was one of the means adopted for keeping the members together and rendering their studies easy and pleasant.

A list of some of the questions discussed by the Junto has been preserved, from which a few are given as specimens :

"Is sound an entity or body?

"How may the phenomena of vapors be explained?

"Is self-interest the rudder that steers mankind?

"Which is the best form of government, and what was that form which first prevailed among mankind?

"Can any one particular form of government suit all mankind?

"What is the reason that the tides rise higher in the Bay of Fundy than in the Bay of Delaware?"

The young men who every Friday evening debated such questions as these were certainly acquiring an education which was not altogether an inferior substitute for that furnished by our modern institutions endowed with millions of dollars and officered by plodding professors prepared by years of exhaustive study. But the plodding professors and the modern institutions are necessary, because young men, as a rule, cannot educate themselves. The Junto could not have existed without Franklin. He inspired and controlled it. His personality and energy pervaded it, and the eleven other members were but clay in his hands. His rare precocity and enthusiasm inspired a love for and an interest in study which money, apparatus, and professors often fail to arouse.

The Junto debated the question of paper money, which was then agitating the Province of Pennsylvania, and Franklin was led to write and publish a pamphlet called "A Modest Inquiry into the Nature and Necessity of a Paper Currency," a very crude performance, showing the deficiencies of his self-education. The use of the word modest in the title was in pursuance of the shrewd plan he had adopted of affecting great humility in the expression of his opinions. But his description in his Autobiography of the effect of this pamphlet is by no means either modest or humble :

" It was well received by the common people in general ; but the rich men disliked it, for it increased and strengthened the clamor for more money, and they happening to have no writers among them that were able to answer it their opposition slackened, and the point was carried by a majority in the House."

In other words, he implies that the boyish debate of twelve young workingmen, resulting in the publication of a pamphlet by one of them, was the means of passing the Pennsylvania paper-money act of 1729. His biographers have echoed his pleasant delusion, and this pamphlet, which in reality contains some of the most atrocious fallacies in finance and political economy, has been lauded as a wonder, the beginning of modern political economy, and the source from which Adam Smith stole the material for his "Wealth of Nations."*

In spite of all his natural brightness and laudable

---

* Pennsylvania : Colony and Commonwealth, p. 80.

efforts for his own improvement, he was but half educated and full of crude enthusiasm. He was only twenty-three, and nothing more, could be expected.

Fifteen or twenty years afterwards, with added experience, Franklin became a very different sort of person. The man of forty, laboriously investigating science, discovering the secrets of electricity, and rejecting everything that had not been subjected to the most rigid proof, bore but little resemblance to the precocious youth of twenty-three, the victim of any specious sophism that promised a millennium. But he never fully apologized to the world for his paper-money delusion, contenting himself with saying in his Autobiography, "I now think there are limits beyond which the quantity may be hurtful."

Three years after the publication of his pamphlet on paper money he began to study modern languages, and soon learned to read French, Italian, and Spanish. An acquaintance who was also studying Italian often tempted him to play chess. As this interfered with the Italian studies, Franklin arranged with him that the victor in any game should have the right to impose a task, either in grammar or translation; and as they played equally, they beat each other into a knowledge of the language.

After he had become tolerably well acquainted with these modern languages he happened one day to look into a Latin Testament, and found that he could read it more easily than he had supposed. The modern languages had, he thought, smoothed the way for him, and he immediately began to study Latin, which had been dropped ever since, as a little boy, he had spent a year in the Boston Grammar School.

From this circumstance he jumped to the conclusion that the usual method pursued in schools of studying Latin before the modern languages was all wrong. It would be better, he said, to begin with the French, proceed to the Italian, and finally reach the Latin. This would be beginning with the easiest first, and would also have the advantage that if the pupils should quit the study of languages, and never arrive at the Latin, they would have acquired another tongue or two which, being in modern use, might be serviceable to them in after-life.

This suggestion, though extravagantly praised, has never been adopted, for the modern languages are now taught contemporaneously with Latin. It was an idea founded exclusively on a single and very unusual experience, without any test as to its general applicability. But all Franklin's notions of education were extremely radical, because based on his own circumstances, which were not those of the ordinary youth, to whom all systems of education have to be adapted.

He wished to entirely abolish Latin and Greek. They had been useful, he said, only in the past, when they were the languages of the learned and when all books of science and important knowledge were written in them. At that time there had been a reason for learning them, but that reason had now passed away. English should be substituted for

them, and its systematic study would give the same
knowledge of language-structure and the same mental training that were supposed to be attainable only
through Latin and Greek. His own self-education
had been begun in English. He had analyzed and
rewritten the essays in Addison's *Spectator*, and,
believing that in this way he had acquired his own
most important mental training, he concluded that
the same method should be imposed on every one.
He wished to set up the study of that author and
of Pope, Milton, and Shakespeare as against Cicero,
Virgil, and Homer.

One of our most peculiar American habits is
that every one who has a pet fancy or experience
immediately wants it adopted into the public school
system.   We not uncommonly close our explanation of something that strikes us as very important
by declaring, "and I would have it taught in the
public schools." It has even been suggested that
the game of poker should be taught as tending to
develop shrewdness and observation.

Franklin's foundation for all education was English.   He would have also French, German, or
Italian, and practical subjects,—natural science, as-
tronomy, history, government, athletic sports, good
manners, good morals, and other topics ; for when
one is drawing up these ideal schemes without a
particle of practical experience in teaching it is so
easy to throw in one thing after another which seems
noble or beautiful for boys and girls to know.   But
English he naturally thought from his own experience was the gate-way to everything.

In the course of his life Franklin received the honorary degree of doctor of laws from Harvard, Yale, Oxford, Edinburgh, and St. Andrew's, and he founded a college. It has been said in support of his peculiar theories of education that when, in 1776, the Continental Congress, which was composed largely of college graduates, was considering who should be sent as commissioner to France, the only member who knew enough of the language to be thoroughly eligible was the one who had never been near a college except to receive honorary degrees for public services he had performed without the assistance of a college training.

This is, of course, an interesting statement; but as an argument it is of no value. Franklin could read French, but could not speak it, and he had to learn to do so after he reached France. By his own confession he never was able to speak it well, and disregarded the grammar altogether,—a natural consequence of being self-taught. John Adams and other members of the Congress could read French as well as Franklin; and when, in their turn, they went to France, they learned to speak it as fluently as he.

In 1743 Franklin attempted to establish an academy in Philadelphia. The higher education was very much neglected at that time in the middle colonies. The nearest colleges were Harvard and Yale, far to the north in New England, and William and Mary, far to the south in Virginia. The Presbyterians had a few good schools in Pennsylvania of almost the grade of academies, but none in

Philadelphia. The Quakers, as a class, were not interested in colleges or universities, and confined their efforts to elementary schools. People were alarmed at the ignorance in which not only the masses but even the sons of the best citizens were growing up, and it was the general opinion that those born in the colony were inferior in intelligence to their fathers who had emigrated from England.

Franklin's efforts failed in 1743 because there was much political agitation in the province and because of the preparations for the war with Spain in which England was about to engage ; but in 1749 he renewed his attempt, and was successful. He was then a man of forty-three, had been married thirteen years, and had children, legitimate and illegitimate, to be educated. The Junto supported him, and in aid of his plan he wrote a pamphlet called "Proposals relating to the Education of Youth in Pennsylvania."

In this pamphlet he could not set forth his extreme views of education because even the most liberal people in the town were not in favor of them. Philadelphia was at that time the home of liberal ideas in the colonies. Many people were in favor of altering the old system of education and teaching science and other practical subjects in addition to Latin and Greek ; but they did not favor abolishing the study of these languages, and they could not see the necessity of making English so all-important as Franklin wished. He was compelled, therefore, to conform his arguments to the opinions of those from whom he expected subscriptions, and he did this with his usual discretion, making, however, the English branches as important as was possible under the circumstances.

The result of the pamphlet was that five thousand pounds were subscribed, and the academy started within a year, occupying a large building on Fourth Street, south of Arch, which had been built for the use of George Whitefield, the famous English preacher. It supplied a real need of the community and had plenty of pupils. Within six years it obtained a charter from the proprietors of the province, and became a college, with an academy and a charitable school annexed.

A young Scotchman, the Rev. William Smith, was appointed to govern the institution, and was called the provost. He had very advanced opinions on education, holding much the same views as were expressed in Franklin's proposals ; but he was not in accord with Franklin's extreme ideas.* Those who intended to become lawyers, doctors, or clergymen should be taught to walk in the old paths and to study Latin and Greek ; but the rest were to be deluged with a knowledge of accounts, mathematics, oratory, poetry, chronology, history, natural and mechanic philosophy, agriculture, ethics, physics, chemistry, anatomy, modern languages, fencing, dancing, religion, and everything else that by any chance might be useful.

Thus the academy founded by Franklin became

* Pennsylvania : Colony and Commonwealth, p. 141.

the College of Philadelphia, and as managed by Provost Smith it was a very good one and played a most interesting part in the life and politics of the colony. Its charter was revoked and its property confiscated during the Revolution, and another college was created, called the University of the State of Pennsylvania, which was worthless. Eleven years afterwards the old college was restored to its rights, and soon after that it was combined with the State University, and the union of the two produced the present University of Pennsylvania.* It should, however, have been called Franklin University, which would have been in every way a better name.

---

* **Pennsylvania :** Colony and Commonwealth, pp. 374–377, 381.

III

RELIGION AND MORALS

FRANKLIN'S father and mother were Massachusetts Puritans who, while not conspicuously religious, attended steadily to their religious duties. They lived in Milk Street, Boston, near the Old South Church, and little Benjamin was carried across the street the day he was born and baptized in that venerable building.

He was born on Sunday, January 6, 1706 (Old Style), and if it had occurred in one of the Massachusetts towns where the minister was very strict, baptism might have been refused, for some of the Puritans were so severe in their views of Sabbath-keeping that they said a child born on the Sabbath must have been conceived on the Sabbath, and was therefore hopelessly unregenerate.*

These good men would have found their theory fully justified in Franklin, for he became a terrible example of the results of Sabbath birth and begetting. As soon as opportunity offered he became a most persistent Sabbath-breaker. While he lived with his parents he was compelled to go to church; but when apprenticed to his elder brother, and living away from home, he devoted Sunday to reading and

---

* Men, Women, and Manners in Colonial Times, vol. i. p. 210.

study. He would slip off to the printing-office and spend nearly the whole day there alone with his books; and during a large part of his life Sunday was to him a day precious for its opportunities for study rather than for its opportunities for worship.

His persistence in Sabbath-breaking was fortified by his entire loss of faith in the prevailing religion.

"I had been religiously educated as a Presbyterian; and tho' some of the dogmas of that persuasion, such as *the eternal decrees of God, election, reprobation,* etc., appeared to me unintelligible, others doubtful, and I early absented myself from the public assemblies of the sect, Sunday being my studying day, I never was without some religious principles. I never doubted, for instance, the existence of the Deity; that he made the world and governed it by his Providence; that the most acceptable service of God was the doing good to man; that our souls are immortal; and that all crime will be punished and virtue rewarded, either here or hereafter." (Bigelow's Works of Franklin, vol. i. p. 172.)

It will be observed that he speaks of himself as having been educated a Presbyterian, a term which in his time was applied to the Puritans of Massachusetts. We find Thomas Jefferson also describing the New Englanders as Presbyterians, and in colonial times the Quakers in Pennsylvania used the same term when speaking of them. But they were not Presbyterians in the sense in which the word is now used, and their religion is usually described as Congregationalism.

In the earlier part of his Autobiography Franklin describes more particularly how he was led away from the faith of his parents. Among his father's books were some sermons delivered on the Boyle foundation, which was a fund established at Oxford,

England, by Robert Boyle for the purpose of having discourses delivered to prove the truth of Christianity. Franklin read some of these sermons when he was only fifteen years old, and was very much interested in the attacks made in them on the deists, the forerunners of the modern Unitarians. He thought that the arguments of the deists which were quoted to be refuted were much stronger than the attempts to refute them.

Shaftesbury and Collins were the most famous deistical writers of that time. Their books were in effect a denial of the miraculous part of Christianity, and whoever accepted their arguments was left with a belief only in God and the immortality of the soul, with Christianity a code of morals and beautiful sentiments instead of a revealed religion. From reading quotations from these authors Franklin was soon led to read their works entire, and they profoundly interested him. Like their successors, the Unitarians, they were full of religious liberty and liberal, broad ideas on all subjects, and Franklin's mind tended by nature in that direction.

It seems that Franklin's brother James was also a liberal. He had been employed to print a little newspaper, called the *Boston Gazette*, and when this work was taken from him, he started a newspaper of his own, called the *New England Courant*. His apprentice, Benjamin, delivered copies of it to the subscribers, and before long began to write for it.

The *Courant*, under the guidance of James Franklin and his friends, devoted itself to ridiculing the

government and religion of Massachusetts. A description of it, supposed to have been written by
Cotton Mather, tells us that it was "full-freighted
with nonsense, unmanliness, raillery, profaneness,
immorality, arrogance, calumnies, lies, contradic-
tions, and what not, all tending to quarrels and
divisions and to debauch and corrupt the minds
and manners of New England." Among other
things, the *Courant*, as Increase Mather informs us,
was guilty of saying that "if the ministers of God
approve of a thing, it is a sign it is of the devil;
which is a horrid thing to be related." Its printer
and editor was warned that he would soon, though
a young man, have to appear before the judgment-
seat of God to answer for things so vile and abomi-
nable.

Some of the Puritan ministers, under the lead of
Cotton Mather, were at that time trying to introduce
inoculation as a preventive of small-pox, and for
this the *Courant* attacked them. It attempted to
make a sensation out of everything. Increase
Mather boasted that he had ceased to take it. To
which the *Courant* replied that it was true he was
no longer a subscriber, but that he sent his grandson every week to buy it. It was a sensational
journal, and probably the first of its kind in this
country. People bought and read it for the sake
of its audacity. It was an instance of liberalism
gone mad and degenerated into mere radicalism and
negation.

Some of the articles attributed to Franklin, and
which were in all probability written by him, were

violent attacks on Harvard College, setting forth
the worthlessness of its stupid graduates, nearly all
of whom went into the Church, which is described
as a temple of ambition and fraud controlled by
money.   There is a touch of what would now be
called Socialism or Populism in these articles, and
it is not surprising to find the author of them afterwards writing a pamphlet in favor of an inflated
paper currency.

The government of Massachusetts allowed the
Courant to run its wicked course for about a year,
and then fell upon it, imprisoning James Franklin for
a month in the common jail.   Benjamin conducted
the journal during the imprisonment of his brother,
who was not released until he had humbly apologized.   The *Courant* then went on, and was worse
than ever, until an order of council was issued for-
bidding its publication, because it had mocked religion, brought the Holy Scriptures into contempt,
and profanely abused the faithful ministers of God,
as well as His Majesty's government and the government of the province.

The friends of James Franklin met and decided
that they would evade the order of council.   James
would no longer print the paper, but it should be
issued in the name of Benjamin.   So Benjamin's
papers of apprenticeship were cancelled, lest it should
be said that James was still publishing the paper
through his apprentice.   And, in order to retain
Benjamin's services, James secured from him secret
articles of apprenticeship.   A little essay on " Hat
Honor" which appeared in the *Courant* soon after-

wards is supposed to have been written by Benjamin and is certainly in his style.

> " In old Time it was no disrespect for Men and Women to be called by their own Names : *Adam* was never called *Master* Adam ; we never read of Noah *Esquire*, Lot *Knight* and *Baronet*, nor the *Right Honourable* Abraham, Viscount of Mesopotamia, *Baron* of Canaan ; no, no, they were plain Men, honest Country Grasiers, that took care of their Families and Flocks. Moses was a great Prophet, and *Aaron* a priest of the Lord ; but we never read of the. *Reverend* Moses, nor the Right Reverend Father in God Aaron, by Divine Providence, *Lord Arch-Bishop* of Israel ; Thou never sawest *Madam* Rebecca in the Bible, my *Lady* Rachel : nor Mary, tho' a Princess of the Blood after the death of *Joseph*, called the Princess Dowager of Nazareth."

This was funny, irreverent, and reckless, and shows a mind entirely out of sympathy with its surroundings. In after-years Franklin wrote several humorous parodies on the Scriptures, but none that was quite so shocking to religious people as this one.

The *Courant*, however, was not again molested ; but Franklin quarrelled with his brother James, and was severely beaten by him. Feeling that James dare not make public the secret articles of apprenticeship, he resolved to leave him, and was soon on his way to Philadelphia, as has been already related.

He had been at war with the religion of his native province, and, though not yet eighteen years old, had written most violent attacks upon it. It is not likely that he would have prospered if he had remained in Boston, for the majority of the people were against him and he was entirely out of sympathy with the prevailing tone of thought. He would have become

a social outcast devoted to mere abuse and negation. A hundred years afterwards the little party
of deists who gave support to the *Courant* increased
so rapidly that their opinions, under the name of
Unitarianism, became the most influential religion
of Massachusetts.* If Franklin had been born in
that later time he would doubtless have grown and
flourished on his native soil along with Emerson
and Channing, Lowell and Holmes, and with them
have risen to greatness. But previous to the Revolution his superb faculties, which required the
utmost liberty for their expansion, would have been
starved and stunted in the atmosphere of intolerance
and repression which prevailed in Massachusetts.

After he left Boston, his dislike for the religion of
that place, and, indeed, for all revealed religion,
seems to have increased. In London we find him
writing the pamphlet "Liberty and Necessity,"
described in the previous chapter, and adopting what
was in effect the position of Voltaire,—namely, an
admission of the existence of some sort of God,
but a denial of the immortality of the soul. He
went even beyond Voltaire in holding that, inasmuch as God was omnipotent and all-wise, and had
created the universe, whatever existed must be right,
and vice and virtue were empty distinctions.

I have already told how this pamphlet brought
him to the notice of a certain Dr. Lyons, who had
himself written a sceptical book, and who introduced
Franklin to other philosophers of the same sort who

---

* Men, Women, and Manners in Colonial Times, vol. i. p. 222.

met at an inn called The Horns. But, in spite of their influence, Franklin began to doubt the principles he had laid down in his pamphlet. He had gone so far in negation that a reaction was started in his mind. He tore up most of the hundred copies of "Liberty and Necessity," believing it to be of an evil tendency. Like most of his writings, however, it possessed a vital force of its own, and some one printed a second edition of it.

His morals at this time were, according to his own account, fairly good. He asserts that he was neither dishonest nor unjust, and we can readily believe him, for these were not faults of his character. In his Autobiography he says that he passed through this dangerous period of his life "without any willful gross immorality or injustice that might have been expected from my want of religion." In the first draft of the Autobiography he added, "some foolish intrigues with low women excepted, which from the expense were rather more prejudicial to me than to them." But in the revision these words were crossed out.*

On the voyage from London to Philadelphia he kept a journal, and in it entered a plan which he had formed for regulating his future conduct, no doubt after much reflection while at sea. Towards the close of his life he said of it, "It is the more remarkable as being formed when I was so young and yet being pretty faithfully adhered to quite thro' to old age." This plan was not found in the

---

* Bigelow's Works of Franklin, vol. i. p. 180.

journal, but a paper which is supposed to contain it was discovered and printed by Parton in his "Life of Franklin." It recommends extreme frugality until he can pay his debts, truth-telling, sincerity, devotion to business, avoidance of all projects for becoming suddenly rich, with a resolve to speak ill of no man, but rather to excuse faults. Revealed religion had, he says, no weight with him; but he had become convinced that "truth, sincerity, and integrity in dealings between man and man were of the utmost importance to the felicity of life."

Although revealed religion seemed of no importance to him, he had begun to think that, "though certain actions might not be bad because they were forbidden by it, or good because it commanded them, yet probably those actions might be forbidden because they were bad for us or commanded because they were beneficial to us in their own natures, all the circumstances of things considered."

It was in this way that he avoided and confuted his own argument in the pamphlet "Liberty and Necessity." He had maintained in it that God must necessarily have created both good and evil. And as he had created evil, it could not be considered as something contrary to his will, and therefore forbidden and wrong in the sense in which it is usually described. If it was contrary to his will it could not exist, for it was impossible to conceive of an omnipotent being allowing anything to exist contrary to his will, and least of all anything which was evil as well as contrary to his will. What we call evil, therefore, must be no worse than good, because both are created by an all-wise, omnipotent being.

This argument has puzzled many serious and earnest minds in all ages, and Franklin could never entirely give it up. But he avoided it by saying that "probably" certain actions "might be forbidden," because, "all the circumstances of things considered," they were bad for us, or they might be commanded because they were beneficial to us. In other words, God created evil as well as good ; but for some reason which we do not understand he has forbidden us to do evil and has commanded us to do good. Or, he has so arranged things that what we call evil is injurious to us and what we call good is beneficial to us.

This was his eminently practical way of solving the great problem of the existence of evil. It will be said, of course, that it was simply exchanging one mystery for another, and that one was as incomprehensible as the other. To which he would probably have replied that his mystery was the pleasanter one, and, being less of an empty, dry negation and giving less encouragement to vice, was more comforting to live under, "all the circumstances of things considered."

He says that he felt himself the more confirmed in this course because his old friends Collins and Ralph, whom he had perverted to his first way of thinking, went wrong, and injured him greatly without the least compunction. He also recollected the contemptible conduct of Governor Keith towards him, and Keith was another free-thinker. His own conduct while under the influence of arguments like those in "Liberty and Necessity" had been by no means above reproach. He had wronged Miss Read, whose affections he had won, and he had embezzled Mr. Vernon's money. So he began to suspect, he tells us, that his early doctrine, "tho' it might be true, was not very useful."

When back again in Philadelphia and beginning to prosper a little, he set himself more seriously to the task of working out some form of religion that would suit him. He must needs go to the bottom of the subject ; and in this, as in other matters, nothing satisfied him unless he had made it himself. In the year 1728, when he was twenty-two years old, he framed a creed, a most curious compound, which can be given no other name than Franklin's creed.

Having rejected his former negative belief as not sufficiently practical for his purposes, and having once started creed-building, he was led on into all sorts of ideas, which it must be confessed were no better than those of older creed-makers, and as difficult to believe as anything in revealed religion. But he would have none but his own, and its preparation was, of course, part of that mental training which, consciously or unconsciously, was going on all the time.

He began by saying that he believed in one Supreme Being, the author and father of the gods,— for in his system there were beings superior to man, though inferior to God. These gods, he thought, were probably immortal, or possibly were changed and others put in their places. Each of them had a glorious sun, attended by a beautiful and admirable system of planets. God the Infinite Father, required no praise or worship from man, being infinitely above it; but as there was a natural principle in man which inclined him to devotion, it seemed right that he should worship something.

He went on to say that God had in him some of the human passions, and was "not above caring for us, being pleased with our praise and offended when we slight him or neglect his glory;" which was a direct contradiction of what he had previously said about the Creator being infinitely above praise or worship. "As I should be happy," says this bumptious youth of twenty-two, "to have so wise, good, and powerful a Being my friend, let me consider in what manner I shall make myself most acceptable to him."

This good and powerful Being would, he thought, be delighted to see him virtuous, because virtue makes men happy, and the great Being would be pleased to see him happy. So he constructed a sort of liturgy, prefacing it with the suggestion that he ought to begin it with "a countenance that expresses a filial respect, mixed with a kind of smiling that signifies inward joy and satisfaction and admiration,"—a piece of formalism which was rather worse than anything that has been invented by the ecclesiastics he so much despised. At one point in the liturgy he was to sing Milton's hymn to the Creator; at another point "to read part of some such book as Ray's Wisdom of God in the Creation, or

Blackmore on the Creation." Then followed his prayers, of which the following are specimens :

"O Creator, O Father, I believe that thou art Good, and that thou art pleased with the pleasure of thy children.
"Praised be thy name for ever."

. . . .

"That I may be preserved from Atheism, and Infidelity, Impiety and Profaneness, and in my Addresses to thee carefully avoid Irreverence and Ostentation, Formality and odious Hypocrisy.
"Help me, O Father.
"That I may be just in all my Dealings and temperate in my pleasures, full of Candour and Ingenuity, Humanity and Benevolence.
"Help me, O Father."

He was doing the best he could, poor boy! but as a writer of liturgies he was not a success. His own liturgy, however, seems to have suited him, and it is generally supposed that he used it for a great many years, probably until he was forty years old. He had it all written out in a little volume, which was, in truth, Franklin's prayer-book in the fullest sense of the word.

Later in life he appears to have dropped the eccentric parts of it and confined himself to a more simple statement. At exactly what period he made this change is not known. But when he was eighty-four years old, and within a few weeks of his death, Ezra Stiles, the President of Yale College, in a letter asking him to sit for his portrait for the college, requested his opinion on religion. In his reply Franklin said, that as to the portrait he was willing it should be painted, but the artist should waste no time, or the man of eighty-four might slip through his fingers. He then gave his creed, which was that there was one God, who governed the world, who should be worshipped, to whom the most acceptable service was doing good to man, and who would deal justly with the immortal souls of men.

"As to Jesus of Nazareth, my opinion of whom you particularly desire, I think his system of morals and his religion, as he left them to us, the best the world ever saw, or is like to see ; but I apprehend it has received various corrupting changes, and I have, with most of the present Dissenters in England, some doubts as to his Divinity ; though it is a question I do not dogmatize upon, having never studied it, and think it needless to busy myself with it now, when I expect soon an opportunity of knowing the truth with less trouble. I see no harm, however, in its being believed, if that belief has the good consequence, as probably it has, of making his doctrines more respected and more observed ; especially as I do not perceive that the Supreme takes it amiss, by distinguishing the unbelievers in his government of the world with any peculiar marks of his displeasure.

"I shall only add, respecting myself, having experienced the goodness of that Being in conducting me prosperously through a long life, I have no doubt of its continuance in the next, though without the smallest conceit of meriting such goodness.

"P. S. I confide, that you will not expose me to criticisms and censures by publishing any part of this communication to you. I have ever let others enjoy their religious sentiments, without reflecting on them for those that appeared to me unsupportable or even absurd. All sects here, and we have a great variety, have experienced my good will in assisting them with subscriptions for the building their new places of worship ; and, as I have never opposed any of their doctrines, I hope to go out of the world in peace with them all."

So Franklin's belief at the close of his life was deism, which was the same faith that he had professed when a boy. From boyish deism he had passed to youthful negation, and from negation returned to deism again. He also in his old age argued out his belief in immortality from the operations he had observed in nature, where nothing is lost; why then should the soul not live?

In the convention that framed the National Constitution in 1787, when there was great conflict of opinion among the members and it seemed doubtful whether an agreement could be reached, he moved that prayers be said by some clergyman every morning, but the motion was lost. In a general way he professed to favor all religions. A false religion, he said, was better than none; for if men were so bad with religion, what would they be without it?

Commenting on the death of his brother John, he said,—

"He who plucks out a tooth, parts with it freely, since the pain goes with it; and he who quits the whole body parts at once with all pains, and possibilities of pains and diseases, which it was liable to or capable of making him suffer. Our friend and we were invited abroad on a party of pleasure, which is to last forever. His chair was ready first, and he is gone before us. We could not all conveniently start together; and why should you and I be grieved at this, since we are soon to follow and know where to find him?"

He not infrequently expressed his views on the future life in a light vein:

"With regard to future bliss, I cannot help imagining that multitudes of the zealously orthodox of different sects who at the last day may flock together in hopes of seeing each other damned, will be disappointed and obliged to rest content with their own salvation."

His wife was an Episcopalian, a member of Christ Church in Philadelphia, and he always encouraged her, as well as his daughter, to attend the services of that church.

"Go constantly to church," he wrote to his daughter after he had started on one of his missions to England, "whoever preaches. The act of devotion in the common prayer book is your principal business there, and if properly attended to, will do more towards mending the heart than sermons generally can do. For they were composed by men of much greater piety and wisdom than our common composers of sermons can pretend to be; and therefore, I wish you would never miss the prayer days; yet I do not mean that you should despise sermons even of the preachers you dislike; for the discourse is often much better than the man, as sweet and clear waters come through very dirty earth."

It does not appear that he himself attended the services of Christ Church, for to the end of his life he was always inclined to use Sunday as a day for study, as he had done when a boy. At one time, soon after he had adopted his curious creed, he was prevailed upon to attend the preaching of a Presbyterian minister for five Sundays successively. But finding that this preacher devoted himself entirely to the explanation of doctrine instead of morals, he left him, and returned, he says, to his own little liturgy.

Not long afterwards another Presbyterian preacher, a young man named Hemphill, came to Philadelphia, and as he was very eloquent and expounded morality rather than doctrine, Franklin was completely captivated, and became one of his regular hearers. We would naturally suppose that a Presbyterian minister able to secure the attention of Franklin was not altogether orthodox, and such proved to be the case. He was soon tried by the synod for wandering from the faith. Franklin supported him, wrote pamphlets in his favor, and secured for him the support of others. But it was soon discovered that the sermons of the eloquent young man had all been stolen from a volume published in England. This was, of course, the end of him, and he lost all his adherents except Franklin, who humorously insisted that he "rather approved of his giving us sermons composed by others, than bad ones of his own manufacture; though the latter was the practice of our common teachers."

Whitefield, the great preacher who towards the middle of the eighteenth century started such a revival of religion in all the colonies, was, of course, a man of too much ability to escape the serious regard of Franklin, who relates that he attended one of his sermons, fully resolved not to contribute to the collection at the close of it. "I had in my pocket," he says, "a handful of copper money, three or four silver dollars, and five pistoles in gold. As he proceeded, I began to soften and concluded to give him the copper. Another stroke of his oratory made me ashamed of that, and determined me to give the silver; and he finished so admirably, that I emptied my pocket wholly into the collector's dish, gold and all."

This seems to have been the only time that Franklin was carried away by preaching. On another occasion, when Whitefield was preaching in Market Street, Philadelphia, Franklin, instead of listening to the sermon, employed himself in estimating the size of the crowd and the power of the orator's voice. He had often doubted what he had read of generals haranguing whole armies, but when he found that Whitefield could easily preach to thirty thousand people and be heard by them all, he was less inclined to be incredulous.

He and Whitefield became fast friends, and Whitefield stayed at his house. In replying to his invitation to visit him, Whitefield answered, "If you make that offer for Christ's sake, you will not miss of the reward." To which the philosopher replied, "Don't let me be mistaken; it was not for Christ's sake, but for your sake." Whitefield often prayed for his host's conversion, but "never," says Franklin, "had the satisfaction of believing that his prayers were heard."

He admitted that Whitefield had an enormous influence, and that the light-minded and indifferent became religious as the result of his revivals. Whether the religion thus acquired was really lasting he has not told us. He was the publisher of Whitefield's sermons and journals, of which great numbers were sold; but he thought that their publication was an injury to their author's reputation, which depended principally upon his wonderful voice and delivery. He commented in his bright way on a sentence in the journal which said that there was no difference between a deist and an atheist. "M. B. is a deist," Whitefield said, "I had almost said an atheist." "He might as well have written," said Franklin, "chalk, I had almost said charcoal."

In spite of his deism and his jokes about sacred things, he enjoyed most friendly and even influential relations with religious people, who might have been supposed to have a horror of him. His conciliatory manner, dislike of disputes, and general

philanthropy led each sect to suppose that he was
on its side, and he made a practice of giving money
to them all without distinction. John Adams said
of him,—

"The Catholics thought him almost a Catholic. The Church of
England claimed him as one of them. The Presbyterians thought
him half a Presbyterian, and the Friends believed him a wet
Quaker."

When in England he was the intimate friend of
the Bishop of St. Asaph, stayed at his house, and
corresponded in the most affectionate way with the
bishop's daughters. At the outbreak of the Revolution he was sent to Canada in company with the
Rev. John Carroll, of Maryland, in the hope of winning over that country to the side of the revolted
colonies. His tendency to form strong attachments
for religious people again showed itself, and he and
Carroll, who was a Roman Catholic priest, became
life-long friends. Eight years afterwards, in 1784,
when he was minister to France, finding that the
papal nuncio was reorganizing the Catholic Church
in America, he urged him to make Carroll a bishop.
The suggestion was adopted, and the first Roman
Catholic bishop of the United States owed his elevation to the influence of a deist.

At the same time the members of the Church of
England in the successfully revolted colonies were
adapting themselves to the new order of things; but,
having no bishops, their clergy were obliged to
apply to the English bishops for ordination. They
were, of course, refused, and two of them applied to

Franklin, who was then in Paris, for advice. It was strange that they should have consulted the philosopher, who regarded bishops and ordinations as mere harmless delusions. But he was a very famous man, the popular representative of their country, and of proverbial shrewdness.

He suggested—doubtless with a sly smile—that the Pope's nuncio should ordain them. The nuncio, though their theological enemy, believed in the pretty delusion as well as they, and his ordination would be as valid as that of the Archbishop of Canterbury. He asked the nuncio, with whom he was no doubt on terms of jovial intimacy, if he would do it; but that functionary was of course obliged to say that such a thing was impossible, unless the gentlemen should first become Roman Catholics. So the philosopher had another laugh over the vain controversies of man.

He carried on the joke by telling them to try the Irish bishops, and, if unsuccessful, the Danish and Swedish. If they were refused, which was likely, for human folly was without end, let them imitate the ancient clergy of Scotland, who, having built their Cathedral of St. Andrew, wanted to borrow some bishops from the King of Northumberland to ordain them a bishop for themselves. The king would lend them none. So they laid the mitre, crosier, and robes of a bishop on the altar, and, after earnest prayers for guidance, elected one of their own members. "Arise," they said to him, "go to the altar and receive your office at the hand of God," And thus he became the first bishop of Scotland. "If the British isles," said Franklin, "were sunk in the sea (and the surface of this globe has suffered greater changes) you would probably take some such method as this." And so he went on enlarging on the topic until he had a capital story to tell Madame Helvetius the next time they flirted and dined together in their learned way.

But his most notable escapade in religion, and one in which his sense of humor seems to have failed him, was his abridgment of the Church of England's "Book of Common Prayer." It seems that in the year 1772, while in England as a representative of the colonies, he visited the country-seat of Sir Francis Dashwood, Lord le Despencer, a reformed rake who had turned deist and was taking a gentlemanly interest in religion. He had been, it is said, a companion of John Wilkes, Bubb Doddington, Paul Whitehead, the Earl of Sandwich, and other reckless characters who established themselves as an order of monks at Medmenham Abbey, where they held mock religious ceremonies, and where the trial of the celebrated Chevalier D'Eon was held to prove his disputed sex. An old book, called "Chrysal, or the Adventures of a Guinea," professes to describe the doings of these lively blades.

Lord Despencer and Franklin decided that the prayer-book was entirely too long. Its prolixity kept people from going to church. The aged and infirm did not like to sit so long in cold churches in winter, and even the young and sinful might attend more willingly if the service were shorter.

Franklin was already a dabster at liturgies. Had

he not, when only twenty-two, written his own creed
and liturgy, compounded of mythology and Christianity? and had he not afterwards, as is supposed,
assisted David Williams to prepare the "Apology
for Professing the Religion of Nature," with a most
reasonable and sensible liturgy annexed? Lord
Despencer had also had a little practice in such matters in his mock religious rites at the old abbey.
Franklin, who was very fond of him, tells of the delightful days he spent at his country-seat, and adds,
"But a pleasanter thing is the kind countenance, the
facetious and very intelligent conversation of mine
host, who having been for many years engaged in
public affairs, seen all parts of Europe, and kept the
best company in the world, is himself the best existing." * I have no doubt that his lordship's experience had been a varied one; but it is a question
whether it was of such a character as to fit him for
prayer-book revision. He, however, went seriously
to work, and revised all of the book except the catechism and the reading and singing psalms, which he
requested Franklin to abridge for him.

The copy which this precious pair went over and
marked with a pen is now in the possession of Mr.
Howard Edwards, of Philadelphia, and is a most
interesting relic. From this copy Lord Despencer
had the abridgment printed at his own expense;
but it attracted no attention in England. All references to the sacraments and to the divinity of the
Saviour were, of course, stricken out and short work

---

* Bigelow's Works of Franklin, vol. v. p. 209.

made of the Athanasian and the Apostles' Creed. Even the commandments in the catechism had the pen drawn through them, which was rather inconsistent with the importance that Franklin attached to morals as against dogma. But both editors, no doubt, had painful recollections on this subject ; and as Franklin would have been somewhat embarrassed by the seventh, he settled the question by disposing of them all.

The most curious mutilation, however, was in the Te Deum, most of which was struck out, presumably by Lord Despencer. The Venite was treated in a similar way by Franklin. The beautiful canticle, " All ye Works of the Lord," which is sometimes used in place of the Te Deum, was entirely marked out. As this canticle is the nearest approach in the prayer-book to anything like the religion of nature, it is strange that it should have suffered. But Franklin, though of picturesque life and character, interested in music as a theory, a writer of verse as an exercise, and a lover of the harmony of a delicately balanced prose sentence, had, nevertheless, not the faintest trace of poetry in his nature.

The book, which is now a very rare and costly relic, a single copy selling for over a thousand dollars, was known in America as " Franklin's Prayer-Book," and he was usually credited with the whole revision, although he expressly declared in a letter on the subject that he had abridged only the catechism and the reading and singing psalms. But he seems to have approved of the whole work, for he wrote the preface

MORNING PRAYER.

Priest. Praise ye the Lord.
Answ. The Lord's Name be praised.

¶ *Then shall be said or sung this Psalm following: Except it be Sunday, whereon another Invitatory is appointed; and on the Nineteenth day of every month it is to be read here, but in the ordinary course of this Psalm.*

Venite, exultemus Domino. Psal. 95.

O Come, let us sing unto the Lord: let us heartily rejoice in the strength of our salvation.

Let us come before his presence with thanksgiving: and shew ourselves glad in him with psalms.

For the Lord is a great God

To him bend are all the corners of the earth

O come, let us worship, and fall down: and kneel before the Lord our Maker.

For he is the Lord our God: and we are the people of his

To day if ye will hear his voice, harden not your hearts

When your fathers tempted me: proved me, and saw my works.

Forty years long

Unto whom I sware in my wrath: that they should not enter into my rest.

Glory be to the Father, and to the Son: and to the Holy Ghost;

As it was in the beginning, is now, and ever shall be

Glory

MORNING PRAYER.

Glory be to the Father, and to the Son

Holy Ghost;

As it was in the beginning, is now, and ever shall be

Te Deum laudamus.

WE praise thee, O God: we acknowledge thee to be the Lord.

All the earth doth worship thee: the Father everlasting.

To thee all Angels cry aloud: the Heavens, and all the Powers therein.

To thee Cherubim, and Seraphim: continually do cry,

Holy, Holy, Holy: Lord God of Sabaoth;

Heaven and earth are full of the Majesty: of thy Glory.

The glorious company of the Apostles: praise thee.

The goodly fellowship of the Prophets: praise thee.

The noble army of Martyrs: praise thee.

The holy Church throughout all the world: doth acknowledge thee;

The Father: of an infinite Majesty;

Thine honourable, true: and only Son;

Also the holy Ghost: the Comforter.

Thou art the King of glory: O Christ.

Thou art the everlasting Son: of the Father.

When thou tookest upon thee to deliver man: thou didst not abhor the Virgin's womb.

When thou hadst overcome the sharpness of death: thou didst open the Kingdom of Heaven to all believers.

Thou

which explains the alterations. A few years after the Revolution, when the American Church was re-organizing itself, the "Book of Common Prayer" was revised and abbreviated by competent hands; and from a letter written by Bishop White it would seem that he had examined the "Franklin Prayer-Book," and was willing to adopt its arrangement of the calendar of holy days.*

The preface which Franklin wrote for the abridgment was an exquisitely pious little essay. It was written as though coming from Lord Despencer, "a Protestant of the Church of England," and a "sincere lover of social worship." His lordship also held "in the highest veneration the doctrines of Jesus Christ," which was a gratifying assurance.

When Franklin was about twenty-two or twenty-three and wrote his curious creed and liturgy, he seems to have been in that not altogether desirable state of mind which is sometimes vulgarly described as "getting religion." He was not the sort of man to be carried away by one of those religious revival excitements of which we have seen so many in our time, but he was as near that state as a person of his intellect could be.

Preaching to him and direct effort at his conversion would, of course, have had no effect on such an original disposition. The revival which he experienced was one which he started for himself, and, besides his creed and liturgy, it consisted of an attempt to arrive at moral perfection.

---

* H. W. Smith's Life of Rev. William Smith, vol. ii. p. 174.

"I wished to live," he says, "without committing any fault at any time; I would conquer all that either natural inclination, custom, or company might lead me into. As I knew or thought I knew what was right and wrong, I did not see why I might not always do the one and avoid the other."

So he prepared his moral code of all the virtues he thought necessary, with his comments thereon, and it speaks for itself:

"1. TEMPERANCE.—Eat not to dullness; drink not to elevation.

"2. SILENCE.—Speak not but what may benefit others or yourself; avoid trifling conversation.

"3. ORDER.—Let all your things have their places; let each part of your business have its time.

"4. RESOLUTION.—Resolve to perform what you ought; perform without fail what you resolve.

"5. FRUGALITY.—Make no expense but to do good to others or yourself; i. e. waste nothing.

"6. INDUSTRY.—Lose no time; be always employed in something useful; cut off all unnecessary actions.

"7. SINCERITY.—Use no hurtful deceit; think innocently and justly; and if you speak, speak accordingly.

"8. JUSTICE.—Wrong none by doing injuries or omitting the benefits that are your duty.

"9. MODERATION.—Avoid extremes; forbear resenting injuries so much as you think they deserve.

"10. CLEANLINESS.—Tolerate no uncleanliness in body, clothes, or habitation.

"11. TRANQUILLITY.—Be not disturbed at trifles, or at accidents common or unavoidable.

"12. CHASTITY.—Rarely use venery but for health or offspring, never to dullness, weakness, or the injury of your own or another's peace or reputation.

"13. HUMILITY.—Imitate Jesus and Socrates."

He thought that he could gradually acquire the habit of keeping all these virtues, and instead of attempting the whole at once, he fixed his attention on one at a time, and when he thought he was master of that, proceeded to the next, and so on. He had arranged them in the order he thought would most facilitate their gradual acquisition, beginning with temperance and proceeding to silence; for the mastery of those which were easiest would help him to attain the more difficult. He has, therefore, left us at liberty to judge which were his most persistent sins.

He had a little book with a page for each virtue, and columns arranged for the days of the week, so that he could give himself marks for failure or success. He began by devoting a week to each virtue, by which arrangement he could go through the complete course in thirteen weeks, or four courses in a year.

His intense moral earnestness and introspection were doubtless inherited from his New England origin. But when he was in the midst of all this creed- and code-making, he records of himself:

" That hard to be governed passion of youth had hurried me frequently into intrigues with low women that fell in my way, which were attended with some expense and great inconvenience, besides a continual risk to my health by a distemper, which of all things I dreaded, though by great good luck I escaped it."

His biographer, Parton, reminds us that his liturgy has no prayer against this vice, and that about a year after the date of the liturgy his illegitimate son William was born. The biographer then goes on to say that Franklin was " too sincere and logical a man to go before his God and ask assistance against a fault which he had not fully resolved to overcome."

There is, however, a prayer in the liturgy against lasciviousness. He had not yet paid Mr. Vernon the money he had embezzled, although he was the author of a prayer asking to be delivered from deceit and fraud, and another against unfaithfulness in trust.*

It is obvious that this inconsistency is very like human nature, especially youthful human nature. There is nothing wonderful in it. It was simply the struggle which often takes place in boys who are both physically and mentally strong. The only thing unusual is that the person concerned has made a complete revelation of it. Such things are generally deeply concealed from the public. But that curious frankness which was mingled with Franklin's astuteness has in his own case opened wide the doors.

It has been commonly stated in his biographies that he had but one illegitimate child, a son; but from a manuscript letter in the possession of the Pennsylvania Historical Society, written by John Foxcroft, February 2, 1772, and never heretofore printed, it appears that he had also an illegitimate daughter, married to John Foxcroft:

"Philadᴬ Feby 2d, 1772.

"Dear Sir

"I have the happiness to acquaint you that your Daughter was safely brot to Bed the 20th ulto and presented me with a sweet little girl, they are both in good spirits and are likely to do very well.

"I was seized with a Giddyness in my head the Day before yesterday wch alarms me a good deal as I had 20 oz of blood taken

---

* Some years afterwards, when he had become prosperous, he restored the money to Mr. Vernon, with interest to date.

JOHN FOXCROFT

from me and took physick wch does not seem in the least to have relieved me.

"I am hardly able to write this. Mrs F joins me in best affections to yourself and compts to Mrs Stevenson and Mr and Mrs Huson.

"I am Dr Sir

"Yrs. affectionately

"JOHN FOXCROFT.

"Mrs Franklin, Mrs Bache, little Ben & Family at Burlington are all well. I had a letter from ye Govr yesterday J. F."

Among the Franklin papers in the State Department at Washington there are copies of a number of letters which Franklin wrote to Foxcroft, and in three of them—October 7, 1772, November 3, 1772, and March 3, 1773—he sends "love to my daughter." There is also in Bigelow's edition of his works* a letter in which he refers to Mrs. Foxcroft as his daughter. The letter I have quoted above was written while Franklin was in England as the representative of some of the colonies, and is addressed to him at his Craven Street lodgings. Foxcroft, who was postmaster of Philadelphia, seems to have been on friendly terms with the rest of Franklin's family.

Mrs. Bache, whom Foxcroft mentions in the letter, was Franklin's legitimate daughter, Sarah, who was married. The family at Burlington was the family of the illegitimate son, William, who was the royal governor of New Jersey. This extraordinarily mixed family of legitimates and illegitimates seems to have maintained a certain kind of harmony.

---

* Vol. v. p. 201.

The son William, the governor, continued the line through an illegitimate son, William Temple Franklin, usually known as Temple Franklin. This condition of affairs enables us to understand the odium in which Franklin was held by many of the upper classes of Philadelphia, even when he was well received by the best people in England and France.

In his writings we constantly find him encouraging early marriages; and he complains of the great number of bachelors and old maids in England. "The accounts you give me," he writes to his wife, " of the marriages of our friends are very agreeable. I love to hear of everything that tends to increase the number of good people." He certainly lived up to his doctrine, and more.

"Men I find to be a sort of beings very badly constructed, as they are generally more easily provoked than reconciled, more disposed to do mischief to each other than to make reparation, much more easily deceived than undeceived, and having more pride and even pleasure in killing than in begetting one another ; for without a blush they assemble in great armies at noonday to destroy, and when they have killed as many as they can they exaggerate the number to augment the fancied glory ; but they creep into corners or cover themselves with the darkness of night when they mean to beget, as being ashamed of a virtuous action." (Bigelow's Works of Franklin, vol. vii. p. 464.)

There has always been much speculation as to who was the mother of Franklin's son, William, the governor of New Jersey ; but as the gossips of Philadelphia were never able to solve the mystery, it is hardly possible that the antiquarians can succeed. Theodore Parker assumed that he must have been the son of a girl whom Franklin would have married if her parents had consented. Her name is unknown, for Franklin merely describes her as a relative of Mrs. Godfrey, who tried to make the match. Parker had no evidence whatever for his supposition. He merely thought it likely ; and, as a Christian minister, it would perhaps have been more to his credit if he had abstained from attacking in this way the reputation of even an unnamed young woman. An English clergyman, Rev. Bennet Allen, writing in the London *Morning Post*, June 1, 1779, when the ill feeling of the Revolution was at its height, says that William's mother was an oyster wench, whom Franklin left to die of disease and hunger in the streets. The gossips, indeed, seem to have always agreed that the woman must have been of very humble origin.

The nearest approach to a discovery has, however, been made by Mr. Paul Leicester Ford, in his essay entitled "Who was the Mother of Franklin's Son?" He found an old pamphlet written during Franklin's very heated controversy with the proprietary party in Pennsylvania when the attempt was made to abolish the proprietorship of the Penn family and make the colony a royal province. The pamphlet, entitled "What is Sauce for a Goose is also Sauce for a Gander," after some general abuse of Franklin, says that the mother of his son was a woman named Barbara, who worked in his house as a servant for ten pounds a year ; that he kept her in that position until her death, when he stole her to the grave in silence without a pall, tomb, or monument. This is, of course, a partisan statement only, and reiterates what was probably the current gossip of the time among Franklin's political opponents.

There have also been speculations in Philadelphia as to who was the mother of Franklin's daughter, the wife of John Foxcroft; but they are mere guesses unsupported by evidence.

From what Franklin has told us of the advice given him when a young man by a Quaker friend, he was at that time exceedingly proud, and also occasionally overbearing and insolent, and this is confirmed by various passages in his early life. But in after-years he seems to have completely conquered these faults. He complains, however, that he never could acquire the virtue of order in his business, having a place for everything and everything in its place. This failing seems to have followed him to the end of his life, and was one of the serious complaints made against him when he was ambassador to France.

But he believed himself immensely benefited by his moral code and his method of drilling himself in it.

" It may be well my posterity should be informed that to this little artifice, with the blessing of God, their ancestor owed the constant felicity of his life, down to his 79th year in which this is written. . . . To Temperance he ascribes his long continued health, and what is still left to him of a good constitution; to Industry and Frugality, the early easiness of his circumstances and acquisition of his fortune, with all that knowledge that enabled him to be a useful citizen, and obtained for him some degree of reputation among the learned; to Sincerity and Justice, the confidence of his country, and the honorable employs it conferred upon him; and to the joint influence of the whole mass of the virtues, even in the imperfect state he was able to acquire then, all that evenness of temper and that cheerfulness in conversation, which makes his company still sought for and agreeable even to his younger acquaintances.''

WILLIAM FRANKLIN, ROYAL GOVERNOR OF NEW JERSEY

At the same time that he was trying to put into practice his moral code, he conceived the idea of writing a book called "The Art of Virtue," in which he was to make comments on all the virtues, and show how each could be acquired. Most treatises of this sort, he had observed, were mere exhortations to be good; but "The Art of Virtue" would point out the means. He collected notes and hints for this volume during many years, intending that it should be the most important work of his life; "a great and extensive project," he calls it, into which he would throw the whole force of his being, and he expected great results from it. He looked forward to the time when he could drop everything else and devote himself to this mighty project, and he received grandiloquent letters of encouragement from eminent men. His vast experience of life would have made it a fascinating volume, and it is to be regretted that public employments continually called him to other tasks.

A young man such as he was is not infrequently able to improve his morals more effectually by marrying than by writing liturgies and codes. He decided to marry about two years after he had begun to discipline himself in his creed and moral precepts. The step seems to have been first suggested to him by Mrs. Godfrey, to whom, with her husband, he rented part of his house and shop. She had a relative who, she thought, would make a good match for him, and she took opportunities of bringing them often together. The girl was deserving, and Franklin began to court her. But he has described the affair so well himself that it would be useless to try to abbreviate it.

" The old folks encouraged me by continual invitations to supper, and by leaving us together, till at length it was time to explain. Mrs. Godfrey managed our little treaty. I let her know that I expected as much money with their daughter as would pay off my remaining debt for the printing-house, which I believe was not then above a hundred pounds. She brought me word they had no such sum to spare ; I said they might mortgage their house in the loan office. The answer to this, after some days, was, that they did not approve the match ; that, on inquiry of Bradford, they had been informed the printing business was not a profitable one ; the types would soon be worn out, and more wanted ; that S. Keimer and D. Harry had failed one after the other, and I should probably soon follow them ; and, therefore, I was forbidden the house and the daughter shut up.''

This the young printer thought was a mere artifice, the parents thinking that the pair were too fond of each other to separate, and that they would steal a marriage, in which event the parents could give or withhold what they pleased. He resented this attempt to force his hand, dropped the whole matter, and as a consequence quarrelled with Mrs. Godfrey, who with her husband and children left his house.

The passage which follows in Franklin's Autobiography implies that his utter inability at this period to restrain his passions directed his thoughts more seriously than ever to marriage, and he was determined to have a wife. It may be well here to comment again on his remarkable frankness. There have been distinguished men, like Rousseau, who were at times morbidly frank. Their frankness, however, usually took the form of a confession which did not add to their dignity. But Franklin never confessed anything ; he told it. His dignity was as natural and as instinctive as Washington's, though of a different kind. His supreme intellect easily avoided all positions in which he would have to confess or make admissions; and, as there was nothing morbid in his character, so there was nothing morbid in his frankness.

The frankness seems to have been closely connected with his serenity and courage. There never was a man so little disturbed by consequences or possibilities. He was quick to take advantage of popular whims, and he would not expose himself unnecessarily to public censure. His letter to President Stiles, of Yale, is an example. Being asked for his religious opinion, he states it fully and without reserve, although knowing that it would be extremely distasteful to the man to whom it was addressed, and, if made public, would bring upon him the enmity of the most respectable people in the country, whose good opinion every one wishes to secure. The only precaution he takes is to ask the president not to publish what he says, and he gives his reasons as frankly as he gives the religious opinion. But if the letter had been published before his death, he would have lost neither sleep nor appetite, and doubtless, by some jest or appeal to human sympathy, would have turned it to good account.

Since his time there have been self-made men in this country who have advanced themselves by professing fulsome devotion to the most popular forms of religion, and they have found this method very useful in their designs on financial institutions or public office. We would prefer them to take Frank-

lin for their model; and they may have all his failings if they will only be half as honest.

But to return to his designs for a wife, which were
by no means romantic. Miss Read, for whom he
had a partiality, had married one Rogers during
Franklin's absence in London. Rogers ill treated
and deserted her, and, dejected and melancholy,
she was now living at home with her mother. She
and Franklin had been inclined to marry before he
went to London, but her mother prevented it. According to his account, she had been in love with
him; but, although he liked her, we do not understand that he was in love. He never seems to have
been in love with any woman in the sense of a romantic or exalted affection, although he flirted with
many, both young and old, almost to the close of
his life.

But now, on renewing his attentions, he found
that her mother had no objections. There was,
however, one serious difficulty, for Mr. Rogers, although he had deserted her, was not known to be
dead, and divorces were but little thought of at
that time. Franklin naturally did not want to add
bigamy to his other youthful offences, and it would
also have required a revision of his liturgy and code.
Rogers had, moreover, left debts which Franklin
feared he might be expected to pay, and he had had
enough of that sort of thing. "We ventured, however," he says, "over all these difficulties, and I
took her to wife September 1, 1730." None of
the inconveniences happened, for neither Rogers nor
his debts ever turned up.

WILLIAM TEMPLE FRANKLIN

Franklin's detractors have always insisted that no marriage ceremony was performed and that he was never legally married. There is no record of such a marriage in Christ Church, of which Mrs. Rogers was a member, and the phrase used, "took her to wife," is supposed to show that they simply lived together, fearing a regular ceremony, which, if Rogers was alive, would convict them of bigamy. The absence of any record of a ceremony is, however, not necessarily conclusive that there was no ceremony of any kind; and the question is not now of serious importance, for they intended marriage, always regarded themselves as man and wife, and, in any event, it was a common-law marriage. Their children were baptized in Christ Church as legitimate children, and in a deed executed three or four years after 1730 they are spoken of as husband and wife.

A few months after the marriage his illegitimate son William was born, and Mr. Bigelow has made the extraordinary statement, " William may therefore be said to have been born in wedlock, though he was not reputed to be the son of Mrs. Franklin." * This is certainly an enlarged idea of the possibilities of wedlock, and on such a principle marriage to one woman would legitimatize the man's illegitimate offspring by all others. It is difficult to understand the meaning of such a statement, unless it is an indirect way of suggesting that William was the son of Mrs. Franklin ; but of this there is no evidence.

Franklin always considered his neglect of Miss

---

* Bigelow's Works of Franklin, vol. iii. p. 216, note.

Read after he had observed her affection for him one of the errors of his life. He had almost forgotten her while in London, and after he returned appears to have shown her no attention, until, by the failure of the match Mrs. Godfrey had arranged for him, he was driven to the determination to marry some one. He believed that he had largely corrected this error by marrying her. "She proved a good and faithful helpmate," he says; "assisted me much by attending the shop; we throve together, and have ever mutually endeavored to make each other happy." She died in 1774, while Franklin was in England.

There is nothing in anything he ever said to show that they did not get on well together. On the contrary, their letters seem to show a most friendly companionship. He addressed her in his letters as "my dear child," and sometimes closed by calling her "dear Debby," and she also addressed him as "dear child." During his absence in England they corresponded a great deal. Her letters to him were so frequent that he complained that he could not keep up with them; and his letters to her were written in his best vein, beautiful specimens of his delicate mastery of language, as the large collection of them in the possession of the American Philosophical Society abundantly shows.

In writing to Miss Catharine Ray, afterwards the wife of Governor Greene, of Rhode Island, who had sent him a cheese, he said,—

"Mrs. Franklin was very proud that a young lady should have so much regard for her old husband as to send him such a present.

We talk of you every time it comes to the table. She is sure you are a sensible girl, and a notable housewife, and talks of bequeathing me to you as a legacy; but I ought to wish you a better, and I hope she will live these hundred years; for we are grown old together, and if she has any faults, I am so used to them that I don't perceive them. As the song says,—

> "'Some faults we have all, & so has my Joan,
> But then they're exceedingly small;
> And, now I'm grown used to them, so like my own,
> I scarcely can see them at all,
> My dear friends,
> I scarcely can see them at all.'

"Indeed I begin to think she has none, as I think of you. And since she is willing I should love you as much as you are willing to be loved by me, let us join in wishing the old lady a long life and a happy one."

While absent at an Indian conference on the frontier, he wrote reprovingly to his wife for not sending him a letter:

"I had a good mind not to write to you by this opportunity; but I never can be ill natured enough even when there is the most occasion. I think I won't tell you that we are well, nor that we expect to return about the middle of the week, nor will I send you a word of news; that's poz. My duty to mother, love to the children, and to Miss Betsey and Gracy. I am your loving husband.

"P. S. I have *scratched out the loving words*, being writ in haste by mistake when I forgot I was angry."

Mrs. Franklin was a stout, handsome woman. We have a description of her by her husband in a letter he wrote from London telling her of the various presents and supplies he had sent home:

"I also forgot, among the china, to mention a large fine jug for beer, to stand in the cooler. I fell in love with it at first sight; for I thought it looked like a fat jolly dame, clean and tidy, with a neat blue and white calico gown on, good natured and lovely, and put me in mind of somebody."

This letter is full of interesting details. He tells her of the regard and friendship he meets with from persons of worth, and of his longing desire to be home again. A full description of the articles sent would be too long to quote entire, but some of it may be given as a glimpse of their domestic life :

"I send you some English china ; viz, melons and hams for a dessert of fruit or the like ; a bowl remarkable for the neatness of the figures, made at Bow, near this city ; some coffee cups of the same ; a Worcester bowl, ordinary. To show the difference of workmanship, there is something from all the china works in England ; and one old true china bason mended, of an odd color. The same box contains four silver salt ladles, newest but ugliest fashion ; a little instrument to core apples ; another to make little turnips out of great ones ; six coarse diaper breakfast cloths ; they are to spread on the tea table, for nobody breakfasts here on the naked table, but on the cloth they set a large tea board with the cups. There is also a little basket, a present from Mrs. Stevenson to Sally, and a pair of garters for you, which were knit by the young lady, her daughter, who favored me with a pair of the same kind ; the only ones I have been able to wear, as they need not be bound tight, the ridges in them preventing their slipping. We send them therefore as a curiosity for the form, more than for the value. Goody Smith may, if she pleases, make such for me hereafter. My love to her."

At the time of the Stamp Act, in 1765, when the Philadelphians were much incensed against Franklin for not having, as they thought, sufficiently resisted, as their agent in England, the passage of the act, the mob threatened Mrs. Franklin's house, and she wrote to her husband :

"I was for nine days kept in a continual hurry by people to remove, and Sally was persuaded to go to Burlington for safety. Cousin Davenport came and told me that more than twenty people had told him it was his duty to be with me. I said I was pleased to receive civility from anybody, so he staid with me some time ;

MRS. FRANKLIN

towards night I said he should fetch a gun or two, as we had none. I sent to ask my brother to come and bring his gun also, so we turned one room into a magazine; I ordered some sort of defense up stairs such as I could manage myself. I said when I was advised to remove, that I was very sure you had done nothing to hurt anybody, nor had I given any offense to any person at all, nor would I be made uneasy by anybody, nor would I stir or show the least uneasiness, but if any one came to disturb me I would show a proper resentment. I was told that there were eight hundred men ready to assist anyone that should be molested."

This letter is certainly written in a homely and pleasant way, not unlike the style of her husband, and other letters of hers have been published at different times possessing the same merit; but they have all been more or less corrected, and in some instances rewritten, before they appeared in print, for she was a very illiterate woman. I have not access to the original manuscript of the letter I have quoted, but I will give another, which is to be found in the collection of the American Philosophical Society, exactly as she wrote it:

October ye 29. 1773.

" MY DEAR CHILD

" I have bin very much distrest a boute as I did not oney letter nor one word from you nor did I hear one word from oney bodey that you wrote to   So I must submit and indever to submit to what I ame to bair I did write by Capt Folkner to you but he is gone doun and when I read it over I did not like it and so if this dont send it I shante like it as I donte send you oney news nor I donte go abrode.

" I shall tell you what consernes myself our yonegest Grandson is the finest child as alive he has had the small Pox and had it very fine and got abrod agen Capt All will tell you a boute him Benj Franklin Beache but as it is so deficall to writ I have desered him to tell you I have sente a squerel for your friend and wish her better luck it is a very fine one I have had very bad luck with two they one killed and another run a way allthou they was bred up tame I have not a caige as I donte know where the man lives that makes them my love to Sally Franklin—my love to all our cousins as thou menthond remember me to Mr and Mrs Weste due you ever hear aney thing of Ninely Evers as was.

.   .   .   .

" I cante write any mor I am your afeckthone wife
                                            " D. FRANKLIN"

She was not a congenial companion for Franklin in most of his tastes and pursuits, in his studies in science and history, or in his political and diplomatic career.   He never appears to have written to her on any of these subjects.   But she helped him, as he has himself said, in the early days in the printing-office, buying rags for the paper and stitching pamphlets. It was her homely, housewifely virtues, handsome figure, good health, and wholesome common sense which appealed to him; and it was a strong appeal, for he enjoyed these earthly comforts fully as much as he did the high walks of learning in which his fame was won.   He once wrote to her, "it was a comfort to me to recollect that I had once been clothed from head to foot in woolen and linen of my wife's manufacture, and that I never was prouder of any dress in my life."

She bore him two children.   The first was a son, Francis Folger Franklin, an unusually bright, handsome boy, the delight of all that knew him.   Franklin had many friends, and seems to have been very much attached to his wife, but this child was the one human being whom he loved with extravagance and devotion.   Although believing in inoculation as a remedy for the small-pox, he seems to have been unable to bear the thought of protecting in this way

MRS. SARAH BACHE

his favorite son ; at any rate, he neglected to take the precaution, and the boy died of the disease when only four years old. The father mourned for him long and bitterly, and nearly forty years afterwards, when an old man, could not think of him without a sigh.

The other child was a daughter, Sarah, also very handsome, who married Richard Bache and has left numerous descendants. His illegitimate son, William, was brought home when he was a year old and cared for along with his other children; and William's illegitimate son, Temple Franklin, was the companion and secretary of his grandfather in England and France. The illegitimate daughter was apparently never brought home, and is not referred to in his writings, except in those occasional letters in which he sends her his love. According to the letter already mentioned as in the collection of the Pennsylvania Historical Society, she was married to John Foxcroft, who was deputy colonial postmaster in Philadelphia. It was well that she was kept away from Franklin's house, for the presence of William appears to have given trouble enough. A household composed of legitimate and illegitimate children is apt to be inharmonious at times, especially when the mother of the legitimate children is the mistress of the house.

Franklin's biographies tell us that Mrs. Franklin tenderly nurtured William. This may be true, and, judging from expressions in her printed letters, she seems to have been friendly enough with him. But from other sources we find that as William grew up she learned to hate him, and this, with some other secrets of the Franklin household, has been described in the diary of Daniel Fisher:

"As I was coming down from my chamber this afternoon a gentlewoman was sitting on one of the lowest stairs which were but narrow, and there not being room enough to pass, she rose up & threw herself upon the floor and sat there. Mr. Soumien & his Wife greatly entreated her to arise and take a chair, but in vain, she would keep her seat, and kept it, I think, the longer for their entreaty. This gentlewoman, whom though I had seen before I did not know, appeared to be Mrs. Franklin. She assumed the airs of extraordinary freedom and great Humility, Lamented heavily the misfortunes of those who are unhappily infected with a too tender or benevolent disposition, said she believed all the world claimed a privilege of troubling her Pappy (so she usually calls Mr. Franklin) with their calamities and distresses, giving us a general history of many such wretches and their impertinent applications to him." (Pennsylvania Magazine of History, vol. xvii. p. 271.)

In the pamphlet called "What is Sauce for a Goose is also Sauce for a Gander," already alluded to, Franklin is spoken of as "Pappy" in a way which seems to show that the Philadelphians knew his wife's nickname for him and were fond of using it to ridicule him.

Afterwards, Daniel Fisher lived in Franklin's house as his clerk, and thus obtained a still more intimate knowledge of his domestic affairs.

"Mr. Soumien had often informed me of great uneasiness and dissatisfaction in Mr. Franklin's family in a manner no way pleasing to me, and which in truth I was unwilling to credit, but as Mrs. Franklin and I of late began to be Friendly and sociable I discerned too great grounds for Mr. Soumien's Reflections, arising solely from the turbulence and jealousy and pride of her disposition. She suspecting Mr. Franklin for having too great an esteem for his son in prejudice of herself and daughter, a young woman of about 12 or 13 years of age, for whom it was visible Mr. Franklin had no less esteem than for his son young Mr. Franklin. I have often seen him pass to and from his father's apartment upon Business (for he does not eat, drink, or sleep in the House) without the least compliment between Mrs. Franklin and him or any sort of notice taken of each other, till one Day as I was sitting with her in the passage when the young Gentleman came by she exclaimed to me (he not hearing) :—

"'Mr. Fisher there goes the greatest Villain upon Earth.'

"This greatly confounded & perplexed me, but did not hinder her from pursuing her Invectives in the foulest terms I ever heard from a Gentlewoman." (Pennsylvania Magazine of History, vol. xvii. p. 276.)

Fisher's descriptions confirm the gossip which has descended by tradition in many Philadelphia families. He found Mrs. Franklin to be a woman of such "turbulent temper" that this and other unpleasant circumstances forced him to leave. Possibly these were some of the faults which her husband speaks of as so exceedingly small and so like his own that he scarcely could see them at all. The presence of her husband's illegitimate son must have been very trying, and goes a long way to excuse her.

All that Franklin has written about himself is so full of a serene philosophic spirit, and his biographers have echoed it so faithfully, that, in spite of his frankness, things are made to appear a little easier than they really were. His life was full of contests, but they have not all been noted, and the sharpness of many of them has been worn off by time. In Philadelphia, where he was engaged in the most bitter partisan struggles, where the details of his life were fully known,—his humble origin, his slow rise, his indelicate jokes, and his illegitimate children,—there were not a few people who cherished a most relentless antipathy towards him which neither his philanthropy nor his philosophic and scientific mind could soften. This bitter feeling against the "old rogue," as they called him, still survives among some of the descendants of the people of his time, and fifty or sixty years ago there were virtuous old ladies living in Philadelphia who would flame into indignation at the mention of his name.

Chief-Justice Allen, who was his contemporary and opponent in politics, described him as a man of "wicked heart," and declared that he had often been a witness of his "envenomed malice." In H. W. Smith's "Life of Rev. William Smith" a great deal of this abuse can be found. Provost Smith and Franklin quarrelled over the management of the College of Philadelphia, and on a benevolent pamphlet by the provost Franklin wrote a verse from the poet Whitehead : *

> "Full many a peevish, envious, slanderous elf
> Is in his works, Benevolence itself
> For all mankind, unknown his bosom heaves,
> He only injures those with whom he lives.
> Read then the man. Does truth his actions guide?
> Exempt from petulance, exempt from pride?
> To social duties does his heart attend—
> As son, as father, husband, brother, friend?
> Do those who know him love him? If they do
> You have my permission—you may love him too."
> (Smith's Life of Rev. William Smith, vol. i. p. 341.)

Provost Smith's biographer resents this attack by giving contemporary opinions of Franklin ; and

---

* This verse Franklin also quotes against Smith in a letter to Miss Stevenson. (Bigelow's Works of Franklin, vol. iii. p. 235.)

a paragraph omitted in the regular edition (page 347 of volume i.), but printed on an extra leaf and circulated among the author's friends, may be quoted as an example. It was, however, not original with Smith's biographer, but was copied with a few changes from Cobbett's attack on Franklin:

"Dr. Benjamin Franklin has told the world in poetry what, in his judgment, my ancestor was. His venerable shade will excuse me, if I tell in prose what, in the judgment of men who lived near a century ago, Dr. Smith was not: He was no almanack maker, nor quack, nor chimney-doctor, nor soap boiler, nor printer's devil, neither was he a deist; and all his children were born in wedlock. He bequeathed no old and irrecoverable debts to a hospital. He never cheated the poor during his life nor mocked them in his death. If his descendants cannot point to his statue over a library, they have not the mortification of hearing him daily accused of having been a fornicator, a hypocrite, and an infidel."

Some of the charges in this venomous statement are in a sense true, but are exaggerated by the manner in which they are presented, an art in which Cobbett excelled. I have in the preceding chapters given sufficient details to throw light on many of them. Franklin was an almanac-maker, a chimney-doctor, and a soap-boiler, but in none of these is there anything to his discredit. As to his irrecoverable debts, it is true that he left them to the Pennsylvania Hospital, saying in his will that, as the persons who owed them were unwilling to pay them to him, they might be willing to pay them to the hospital as charity. They were a source of great annoyance to the managers, and were finally returned to his executors. The statement that he cheated the poor during his life and mocked them in his death is entirely unjustified. He was often generous with his money to people in misfortune, and several such instances can be found in his letters. It is also going too far to say that he was a quack and a hypocrite.

While in England he associated on the most intimate terms with eminent literary and scientific men. Distinguished travellers from the Continent called on him to pay their respects. He stayed at noblemen's country-seats and with the Bishop of St. Asaph. He corresponded with all these people in the most friendly and easy manner ; they were delighted with his conversation and could never see enough of him. In France everybody worshipped him, and the court circles received him with enthusiasm. But in Philadelphia the colonial aristocracy were not on friendly terms with him. He had, of course, numerous friends, including some members of aristocratic families ; but we find few, if any, evidences of that close intimacy and affection which he enjoyed among the best people of Europe.

This hostility was not altogether due to his humble origin or to the little printing-office and stationery store where he sold goose-feathers as well as writing material and bought old rags. These disadvantages would not have been sufficient, for his accomplishments and wit raised him far above his early surroundings, and the colonial society of Philadelphia was not illiberal in such matters. The principal cause of the hostility towards him was his violent opposition to the proprietary party, to which most of the upper classes belonged, and, having this ground

of dislike, it was easy for them to strengthen and excuse it by the gossip about his illegitimate son and
the son's mother kept as a servant in his house.
They ridiculed the small economies he practised,
and branded his religious and moral theorizing as
hypocrisy.

He was very fond of broad jokes, which have
always been tolerated in America under certain
circumstances; but the man who writes them,
especially if he also writes and talks a great deal
about religion and undertakes to improve prayer-
books, gives a handle to his enemies and an opportunity for unfavorable comment. The *Portfolio*, a
Philadelphia journal, of May 23, 1801, representing
more particularly the upper classes of the city, prints
one of his broad letters, and takes the opportunity
to assail him for "hypocrisy, hackneyed deism,
muck-worn economy," and other characteristics of
what it considers humbug and deceit. It has been
suggested that far back in the past one of Franklin's
ancestors might have been French, for his name in
the form Franquelin was at one time not uncommon
in France. This might account for his easy brightness and vivacity, and also, it may be added, for
such letters as he sometimes wrote :

"To Mr. JAMES READ

"Saturday morning Aug 17 '45.
"DEAR J.

"I have been reading your letter over again, and since you desire an answer I sit me down to write you ; yet as I write in the
market, will I believe be but a short one, tho' I may be long about
it. I approve of your method of writing one's mind when one is too
warm to speak it with temper : but being myself quite cool in this
affair I might as well speak as write, if I had opportunity. Your copy

of Kempis must be a corrupt one if it has that passage as you quote it, *in omnibus requiem quaesivi, sed non inveni, nisi in angulo cum libello.* The good father understood pleasure (*requiem*) better, and wrote *in angulo cum puella.* Correct it thus without hesitation."

.   .   .   .

(*Portfolio*, vol. i. p. 165.)

The letter continues the jest in a way that I do not care to quote ; but the last half of it is full of sage and saintly advice.   It is perhaps the only letter which gives at the same time both sides of Franklin's character.   But Sparks and Bigelow in their editions of his works give the last half only, with no indication that the first half has been omitted.

In the same year that he wrote this letter he also wrote his letter of advice to a young man on the choice of a mistress, a copy of which is now in the State Department at Washington, while numerous copies taken from it have been circulated secretly all over the country.   This year (1745) seems to have been his reckless period, for it was about that time that he published "Polly Baker's Speech," which will be given in another chapter.   In the State Department at Washington is also preserved his letter on Perfumes to the Royal Academy of Brussels, which cannot be published under the rules of modern taste, and, in fact, Franklin himself speaks of it as having "too much *grossièreté*" to be borne by polite readers.*

I shall, however, give as much of the letter on the choice of a mistress as is proper to publish.

"June 25th, 1745.

"MY DEAR FRIEND :

"I know of no medicine fit to diminish the violent natural inclinations you mention, and if I did, I think I should not communi-

---

* Bigelow's Works of Franklin, vol. vii. p. 374.

cate it to you. Marriage is the *proper* remedy. It is the most natural state of man, and, therefore, the state in which you are most likely to find solid happiness. Your reasons against entering it at present appear to me not well founded. The circumstantial advantages you have in view of postponing it are not only uncertain, but they are small in comparison with that of the thing itself.

"It is the man and woman united that make the complete human being. Separate she wants his force of body and strength of reason. He her softness, sensibility, and acute discernment. Together they are more likely to succeed in the world. A single man has not nearly the value he would have in a state of union. He is an incomplete animal. He resembles the odd half of a pair of scissors. If you get a prudent, healthy wife, your industry in your profession, with her good economy will be a fortune sufficient.

"But if you will not take this counsel, and persist in thinking a commerce with the sex inevitable, then I repeat my former advice, that in all your amours you should *prefer old women to young ones*. You call this a paradox and demand my reasons. They are these :

"1st. Because they have more knowledge of the world, and their minds are better stored with observations ; their conversation is more improving and more lastingly agreeable.

"2d. Because when women cease to be handsome, they study to be good. To maintain their influence over men, they supply the diminution of beauty by an augmentation of utility. They learn to do a thousand services, small and great, and are the most tender and useful of all friends when you are sick. Thus they continue amiable, and hence there is scarcely such a thing to be found as an old woman who is not a good woman.

"3d. Because there is no hazard of children, which, irregularly produced, may be attended with much inconvenience.

"4th. Because, through more experience, they are more prudent and discreet in conducting an intrigue to prevent suspicion. The commerce with them is therefore safe with regard to your reputation and with regard to theirs. If the affair should happen to be known, considerate people might be rather inclined to excuse an old woman who would kindly take care of a young man, form his manners by her good counsels, and prevent his ruining his health and fortunes among mercenary prostitutes.

"5th. . . .

"6th. . . .

"7th. Because the compunction is less. The having made a

young girl miserable may give you frequent bitter reflections, none of which can attend the making an *old* woman *happy*.

"8th and lastly. . . .

"Thus much for my paradox, but I still advise you to marry directly, being sincerely,

"Your Affectionate Friend,

"B. F."

Franklin, however, was capable of the most courteous gallantry to ladies. In France he delighted the most distinguished women of the court by his compliments and witticisms. When about fifty years old he wrote some letters to Miss Catharine Ray, of Rhode Island, which, as coming from an elderly man to a bright young girl who was friendly with him and told him her love-affairs, are extremely interesting. One of them about his wife we have already quoted. In a letter to him Miss Ray had asked, "How do you do and what are you doing? Does everybody still love you, and how do you make them do so?" After telling her about his health, he said,—

"As to the second question, I must confess (but don't you be jealous), that many more people love me now than ever did before; for since I saw you, I have been able to do some general services to the country and to the army, for which both have thanked and praised me, and say they love me. They say so, as you used to do; and if I were to ask any favors of them, they would, perhaps, as readily refuse me; so that I find little real advantage in being beloved, but it pleases my humor."

On another occasion he wrote to her,—

"Persons subject to the *hyp* complain of the northeast wind as increasing their malady. But since you promised to send me kisses in that wind, and I find you as good as your word, it is to me the gayest wind that blows, and gives me the best spirits. I write this during a northeast storm of snow, the greatest we have had this winter. Your favors come mixed with the snowy fleeces, which are pure as your virgin innocence, white as your lovely bosom, and—as cold. But let it warm towards some worthy young man, and may Heaven bless you both with every kind of happiness."

He had another young friend to whom he wrote pretty letters, Miss Mary Stevenson, daughter of the Mrs. Stevenson in whose house he lived in London when on his diplomatic missions to England. He encouraged her in scientific study, and some of his most famous explanations of the operations of nature are to be found in letters written to her. He had hoped that she would marry his son William, but William's fancy strayed elsewhere.

" PORTSMOUTH, 11 August, 1762.

" MY DEAR POLLY

" This is the best paper I can get at this wretched inn, but it will convey what is intrusted to it as faithfully as the finest. It will tell my Polly how much her friend is afflicted that he must perhaps never again see one for whom he has so sincere an affection, joined to so perfect an esteem ; who he once flattered himself might become his own, in the tender relation of a child, but can now entertain such pleasing hopes no more. Will it tell *how much* he is afflicted ? No, it cannot.

" Adieu, my dearest child. I will call you so. Why should I not call you so, since I love you with all the tenderness of a father ? Adieu. May the God of all goodness shower down his choicest blessings upon you, and make you infinitely happier than that event would have made you. . . ."

(Bigelow's Works of Franklin, vol. iii. p. 209.)

This correspondence with Miss Stevenson continued for a great many years, and there are beautiful letters to her scattered all through his published works. The letters both to her and to Miss Ray became more serious as the two young women grew older and married. Miss Stevenson sought his advice on the question of her marriage, and his reply was as wise and affectionate as anything he ever wrote. She married Dr. Hewson, of London, and they migrated to Philadelphia, where she became the mother of a numerous family.

Franklin had a younger sister, Jane, a pretty girl, afterwards Mrs. Mecom, of whom he was very fond, and he kept up a correspondence with her all his life, sending presents to her at Boston, helping her son to earn a livelihood, and giving her assistance in her old age. Their letters to each other were most homely and loving, and she took the greatest pride in his increasing fame.

His correspondence with his parents was also pleasant and familiar. In one of his letters to his mother he amuses her by accounts of her grand-children, and at the same time pays a compliment to his sister Jane.

"As to your grandchildren, Will is now nineteen years of age, a tall, proper youth, and much of a beau. He acquired a habit of idleness on the Expedition, but begins of late to apply himself to business, and I hope will become an industrious man. He imagined his father had got enough for him, but I have assured him that I intend to spend what little I have myself, if it pleases God that I live long enough; and, as he by no means wants acuteness, he can see by my going on that I mean to be as good as my word.

"Sally grows a fine girl, and is extremely industrious with her needle, and delights in her work. She is of a most affectionate temper, and perfectly dutiful and obliging to her parents, and to all. Perhaps I flatter myself too much, but I have hopes that she will prove an ingenious, sensible, notable and worthy woman like her aunt Jenny." (Bigelow's Works of Franklin, vol. ii. p. 154.)

Over the grave of his parents in the Granary Burial-Ground in Boston he placed a stone, and pre-

pared for it one of those epitaphs in which he was
so skilful and which were almost poems :

Josiah Franklin and Abiah his wife
lie here interred.
They lived together in wedlock fifty-five years ;
and without an estate or any gainful employment,
by constant labour, and honest industry,
(with God's blessing,)
maintained a large family comfortably ;
and brought up thirteen children and seven grandchildren reputably.
From this instance, reader,
be encouraged to diligence in thy calling,
and distrust not Providence.
He was a pious and prudent man,
she a discreet and virtuous woman.
Their youngest son,
in filial regard to their memory,
places this stone.
J. F. born 1655—died 1744,—Æ. 89.
A. F. born 1667—died 1752,—Æ. 85.

IV

BUSINESS AND LITERATURE

FRANKLIN'S ancestors in both America and England had not been remarkable for their success in worldly affairs. Most of them did little more than earn a living, and, being of contented dispositions, had no ambition to advance beyond it. Some of them were entirely contented with poverty. All of them, however, were inclined to be economical and industrious. They had no extended views of business enterprise, and we find none of them among the great merchants or commercial classes who were reaching out for the foreign trade of that age. Either from lack of foresight or lack of desire, they seldom selected very profitable callings. They took what was nearest at hand—making candles or shoeing horses—and clung to it persistently.

Franklin advanced beyond them only because all their qualities of economy, thrift, industry, and serene contentedness were intensified in him. His choice of a calling was no better than theirs, for printing was not a very profitable business in colonial times, and was made so in his case only by his unusual sagacity.

I have already described his adventures as a young printer, and how he was sent on a wild-goose chase to London by Governor Keith, of Pennsylvania. I have also told how on his return to Philadelphia he gave up printing and became the clerk of Mr. Denham. He liked Mr. Denham and the clerkship, and never expected to return to his old calling. If Mr. Denham had lived, Franklin might have become a renowned Philadelphia merchant and financier, like Robert Morris, an owner of ships and cargoes, a trader to India and China, and an outfitter of privateers. But this sudden change from the long line of his ancestry was not to be. Nature, as if indignant at the attempt, struck down both Denham and himself with pleurisy within six months of their association in business. Denham perished, and Franklin, after a narrow escape from death, went back reluctantly to set type for Keimer.

He was now twenty-one, a good workman, with experience on two continents, and Keimer made him foreman of his printing-office. Within six months, however, his connection with Keimer was ended by a quarrel, and one of the workmen, Hugh Meredith, suggested that he and Franklin should set up in the printing business for themselves, Meredith to furnish the money through his father, and Franklin to furnish the skill. This offer was eagerly accepted; but as some months would be required to obtain type and materials from London, Franklin's quarrel with Keimer was patched up and he went back to work for him.

In the spring of 1728 the type arrived. Franklin parted from Keimer in peace, and then with Meredith sprung upon him the surprise of a rival printing establishment. They rented a house for twenty-four pounds a year, and to help pay it took in Mr. and Mrs. Thomas Godfrey as lodgers. But their money was all spent in getting started, and they had a hard struggle. Their first work was a translation of a Dutch history of the Quakers. Franklin worked late and early. People saw him still employed as they went home from their clubs late at night, and he was at it again in the morning before his neighbors were out of bed.

There were already two other printing-offices, Keimer's and Bradford's, and hardly enough work for them. The town prophesied failure for the firm of Franklin & Meredith; and, indeed, their only hope of success seemed to be in destroying one or both of their rivals, a serious undertaking for two young men working on borrowed capital. There was so little to be made in printing at that time that most of the printers were obliged to branch out into journalism and to keep stationery stores. Franklin resolved to start a newspaper, but, unfortunately, told his secret to one of Keimer's workmen, and Keimer, to be beforehand, immediately started a newspaper of his own, called *The Universal Instructor in all Arts and Sciences and the Pennsylvania Gazette.*

Franklin was much disgusted, and in resentment, as he tells us, and to counteract Keimer, began writing amusing letters for the other newspaper of the town, Bradford's *Mercury.* His idea was to crush Keimer's paper by building up Bradford's until he could have one of his own. His articles, which were signed "Busy Body," show the same talent for humor that he had displayed in Boston a

THE

Pennſylvania *GAZETTE.*

Containing the freſheſt Advices Foreign and Domeſtick.

From Thurſday, September 25. to Thurſday, October 2. 1729.

---

*T*HE Pennſylvania Gazette *being now to be carry'd on by other Hands, the Reader may expect ſome Account of the Method we deſign to proceed in.*

Upon a View of Chambers's great Dictionaries, from whence were taken the Materials of the Univerſal Inſtructor *in all Arts and Sciences, which uſually made the Firſt Part of this Paper, we find that beſides their containing many Things abſtruſe or inſignificant to us, it will probably be fifty Years before the Whole can be gone thro' in this Manner of Publication. There are likewiſe in thoſe Books continual References from Things under one Letter of the Alphabet to thoſe under another, which relate to the ſame Subject, and are neceſſary to explain and compleat it ; theſe taken in their Turn may perhaps be Ten Years diſtant ; and ſince it is likely that they who deſire to acquaint themſelves with any particular Art or Science, would gladly have the whole before them in a much leſs Time, we believe our Readers will not think ſuch a Method of communicating Knowledge to be a proper One.*

However, tho' we do not intend to continue the Publication of thoſe Dictionaries in a regular Alphabetical Method, as has hitherto been done ; yet as ſeveral Things exhibited from them in the Courſe of theſe Papers, have been entertaining to ſuch of the Curious, who never had and cannot have the Advantage of good Libraries ; and as there are many Things ſtill behind, which being in this Manner made generally known, may perhaps become of conſiderable Uſe, by giving ſuch Hints to the excellent natural Genius's of our Country, as may contribute either to the Improvement of our preſent Manufactures, or towards the Invention of new Ones ; we propoſe from Time to Time to communicate ſuch particular Parts as appear to be of the moſt general Conſequence.

As to the Religious Courtſhip, Part of which has been retail'd to the Publick in theſe Papers, the Reader may be inform'd, that the whole Book will probably in a little Time be printed and bound up by it ſelf ; and thoſe who approve of it, will doubtleſs be better pleas'd to have it entire, than in this broken interrupted Manner.

There are many who have long deſired to ſee a good News-Paper in Pennſylvania, and we hope thoſe Gentlemen who are able, will contribute towards the making This ſuch. We ask Aſſiſtance, becauſe we are fully ſenſible, that to publiſh a good News-Paper is not ſo eaſy an Undertaking as many People imagine it to be. The Author of a Gazette (in the Opinion of the Learned) ought to be qualified with an extenſive Acquaintance with Languages, a great Eaſineſs and Command of Writing and Relating Things cleanly and intelligibly, and in few Words ; he ſhould be able to ſpeak of War both by Land and Sea ; be well acquainted with Geography, with the Hiſtory of the Time, with the ſeveral Intereſts of Princes, and States, the Secrets of Courts, and the Manners and Cuſtoms of all Nations. Men thus accompliſh'd are very rare in this remote Part of the World ; and it would be well if the Writer of theſe Papers could make up among his Friends what is wanting in himſelf.

Upon the Whole, we may aſſure the Publick, that as far as the Encouragement we meet with will enable us, no Care and Pains ſhall be omitted, that may make the Pennſylvania Gazette as agreeable and uſeful an Entertainment as the Nature of the Thing will allow.

The Following is the laſt Meſſage ſent by his Excellency Governour Burnet, to the Houſe of Repreſentatives in Boſton.

Gentlemen of the Houſe of Repreſentatives,

*I*T is not with ſo vain a Hope as to convince you, that I take the Trouble to anſwer your Meſſages, but, if poſſible, to open the Eyes of the deluded People whom you repreſent, and whom you are at ſo much Pains to keep in Ignorance of the true State of their Affairs. I need not go further for an undeniable Proof of this Endeavour to blind them, than your ordering the Letter of Meſſieurs Wilks and Belcher of the 7th of June laſt to your Speaker to be publiſhed This Letter (I ſaid (in Page 1 of your Votes) to incloſe a Copy of the Report of the Lords of the Committee of His Majeſty's Privy Council, with His Majeſty's Approbation and Order thereon in Council , Yet theſe Gentlemen had at the ſame time the unparallell'd Preſumption to write to the Speaker in this Manner ; You'll obſerve by the Concluſion, that it is propoſed to be the Conſequence of your not complying with His Majeſty's Inſtruction, that the whole Matter to be laid

---

FRONT PAGE OF THE FIRST NUMBER OF THE "PENNSYLVANIA GAZETTE," PUBLISHED BY FRANKLIN AND MEREDITH

few years before, when he wrote for his brother's newspaper over the name "Silence Dogood;" but there is a great difference in their tone. No ridicule of the prevailing religion or hatred of those in authority appears in them. The young man evidently found Philadelphia more to his taste than Boston, and was not at war with his surroundings. The "Busy Body" papers are merely pleasant raillery at the failings of human nature in general, interspersed with good advice, something like that which he soon afterwards gave in "Poor Richard."

Keimer tried to keep his journal going by publishing long extracts from an encyclopædia which had recently appeared, beginning with the letter A, and he tried to imitate the wit of the "Busy Body." But he merely laid himself open to the "Busy Body's" attacks, who burlesqued and ridiculed his attempts, and Franklin in his Autobiography gives himself the credit of having drawn public attention so strongly to Bradford's *Mercury* that Keimer, after keeping his *Universal Instructor* going on only ninety subscribers for about nine months, gave it up. Franklin & Meredith bought it in and thus disposed of one of their rivals. That rival, being incompetent and ignorant, soon disposed of himself by bankruptcy and removal to the Barbadoes. Franklin continued the publication of the newspaper under the title of the *Pennsylvania Gazette;* but it was vastly improved in every way,—better type, better paper, more news, and intelligent, well-reasoned articles on public affairs instead of Keimer's stupid prolixity.

An article written by Franklin on that great question of colonial times, whether the Legislature of each colony should give the governor a fixed salary or pay him only at the end of each year, according as he had pleased them, attracted much attention. It was written with considerable astuteness, and, while upholding the necessity of the governor's dependence on the Legislature, was careful not to give offence to those who were of a different opinion. The young printers also won favor by reprinting neatly and correctly an address of the Assembly to the governor, which Bradford had previously printed in a blundering way. The members of the Assembly were so pleased with it that they voted their printing to Franklin & Meredith for the ensuing year. These politicians, finding that Franklin knew how to handle a pen, thought it well, as a matter of self-interest, to encourage him.

The two young men were kept busily employed, yet found it very difficult to make both ends meet, although they did everything themselves, not having even a boy to assist them. Meredith's father, having suffered some losses, could lend them but half of the sum they had expected from him. The merchant who had furnished them their materials grew impatient and sued them. They succeeded in staying judgment and execution for a time, but fully expected to be eventually sold out by the sheriff and ruined.

At this juncture two friends of Franklin came to him and offered sufficient money to tide over his difficulties if he would get rid of Meredith, who was intemperate, and take all the business on himself. This he succeeded in doing, and with the money supplied by his friends paid off his debts and added a stationery shop, where he sold paper, parchment, legal blanks, ink, books, and, in time, soap, goose-feathers, liquors, and groceries; he also secured the printing of the laws of Delaware, and, as he says, went on swimmingly. Soon after this he married Miss Read, and he has left us an account of how they lived together:

"We kept no idle servants, our table was plain and simple, our furniture of the cheapest. For instance, my breakfast was for a long time bread and milk (no tea), and I ate it out of a twopenny earthen porringer, with a pewter spoon. But mark how luxury will enter families, and make a progress in spite of principle: being called one morning to breakfast, I found it in a china bowl, with a spoon of silver! They had been bought for me without my knowledge by my wife, and had cost her the enormous sum of three and twenty shillings, for which she had no other excuse or apology to make but that she thought *her* husband deserved a silver spoon and china bowl as well as any of his neighbors."

A story is told on the Eastern Shore of Maryland of a young man who called one evening on an old farmer to ask him how it was that he had become rich.

"It is a long story," said the old man, "and while I am telling it we might as well save the candle," and he put it out.

"You need not tell it," said the youth. "I see."

Franklin's method was the one that had always been practised by his ancestors, and with his wider intelligence and great literary ability it was sure to succeed. The silver spoons slowly increased until in the course of years, as he tells us, the plate in his house was "augmented gradually to several hundred pounds in value."

His newspaper, the *Pennsylvania Gazette*, was the best in the colonies. Besides the ordinary news and advertisements, together with little anecdotes and squibs which he was always so clever in telling, he printed in it extracts from *The Spectator* and various moral writers, articles from English newspapers, as well as articles of his own which had been previously read to the Junto. He also published long poems by Stephen Duck, now utterly forgotten; but he was then the poet laureate and wrote passable verse. He carefully excluded all libelling and personal abuse; but what would now be considered indelicate jests were not infrequent. These broad jokes, together with witticisms at the expense of ecclesiastics, constituted the stock amusements of the time, as the English literature of that period abundantly shows.

Opening one of the old volumes of his *Gazette* at random, we find for September 5, 1734, a humorous account of a lottery in England, by which, to encourage the propagation of the species, all the old maids of the country are to be raffled for. Turning over the leaves, we find the humorous will of a fellow who, among other queer bequests, leaves his body "as a very wholesome feast to the worms of his family vault." In another number an account is given of some excesses of the Pope, with a Latin verse and its translation which had been pasted on Pasquin's statue :

BUSINESS AND LITERATURE

"Omnia Venduntur imo
Dogmata Christi
Et ne me vendunt, evolo.
Roma Vale."

"Rome all things sells, even doctrines old and new.
I'll fly for fear of sale; so Rome adieu."

In the number for November 7, 1734, we are given "The Genealogy of a Jacobite."

"The Devil *begat* Sin, Sin *begat* Error, Error *begat* Pride, Pride *begat* Hatred, Hatred *begat* Ignorance, Ignorance *begat* Blind Zeal, Blind Zeal *begat* Superstition, Superstition *begat* Priestcraft, Priestcraft *begat* Lineal Succession, Lineal Succession *begat* Indelible Character, Indelible Character *begat* Blind Obedience, Blind Obedience *begat* Infallibility, Infallibility *begat* the Pope and his Brethren in the time of Egyptian Darkness, the Pope *begat* Purgatory, Purgatory *begat* Auricular Confession, Auricular Confession *begat* Renouncing of Reason, Renouncing of Reason *begat* Contempt of Scriptures, Contempt of the Scriptures *begat* Implicit Faith, Implicit Faith *begat* Carnal Policy, Carnal Policy *begat* Unlimited Passive Obedience, Unlimited Passive Obedience *begat* Non-Resistance, Non-Resistance *begat* Oppression, Oppression *begat* Faction, Faction *begat* Patriotism, Patriotism *begat* Opposition to all the Measures of the Ministry, Opposition *begat* Disaffection, Disaffection *begat* Discontent, Discontent *begat* a Tory, and a Tory *begat* a Jacobite, with Craftsman and Fog and their Brethren on the Body of the Whore of Babylon when she was deemed past child bearing."

Franklin's famous "Speech of Polly Baker" is supposed to have first appeared in the *Gazette*. This is a mistake, but it was reprinted again and again in American newsapers for half a century.

"The Speech of Miss Polly Baker before a Court of Judicatory, in New England, where she was prosecuted for a fifth time, for having a Bastard Child; which influenced the Court to dispense with her punishment, and which induced one of her judges to marry her the next day—by whom she had fifteen children.

"May it please the honourable bench to indulge me in a few words : I am a poor, unhappy woman, who have no money to fee lawyers to plead for me, being hard put to it to get a living. . . . Abstracted from the law, I cannot conceive (may it please your honours) what the nature of my offence is. I have brought five children into the world, at the risque of my life ; I have maintained them well by my own industry, without burthening the township, and would have done it better, if it had not been for the heavy charges and fines I have paid. Can it be a crime (in the nature of things, I mean) to add to the King's subjects, in a new country that really needs people ? I own it, I should think it rather a praiseworthy than a punishable action. I have debauched no other woman's husband, nor enticed any youth ; these things I never was charged with ; nor has any one the least cause of complaint against me, unless, perhaps, the ministers of justice, because I have had children without being married, by which they have missed a wedding fee. But can this be a fault of mine ? I appeal to your honours. You are pleased to allow I don't want sense ; but I must be stupefied to the last degree, not to prefer the honourable state of wedlock to the condition I have lived in. I always was, and still am willing to enter into it ; and doubt not my behaving well in it ; having all the industry, frugality, fertility, and skill in economy appertaining to a good wife's character. I defy any one to say I ever refused an offer of that sort ; on the contrary, I readily consented to the only proposal of marriage that ever was made me, which was when I was a virgin, but too easily confiding in the person's sincerity that made it, I unhappily lost my honour by trusting to his ; for he got me with child, and then forsook me.

"That very person, you all know ; he is now become a magistrate of this country ; and I had hopes he would have appeared this day on the bench, and have endeavoured to moderate the Court in my favour ; then I should have scorned to have mentioned it, but I must now complain of it as unjust and unequal, that my betrayer, and undoer, the first cause of all my faults and miscarriages (if they must be deemed such), should be advanced to honour and power in the government that punishes my misfortunes with stripes and infamy. . . . But how can it be believed that Heaven is angry at my having children, when to the little done by me towards it, God has been pleased to add his divine skill and admirable workmanship in the formation of their bodies, and crowned the whole by furnishing them with rational and immortal souls ? Forgive me, gentlemen, if I talk a little extravagantly on these matters : I am no divine, but if you, gentlemen, must be making laws, do not turn natural and useful actions into crimes by your prohibitions. But take into your wise consideration the great and growing number of bachelors in the country, many of whom, from the mean fear of the expense of a family, have never sincerely and honestly courted a woman in their lives ; and by their manner of living leave unproduced (which is little better than murder) hundreds of their posterity to the thousandth generation. Is not this a greater offence against the public good than mine? Compel them, then, by law, either to marriage, or to pay double the fine of fornication every year. What must poor young women do, whom customs and nature forbid to solicit the men, and who cannot force themselves upon husbands, when the laws take no care to provide them any, and yet severely punish them if they do their duty without them ; the duty of the first and great command of nature and nature's God, increase and multiply ; a duty, from the steady performance of which nothing has been able to deter me, but for its sake I have hazarded the loss of the public esteem, and have frequently endured public disgrace and punishment ; and therefore ought, in my humble opinion, instead of a whipping, to have a statue erected to my memory.''

A newspaper furnishing the people with so much information and sound advice, mingled with broad stories, bright and witty, and appealing to all the human passions,—in other words, so thoroughly like Franklin,—was necessarily a success. It was, however, a small affair,—a single sheet which, when folded, was about twelve by eighteen inches,—and it appeared only twice a week.

It differed from other colonial newspapers chiefly in its greater brightness and in the literary skill shown in its preparation. But attempts have been made to exaggerate its merits, and Parton declares that in it Franklin "originated the modern system of business advertising" and that "he was the first man who used this mighty engine of publicity as we now use it." A careful examination of the

Gazette and the other journals of the time fails to disclose any evidence in support of this extravagant statement. The advertisements in the *Gazette* are like those in the other papers,—runaway servants and slaves, ships and merchandise for sale, articles lost or stolen. On the whole, perhaps more advertisements appear in the *Gazette* than in any of the others, though a comparison of the *Gazette* with Bradford's *Mercury* shows days when the latter has the greater number.

Franklin advertised rather extensively his own publications, and the lamp-black, soap, and "ready money for old rags" which were to be had at his shop, for the reason, doubtless, that, being owner of both the newspaper and the shop, the advertisements cost him nothing. This is the only foundation for the tale of his having originated modern advertising. His advertisements are of the same sort that appeared in other papers, and there is not the slightest suggestion of modern methods in them.

Parton also says that Franklin "invented the plan of distinguishing advertisements by means of little pictures which he cut with his own hands." If he really was the inventor of this plan, it is strange that he allowed his rival Bradford to use it in the *Mercury* before it was adopted by the *Gazette*. No cuts appear in the advertisements in the *Gazette* until May 30, 1734; but the *Mercury's* advertisements have them in the year 1733.

Franklin made no sudden or startling changes in the methods of journalism; he merely used them effectively. His reputation and fortune were increased by his newspaper, but his greatest success came from his almanac, the immortal "Poor Richard."

In those days almanacs were the literature of the masses, very much as newspapers are now. Everybody read them, and they supplied the place of books to those who would not or could not buy these means of knowledge. Every farm-house and hunter's cabin had one hanging by the fireplace, and the rich were also eager to read afresh every year the weather forecasts, receipts, scraps of history, and advice mingled with jokes and verses.

Every printer issued an almanac as a matter of course, for it was the one publication which was sure to sell, and there was always more or less money to be made by it. While Franklin and Meredith were in business they published their almanac annually, and it was prepared by Thomas Godfrey, the mathematician, who with his wife lived in part of Franklin's house. But, as has been related, Mrs. Godfrey tried to make a match between Franklin and one of her relatives, and when that failed the Godfreys and Franklin separated, and Thomas Godfrey devoted his mathematical talents to the preparation of Bradford's almanac.

This was in the year 1732, and the following year Franklin had no philomath, as such people were called, to prepare his almanac. A great deal depended on having a popular philomath. Some of them could achieve large sales for their employer, while others could scarcely catch the public attention at all. Franklin's literary instinct at once suggested the plan of creating a philomath out of his own imagination, an ideal one who would achieve the highest possibilities of the art. So he wrote his own almanac, and announced that it was prepared by one Richard Saunders, who for short was called "Poor Richard," and he proved to be the most wonderful philomath that ever lived.

As Shakespeare took the suggestions and plots of his plays from old tales and romances, endowing his spoils by the touch of genius with a life that the originals never possessed, so Franklin plundered right and left to obtain material for the wise sayings of "Poor Richard." There was, we are told, a Richard Saunders who was the philomath of a popular English almanac called "The Apollo Anglicanus," and another popular almanac had been called "Poor Robin;" but "Poor Richard" was a real creation, a new human character introduced to the world like Sir Roger de Coverley.

Novel-writing was in its infancy in those days, and Bunyan's "Pilgrim's Progress," Addison's character of Sir Roger, and the works of Richardson, Fielding, and Smollett were the only examples of this new literature. That beautiful sentiment that prompts children to say, "Tell us a story," and which is now fed to repletion by trash, was then primitive, fresh, and simple. Franklin could have written a novel in the manner of Fielding, but he had no inclination for such a task. He took more naturally and easily to creating a single character somewhat in the way Sir Roger de Coverley was created by

Poor Richard, 1733.

AN

Almanack

For the Year of Chrift

1733,

Being the Firft after LEAP YEAR:

And makes fince the Creation Years

By the Account of the Eaftern *Greeks*	7241
By the Latin Church, when ☉ ent. ♈	6932
By the Computation of *W. W*	5742
By the *Roman* Chronology	5682
By the *Jewiſh* Rabbies	5494

Wherein is contained

The Lunations, Eclipfes, Judgment of the Weather, Spring Tides, Planets Motions & mutual Afpects, Sun and Moon's Rifing and Setting, Length of Days, Time of High Water, Fairs, Courts, and obfervable Days

Fitted to the Latitude of Forty Degrees, and a Meridian of Five Hours Weft from *London*, but may without fenfible Error, ferve all the adjacent Places, even from *Newfoundland* to *South-Carolina.*

By RICHARD SAUNDERS, Philom.

PHILADELPHIA:

Printed and fold by *B. FRANKLIN*, at the New Printing Office near the Market.

The Third Impreſſion.

Addison, whose essays he had rewritten so often for practice.

Sir Roger was so much of a gentleman, there were so many delicate touches in him, that he never became the favorite of the common people. But "Poor Richard" was the Sir Roger of the masses ; he won the hearts of high and low. In that first number for the year 1733 he introduces himself very much after the manner of Addison.

"COURTEOUS READER,

"I might in this place attempt to gain thy favor by declaring that I write almanacks with no other view than that of the public good, but in this I should not be sincere ; and men are now-a-days too wise to be deceived by pretences, how specious soever. The plain truth of the matter is, I am excessive poor, and my wife, good woman, is, I tell her, excessive proud ; she cannot bear, she says, to sit spinning in her shift of tow, while I do nothing but gaze at the stars ; and has threatened more than once to burn all my books and rattling traps (as she calls my instruments) if I do not make some profitable use of them for the good of my family. The printer has offered me some considerable share of the profits, and I have thus begun to comply with my dame's desire."

There was a rival almanac, of which the philomath was Titan Leeds. "Poor Richard" affects great friendship for him, and says that he would have written almanacs long ago had he not been unwilling to interfere with the business of Titan. But this obstacle was soon to be removed.

"He dies by my calculation," says "Poor Richard," "made at his request, on Oct. 17, 1733, 3 ho., 29 m., P. M., at the very instant of the ♂ of ☉ and ☿. By his own calculation he will survive till the 26th of the same month. This small difference between us we have disputed whenever we have met these nine years past ; but at length he is inclinable to agree with my judgment. Which of us is most exact, a little time will now determine."

In the next issue "Poor Richard" announces that his circumstances are now much easier. His wife has a pot of her own and is no longer obliged to borrow one of a neighbor; and, best of all, they have something to put in it, which has made her temper more pacific. Then he begins to tease Titan Leeds. He recalls his prediction of his death, but is not quite sure whether it occurred; for he has been prevented by domestic affairs from being at the bedside and closing the eyes of his old friend. The stars have foretold the death with their usual exactitude; but sometimes Providence interferes in these matters, which makes the astrologer's art a little uncertain. But on the whole he thinks Titan must be dead, "for there appears in his name, as I am assured, an Almanack for the year 1734 in which I am treated in a very gross and unhandsome manner; in which I am called a false predicter, an ignorant, a conceited scribbler, a fool, and a lyar;" and he goes on to show that his good friend Titan would never have treated him in this way.

The next year he is still making sport of Titan, the deceased Titan, and the ghost of Titan, "who pretends to be still living, and to write Almanacks in spight of me;" and he proves again by means of the funniest arguments that he must be dead. Another year he devotes several pages of nonsense to disproving the charge that "Poor Richard" is not a real person. He ridicules astrology and weather forecasting by pretending to be very serious over it. At any rate, he says, "we always hit the day of the month, and that I suppose is esteemed one of the most useful things in an Almanack." He and his good old wife are getting on now better than ever; and the almanac for 1738 is prepared by Mistress Saunders herself, who rails at her husband and makes queer work with eclipses and forecasting. Then in the number for 1740 Titan writes a letter to "Poor Richard" from the other world.

Besides the formal essays or prefaces which appeared in each number, there were numerous verses, paragraphs of admirable satire on the events of the day or the weaknesses of human nature, and those prudential maxims which in the end became the most famous of all. As we look through a collection of these almanacs for an hour or so we seem to have lived among the colonists, who were not then Americans, but merry Englishmen, heavy eaters and drinkers, full of broad jokes, whimsical, humorous ways, and forever gossiping with hearty good nature over the ludicrous accidents of life, the love-affairs, the married infelicities, and the cuckolds. It is the freshness, the sap, and the rollicking happiness of old English life.

> "Old Batchelor would have a wife that's wise,
>   Fair, rich and young a maiden for his bed;
> Not proud, nor churlish, but of faultless size,
>   A country housewife in the city bred.
>   He's a nice fool and long in vain hath staid;
>   He should bespeak her, there's none ready made."

"Never spare the parson's wine, nor the baker's pudding."

"Ne'er take a wife till thou hast a house (and a fire) to put her in."

" My love and I for kisses play'd,
   She would keep stakes, I was content,
But when I won, she would be paid,
   This made me ask her what she meant :
      Quoth she, since you are in the wrangling vein
      Here take your kisses, give me mine again."

" Who has deceived thee so oft as thyself?"

" There is no little enemy."

" *Of the Eclipses this year.*

" During the first visible eclipse Saturn is retrograde : For which reason the crabs will go sidelong and the ropemakers backward. The belly will wag before, and the —— will sit down first. . . . When a New Yorker thinks to say THIS he shall say DISS, and the People in New England and Cape May will not be able to say Cow for their Lives, but will be forc'd to say KEOW by a certain involuntary Twist in the Root of their Tongues. . . ."

" Many dishes many diseases."

" Let thy maid servant be faithful, strong and homely."

" Here I sit naked, like some fairy elf ;
   My seat a pumpkin ; I grudge no man's pelf,
   Though I've no bread nor cheese upon my shelf,
     I'll tell thee gratis, when it safe is
   To purge, to bleed, or cut thy cattle or—thyself."

" Necessity never made a good bargain."

" A little house well filled, a little field well till'd and a little wife well will'd are great riches."

" *Of the Diseases this year.*

" This Year the Stone-blind shall see but very little ; the Deaf shall hear but poorly ; and the Dumb shan't speak very plain. And it's much, if my Dame Bridget talks at all this Year. Whole Flocks, Herds and Droves of Sheep, Swine and Oxen, Cocks and Hens, Ducks and Drakes, Geese and Ganders shall go to Pot ; but the Mortality will not be altogether so great among Cats, Dogs and Horses. . . ."

" Of the Fruits of the Earth.

"I find that this will be a plentiful Year of all manner of good Things, to those who have enough; but the Orange Trees in Greenland will go near to fare the worse for the Cold. As for Oats, they'll be a great Help to Horses. . . ."

"Lend money to an enemy, and thou'lt gain him; to a friend, and thou'lt lose him."

"Keep your eyes wide open before marriage, half shut afterwards."

"It is hard for an empty sack to stand uprignt."

For twenty years and more "Poor Richard" kept up this continuous stream of fun, breaking forth afresh every autumn,—sound, wholesome, dealing with the real things and the elemental joys of life, and expressed in that inimitable language of which Franklin was master. In this way was built up the greater part of his wonderful reputation, which in some of its manifestations surprises us so much. Such a reputation is usually of long growth ; one or two conspicuous acts will not achieve it. But the man who every year for nearly a generation delighted every human being in the country, from the ploughman and hunter to the royal governors, was laying in store for himself a sure foundation of influence.

The success of "Poor Richard" was immediate. The first number of it went through several editions, and after that the annual sales amounted to about ten thousand copies. For the last number which Franklin prepared for the year 1758, before he turned over the enterprise to his partner, he wrote a most happy preface. It was always his habit, when a controversy or service he was engaged in was finished, to summarize the whole affair in a way that strengthened his own position and left an indelible impression which all the efforts of his enemies could not efface. Accordingly, for this last preface he invented a homely, catching tale that enabled him to summarize all the best sayings of "Poor Richard" for the last twenty-five years.

"I stopt my Horse lately where a great Number of people were collected at a Vendue of Merchant Goods. The Hour of Sale not being come, they were conversing on the Badness of the Times, and one of the Company call'd to a plain clean old Man, with white Locks, 'Pray, Father Abraham, what think you of the Times? Won't these heavy Taxes quite ruin the Country? How shall we be ever able to pay them? What would you advise us to?'—Father Abraham stood up, and reply'd, 'If you'd have my Advice, I'll give it you in short, for a Word to the Wise is enough, and many Words won't fill a Bushel, as Poor Richard says.' They join'd in desiring him to speak his Mind, and gathering round him, he proceeded as follows:

"'Friends,' says he, 'and neighbours, the Taxes are indeed very heavy, and if those laid on by the Government were the only Ones we had to pay, we might more easily discharge them; but we have many others, and much more grievous to some of us. We are taxed twice as much by our Idleness, three times as much by our Pride, and four times as much by our Folly, and from these Taxes the Commissioners cannot ease or deliver us by allowing an Abatement. However let us hearken to good Advice, and something may be done for us; God helps them that help themselves, as Poor Richard says in his Almanack of 1733.

"'It would be thought a hard Government that should tax its People one tenth Part of their Time, to be employed in its Service. But Idleness taxes many of us much more, if we reckon all that is spent in absolute Sloth, or doing of nothing, with that which is spent in idle Employments or Amusements, that amount to nothing. Sloth, by bringing on Diseases absolutely shortens Life. Sloth, like Rust, consumes faster than Labour wears, while the used Key is always bright, as Poor Richard says. But dost thou love Life, then do not squander Time, for that's the Stuff Life is made of, as poor Richard says.— How much more than is necessary do we spend in Sleep! forgetting that The Sleeping Fox catches no Poultry, and that there will be sleeping enough in the Grave, as Poor Richard says. If Time be of all Things the most precious, wasting of Time must be, as Poor Richard says, the greatest Prodigality, since, as he elsewhere tells us, Lost Time is never found again; and what we call Time-enough, always proves little enough. Let us then be up and doing, and doing to the Purpose; so by Diligence shall we do more with less Perplexity. Sloth makes all Things difficult, but Industry all Things easy, as Poor Richard says; and He that riseth late, must trot all Day, and shall scarce overtake his Business at night. While Laziness travels so slowly, that Poverty soon overtakes him, as we read in Poor Richard, who adds, Drive thy Business, let that not drive thee; and Early to Bed, and early to rise, makes a Man healthy, wealthy, and wise.

. . . .

" ' So much for Industry, my Friends, and Attention to one's own Business; but to these we must add Frugality, if we would make our Industry more certainly successful. A man may, if he knows not how to save as he gets, Keep his nose all his life to the Grindstone, and die not worth a Groat at last.

. . . .

" ' And now to conclude, Experience keeps a dear School, but Fools will learn in no other, and scarce in that; for it is true, we may give Advice, but we cannot give Conduct, as Poor Richard says: However, remember this, They that won't be counselled, can't be helped, as Poor Richard says : and farther, That if you will not hear Reason, she'll surely wrap your Knuckles.'

" Thus the old Gentleman ended his Harangue. The People heard it, and approved the Doctrine, and immediately practised the contrary, just as if it had been a common Sermon; for the Vendue opened and they began to buy extravagantly, notwithstanding all his Cautions and their own Fear of Taxes."

. . . .

This speech of the wise old man at the auction, while perhaps not so interesting to us now as are some other parts of " Poor Richard," was a great hit in its day ; in fact, the greatest Franklin ever made. Before it appeared " Poor Richard's" reputation was confined principally to America, and without this final speech might have continued within those limits. But the "clean old Man, with white locks" spread the fame of "Poor Dick" over the whole civilized world. His speech was reprinted on broadsides in England to be fastened to the sides of houses, translated into French, and bought by the clergy and gentry for distribution to parishioners and tenants. Mr. Paul Leicester Ford, in his excellent little volume, "The Sayings of Poor Richard," has summarized its success. Seventy editions of it have been printed in English, fifty-six in French, eleven in German, and nine in Italian. It has also been translated into Spanish, Danish, Swedish, Welsh, Polish, Gaelic, Russian, Bohemian, Dutch, Catalan, Chinese, and Modern Greek, reprinted at least four hundred times, and still lives.

It was quite common a hundred years ago to charge Franklin with being an arrant plagiarist. It is true that the sayings of "Poor Richard" and a great deal that went to make up the almanac were taken from Rabelais, Bacon, Rochefoucauld, Ray Palmer, and any other sources where they could be found or suggested. But "Poor Richard" changed and rewrote them to suit his purpose, and gave most of them a far wider circulation than they had before.

More serious charges have, however, been made, and they are summarized in Davis's "Travels in America," * which was published in 1803. I have already noticed one of these,—the charge that his letter on air-baths was taken from Aubrey's "Miscellanies,"—which, on examination, I cannot find to be

---

* Pp. 209–217.

sustained. Davis also charges that Franklin's famous epitaph on himself was taken from a Latin one by an Eton school-boy, published with an English translation in the *Gentleman's Magazine* for February, 1736. Franklin's epitaph is already familiar to most of us:

The Body
of
Benjamin Franklin
Printer
(Like the cover of an old book
Its contents torn out
And stript of its lettering and gilding)
Lies here, food for worms.
But the work shall not be lost
For it will (as he believed) appear once more
In a new and more elegant edition
Revised and corrected
by
The Author.

The Eton boy's was somewhat like it:

Vitæ Volumine peracto
Hic Finis Jacobi Tonson
Perpoliti Sociorum Principis;
Qui Velut Obstetrix Musarum
In Lucem Edivit
Fœlices Ingenii Partus.
Lugete, Scriptorum chorus,
Et Frangite Calamos;
Ille vester, Margine Erasus, deletur!
Sed hæc postrema Inscriptio
Huic primæ Mortis Paginæ
Imprimatur,
Ne Prælo Sepulchri Commissus,
Ipse Editor careat Titulo:
Hic Jacet Bibliopola
Folio vitæ delapso
Expectans novam Editionem
Auctiorem et Emendatiorem.

One of these productions might certainly have been suggested by the other. But Franklin's grandson, William Temple Franklin, who professed to have the original in his possession, in his grandfather's handwriting, said that it was dated 1728, and it is printed with that date in one of the editions of Franklin's works. If this date is correct, it would be too early for the epitaph to have been copied from the one in the *Gentleman's Magazine* for February, 1736. It might be said that possibly the Eton boy knew of Franklin's epitaph ; but I cannot find that it was printed or in any way made public before 1736. There is no reason why both should not be original, for everybody wrote epitaphs in that century.

Franklin has been credited by one of his biographers with the invention of the comic epitaph, and Smollett's famous inscription on Commodore Trunnion's tomb in "Peregrine Pickle" is described as a mere imitation of Franklin's epitaph on himself. But there is no evidence that Smollett had seen Franklin's production before "Peregrine Pickle" was published in 1750, and it was not necessary that he should. There were plenty of similar productions long before that time. Franklin's own *Gazette*, January 6 to January 15, 1735/6, gives a very witty inscription on a dead greyhound, which is described as cut on the walls of Lord Cobham's gardens at Stow. In writing comic epitaphs Franklin was merely following the fashion of his time, and he was hardly as good at it as Smollett.

He has himself told us the source of one of his best short essays, "The Ephemera," a beautiful little allegory which he wrote to please Madame Brillon in Paris. In a letter to William Carmichael, of June 17, 1780, he describes the circumstances under which it was written, and says that "the thought was partly taken from a little piece of some unknown writer, which I met with fifty years since in a newspaper."* It was in this way that he worked over old material for "Poor Richard." Everything he had read seemed capable of supplying suggestions, and it must be said that he usually improved on the work of other men.

He was very fond of paraphrasing the Bible as a humorous task and also to show what he conceived to be the meaning of certain passages.) He altered the wording of the Book of Job so as to make it a satire on English politics. He did it cleverly, and it was amusing ; but it was a very cheap sort of humor.

His most famous joke of this kind was his " Parable against Persecution." He had learned it by heart, and when he was in England, and the discussion turned on religious liberty, he would open the Bible and read his parable as the last chapter in Genesis. The imitation of the language of Scripture was perfect, and the parable itself was so interesting and striking that every one was delighted with it. His guests would wonder and say that they had never known there was such a chapter in Genesis.

The parable was published and universally admired, but when it appeared in the *Gentleman's Magazine* some one very quickly discovered that it had been taken from Jeremy Taylor's Polemical Dis-

---

* Bigelow's Franklin from His Own Writings, vol. ii. p. 511.

courses, and there was a great discussion over it. Franklin afterwards said, in a letter to Mr. Vaughan, that he had taken it from Taylor; and John Adams said that he never pretended that it was original.* It is interesting to see how cleverly he improved on Taylor's language:

TAYLOR.	FRANKLIN.
"When Abraham sat at his tent door according to his custom, waiting to entertain strangers, he espied an old man stooping and leaning on his staff; weary with age and travel, coming towards him, who was an hundred years old. He received him kindly, washed his feet, provided supper, and caused him to sit down; but observing that the old man ate and prayed not, nor begged for a blessing on his meat, he asked him why he did not worship the God of heaven? The old man told him, that he worshipped the fire only and acknowledged no other god. At which answer Abraham grew so zealously angry, that he thrust the old man out of his tent, and exposed him to all the evils of the night and an unguarded condition. When the old man was gone, God called to Abraham, and asked him where the stranger was? He replied, I thrust him away, because he did not worship thee. God answered	"¶ 1 And it came to pass after these things, that Abraham sat in the door of his tent, about the going down of the sun. ¶ 2 And behold a man, bent with age, coming from the way of the wilderness leaning on his staff. ¶ 3 And Abraham rose and met him, and said unto him: Turn in, I pray thee, and wash thy feet, and tarry all night; and thou shalt arise early in the morning and go on thy way. ¶ 4 But the man said, Nay, for I will abide under this tree. ¶ 5 And Abraham pressed him greatly: so he turned and they went into the tent, and Abraham baked unleavened bread, and they did eat. ¶ 6 And when Abraham saw that the man blessed not God he said unto him, wherefore dost thou not worship the Most High God, Creator of heaven and earth? ¶ 7 And the man answered, and said, I do not worship thy God, neither do I call upon his name; for I have made to myself a god, which abideth in my

* Bigelow's Works of Franklin, vol. v. p. 376; also vol. x. p. 78; Adams's Works, vol. i. p. 659.

him, I have suffered him these hundred years, although he dishonoured me; and couldst not thou endure him one night, and when he gave thee no trouble? Upon this, saith the story, Abraham fetched him back again, and gave him hospitable entertainment and wise instruction. Go thou and do likewise and thy charity will be rewarded by the God of Abraham."

house and provideth me with all things. ¶ 8 And Abraham's zeal was kindled against the man; and he arose and fell upon him, and drove him forth with blows into the wilderness. ¶ 9 And at midnight God called unto Abraham saying, Abraham, where is the stranger? ¶ 10 And Abraham answered and said, Lord, he would not worship thee, neither would he call upon thy name; therefore have I driven him out from before my face into the wilderness. ¶ 11 And God said, have I borne with him these hundred and ninety and eight years, and nourished him, and Cloathed him, notwithstanding his rebellion against me; and couldest not thou, who art thyself a sinner, bear with him one night? ¶ 12 And Abraham said, Let not the anger of the Lord wax hot against his servant; lo, I have sinned; forgive me I pray thee. ¶ 13 And Abraham arose and went forth into the wilderness and sought diligently for the man and found him, and returned with him to the tent; and when he had entreated him kindly, he sent him away on the morrow with gifts. ¶ 14 And God spake unto Abraham, saying, For this thy sin shall thy seed be afflicted four hundred years in a strange land. ¶ 15 But for thy repentance will I deliver them; and they shall come forth with power and gladness of heart, and with much substance."

The parable was, indeed, older than Taylor for Taylor said he had found it in " The Jews' Book," and at length it was discovered in a Latin dedication of a rabbinical work, called "The Rod of Judah," published at Amsterdam in 1651, which ascribed the parable to the Persian poet Saadi. None of them, however, had thought of introducing it into the Old Testament, nor had they told it so well as Franklin, who gave it a new currency, and it was reprinted as a half-penny tract and also in Lord Kames's "Sketches of the History of Man."

While on this question of plagiarism it may be said that Franklin's admirable style was in part modelled on that of the famous Massachusetts divine, Cotton Mather, whom he had known and whose books he had read in his boyhood. The similarity is, indeed, quite striking, and for vigorous English he could hardly have had a better model. But he improved so much on Mather that his style is entirely his own. It is the most effective literary style ever used by an American. Nearly one hundred and fifty years have passed since his Autobiography was written, yet it is still read with delight by all classes of people, has been called for at some public libraries four hundred times a year, and shows as much promise of immortality as the poems of Longfellow or the romances of Hawthorne.

Besides his almanac and newspaper, Franklin extended his business by publishing books, consisting mostly of religious tracts and controversies. He also imported books from England, and sold them along with the lamp-black, soap, and groceries contained in

that strange little store and printing-office on Market
Street. He sent one of his journeymen to Charleston to establish a branch printing-office, of which
Franklin was to pay one-third of the expense and
receive one-third of the profits. After continuing
in this manner some five years, the Legislature of
the province in 1736 elected him clerk of that body,
which enabled him to retain the printing of the
notes, laws, paper money, and other public jobs,
which he tells us were very profitable.

The next year Colonel Spotswood, Postmaster-
General of the colonies, made him deputy postmaster of Philadelphia. This appointment reinforced
his other occupations. He could collect news for
his *Gazette* more easily, and also had greater facili-
ties for distributing it to his subscribers. In those
days the postmaster of a town usually owned a
newspaper, because he could have the post-riders
distribute copies of it without cost, and he did not
allow them to carry any newspaper but his own.
Franklin had been injured by the refusal of his pre-
decessor to distribute his *Gazette ;* but when he
became postmaster, finding his subscriptions and
advertisements much increased and his competitor's
newspaper declining, he magnanimously refused to
retaliate, and allowed his riders to carry the rival
journal.

How much money Franklin actually made in his
business is difficult to determine, although many
guesses have been made. He was, it would seem,
more largely and widely engaged than any other
printer in the colonies, for nearly all the important

printing of the middle colonies and a large part of that of the southern colonies came to his office. He made enough to retire at forty-two years of age, having been working for himself only twenty years.

On retiring he turned over his printing and publishing interest to his foreman, David Hall, who was to carry on the business in his own way, but under the firm name of Franklin & Hall, and to pay Franklin a thousand pounds a year for eighteen years, at the end of which time Hall was to become sole proprietor. This thousand pounds which Franklin was to receive may be looked upon as an indication that before his retirement the business was yielding him annually something more than that sum, possibly almost two thousand pounds, as some have supposed.

He never again engaged actively in any gainful trade, and his retirement seems to have been caused by the passion for scientific research which a few years before had seized him, and by that trait of his character which sometimes appears in the form of a sort of indolence and at other times as a wilful determination to follow the bent of his inclinations and pleasures. Although extremely economical and thrifty in practice as well as in precept, he had very little love of money, and took no pleasure in business for mere business' sake. The charges of sordidness and mean penny-wisdom are not borne out by any of the real facts of his life. It is not improbable that just before his retirement he had advanced far enough in his scientific experiments to see dimly in the future the chance of a great discovery and distinction. He certainly went to work with a will as soon as he got rid of the cares of the printing-office, and in a few years was rewarded.

He had invested some of his savings in houses and land in Philadelphia, and the thousand pounds (five thousand dollars) which he was to receive for eighteen years was a very good income in those times, and more than equivalent to ten thousand dollars at the present day. He moved from the bustle of Market Street and his home in the old printing, stationery, and grocery house, and is supposed to have taken a house at the southeast corner of Second and Race Streets. This was at the northern edge of the town, close to the river, where in the summer evenings he renewed his youthful fondness for swimming.

It must be confessed that very few self-made men, conducting a profitable business with the prospect of steady accumulation of money, have willingly resigned it in the prime of life, under the influence of such sentiments as appear to have moved him. But that intense and absolute devotion to business which is the prevailing mood of our times had not then begun in America, and it was rather the fashion to retire.

The years which followed his retirement, and before he became absorbed in political affairs, seem to have had for him a great deal of ideal happiness. He lived like a man of taste and a scholar accustomed to cultured surroundings more than like a self-made man who had battled for forty years with the material world. In writing to his mother, he said,—

"I read a great deal, ride a little, do a little business for myself, now and then for others, retire when I can, and go into company when I please ; so the years roll round, and the last will come, when I would rather have it said, He lived usefully than He died rich."

After his withdrawal from business he remained postmaster of Philadelphia, and in 1753, after he had held that office for sixteen years, he was appointed Postmaster-General of all the colonies, with William Hunter, of Virginia, as his colleague, and he retained this position until dismissed from it by the British government in 1774, on the eve of the Revolution. There was some salary attached to these offices, that of Postmaster-General yielding three hundred pounds. The postmastership of Philadelphia entailed no difficult duties at that time, and his wife assisted him ; but when he was made Postmaster-General he more than earned his salary during the first few years by making extensive journeys through the colonies to reform the system. The salary attached to the office was not to be allowed unless the office produced it ; and during the first four years the unpaid salary of Franklin and his colleague amounted to nine hundred and fifty pounds. He procured faster post-riders, increased the number of mails between important places, made a charge for carrying newspapers, had all newspapers carried by the riders, and reduced some of the rates of postage.

But he was not the founder of the modern post-office system, nor was he the first Postmaster-General of America, as some of his biographers insist. He merely improved the system which he found and increased its revenues as others have done before and since.

The leisure he sought by retirement was enjoyed but a few years. He became more and more involved in public affairs, and soon spent most of his time in England as agent of Pennsylvania or other colonies, and during the Revolution he was in France. There was a salary attached to these offices. As agent of Pennsylvania he received five hundred pounds a year, and when he represented other colonies he received from Massachusetts four hundred, from Georgia two hundred, and from New Jersey one hundred. These sums, together with the thousand pounds a year from Hall, would seem to be enough for a man of his habits; but apparently he used it all, and was often slow in paying his debts.

In a letter written to Mrs. Stevenson in London, while he was envoy to France, he expresses surprise that some of the London tradespeople still considered him their debtor for things obtained from them during his residence there some years before, and he asks Mrs. Stevenson, with whom he had lodged, how his account stands with her. The thousand pounds from Hall ceased in 1766, and after that his income must have been seriously diminished, for the return from his invested savings is supposed to have been only about seven hundred pounds. He appears to have overdrawn his account with Hall, for there is a manuscript letter in the possession of Mr. Howard Edwards, of Philadelphia, written by Hall March 1, 1770, urging Franklin to pay nine hundred and ninety-three pounds which had been due for three years.

He procured for his natural son, William, the royal governorship of New Jersey, and he was diligent all his life in getting government places for relatives. This practice does not appear to have been much disapproved of in his time; he was not subjected to abuse on account of it; and, indeed, nepotism is far preferable to some of the more modern methods.

When Governor of Pennsylvania, after the Revolution, he declined, we are told, to receive any salary for his three years' service, accepting only his expenses for postage, which was high in those times, and amounted in this case to seventy-seven pounds for the three years. This is one of the innumerable statements about him in which the truth is distorted for the sake of eulogy. He did not decline to receive his salary, but he spent it in charity, and we find bequests of it in his will.

As minister to France he had at first five hundred pounds a year and his expenses, and this was paid. He was also promised a secretary at a salary of one thousand pounds a year; but, as the secretary was never sent, he did the work himself with the assistance of his grandson, William Temple Franklin, who was allowed only three hundred pounds a year.

He considered himself very much underpaid for his services in resisting the Stamp Act, for his mission to Canada in 1776 at the risk of his life, and for the long and laborious years which he spent in France. Certainly five hundred pounds a year and expenses was very small pay for his diplomatic work in Paris, but during the last six years of his mission there he received two thousand five hundred pounds a year, which would seem to be sufficient compensation for acting as ambassador, as well as merchant to buy and ship supplies to the United States, and as financial agent to examine and accept innumerable bills of exchange drawn by the Continental Congress (Bigelow's Works of Franklin, vol. ix. p. 127). In 1788, two years before his death, he made a statement of these claims for extra service and sent it to Congress, accompanied by a letter to his friend, Charles Thomson, the secretary.

He thought that Congress should recognize these services by a grant of land, an office, or in some other way, as was the custom in Europe when an ambassador returned from a long foreign service; and he reminded Thomson that both Arthur Lee and John Jay had been rewarded handsomely for similar services. But the old Congress under the Articles of Confederation was then just expiring, and took no notice of his petition; and when the new Congress came in under the Constitution, it does not appear that his claims were presented. It is a mistake to say, however, as some have done, that the United States never paid him for his services and still owes him money. These claims were for extra services which the government had never obligated itself to pay.

He died quite well off for those times, leaving an estate worth, it is supposed, considerably over one hundred thousand dollars. The rapid rise in the value of houses and land in Philadelphia after the Revolution accounts for a part of this sum. He owned five or six large houses in Philadelphia, the printing-house which he built for his grandson, and several small houses. He had also a number of vacant lots in the town, a house and lot in Boston, a tract of land in Nova Scotia, another large tract in Georgia, and still another in Ohio. His personal property, consisting mostly of bonds and money, was worth from sixty to seventy thousand dollars.

V

SCIENCE

THE exact period at which Franklin began to turn
his attention to original researches in science is difficult to determine. There are no traces of such
efforts when he was a youth in Boston. He was not
then interested in science, even in a boyish way.
His instincts at that time led him almost exclusively
in the direction of general reading and the training
of himself in the literary art by verse-writing and by
analyzing the essays of the *Spectator*.

The atmosphere of Boston was completely theological. There was no room, no opportunity, for
science, and no inducement or even suggestion that
would lead to it, still less to original research in it.
We find Franklin in a state of rebellion against the
prevailing tone of thought, writing against it in his
brother's newspaper at the risk of imprisonment, and
in a manner more bitter and violent than anything
he afterwards composed. If he had remained in
Boston it is not likely that he would ever have taken
seriously to science, for all his energies would have
been absorbed in fighting those intolerant conditions
which smothered all scientific inquiries.

In Pennsylvania he found the conditions reversed.
The Quakers and the German sects which made up
the majority of the people of that province in colo-

nial times had more advanced ideas of liberty and free thought than any of the other religious bodies in America, and in consequence science flourished in Pennsylvania long before it gained entrance into the other colonies. The first American medical college, the first hospital, and the first separate dispensary were established there. Several citizens of Philadelphia who were contemporaries of Franklin achieved sufficient reputation in science to make their names well known in Europe.

David Rittenhouse invented the metallic thermometer, developed the construction of the compensation pendulum, and made valuable experiments on the compressibility of water. He became a famous astronomer, constructed an orrery to show the movements of the stars which was an improvement on all its predecessors, and conducted the observations of the transit of Venus in 1769. Pennsylvania was the only one of the colonies that took these observations, which in that year were taken by all the European governments in various parts of the world. The Legislature and public institutions, together with a large number of individuals, assisted in the undertaking, showing what very favorable conditions for science prevailed in the province.*

These were the conditions which seem to have aroused Franklin. Without them his mind tended more naturally to literature, politics, and schemes of philanthropy and reform ; but when his strong

---

* Making of Pennsylvania, chap. ix.

intellect was once directed towards science, he easily excelled in it. Some of the early questions discussed by the Junto, such as " Is sound an entity or body?" and " How may the phenomena of vapors be explained?" show an inclination towards scientific research ; and it is very likely that he studied such subjects more or less during the ten years which followed his beginning business for himself.

In his *Gazette* for December 15, 1737, there is an essay on the causes of earthquakes, summarizing the various explanations which had been given by learned men, and this essay is supposed to have been written by him. Six years afterwards he made what has been usually considered his first discovery, —namely, that the northeast storms of the Atlantic coast move against the wind ; or, in other words, that instead of these storms coming from the northeast, whence the wind blows, they come from the southwest. He was led to this discovery by attempting to observe an eclipse of the moon which occurred on the evening of October 21, 1743 ; but he was prevented by a heavy northeaster which did great damage on the coast. He was surprised to find that it had not prevented the people of Boston from seeing the eclipse. The storm, though coming from the northeast, swept over Philadelphia before it reached Boston. For several years he carefully collected information about these storms, and found in every instance that they began to leeward and were often more violent there than farther to windward.

He seems to have been the first person to observe

these facts, but he took no pains to make his observations public, except in conversation or in letters to prominent men like Jared Eliot, of Connecticut, and these letters were not published until long afterwards. This was his method in all his investigations. He never wrote a book on science; he merely reported his investigations and experiments by letter, usually to learned people in England or France. There were no scientific periodicals in those days. The men who were interested in such things kept in touch with one another by means of correspondence and an occasional pamphlet or book.

During the same period in which he was making observations on northeast storms he invented the "Pennsylvania Fireplace," as he called it, a new sort of stove which was a great improvement over the old methods of heating rooms. He published a complete description of this stove in 1745, and it is one of the most interesting essays he ever wrote. It is astonishing with what pleasure one can still read the first half of this essay written one hundred and fifty years ago on the driest of dry subjects. The language is so clear and beautiful, and the homely personality of the writer so manifest, that one is inclined to lay down the principle that the test of literary genius is the ability to be fascinating about stoves.

He explained the laws of hot air and its movements; the Holland stove, which afforded but little ventilation; the German stove, which was simply an iron box fed from outside, with no ventilating properties; and the great open fireplace fed with huge logs, which required such a draft to prevent the smoke from coming back into the room that the outer door had to be left open,—and if the door was shut the draft would draw the outer air whistling and howling through the crevices of the windows. His " Pennsylvania Fireplace" was what we would now call an open-fireplace stove. It was intended to be less wasteful of fuel than the ordinary fireplace and to give ventilation, while combining the heating power of the German and Holland stoves. It continued in common use for nearly a century, and modified forms of it are still called the Franklin stoves.

One of its greatest advantages was that it saved wood, which, for some time prior to the introduction of coal, had to be brought such a long distance that it was becoming very expensive. Franklin refused to take out a patent for his invention; for he was on principle opposed to patents, and said that as we enjoyed great advantages from the inventions of others, we should be willing to serve them by inventions of our own. He afterwards learned that a London ironmonger made a few changes in the "Pennsylvania Fireplace" and sold it as his own, gaining a small fortune.

Franklin's invention was undoubtedly an improvement on the old methods of heating and ventilation ; but he was not, as has been absurdly claimed, the founder of the "American stove system," for that system very soon departed from his lines and went back to the air-tight stoves of Germany and Holland.

It was not until 1746 or 1747, after he had been making original researches in science for about five years, that he took up the subject of electricity, and he was then forty-one years old. It appears that Mr. Peter Collinson, of London, who was interested in botany and other sciences, and corresponded largely on such subjects, had presented to the Philadelphia Library one of the glass tubes which were used at that time for producing electricity by rubbing them with silk or skin. Franklin began experimenting with this tube, and seems to have been fascinated by the new subject. On March 28, 1747, he wrote to Mr. Collinson thanking him for the tube, and saying that they had observed with its aid some phenomena which they thought to be new.

"For my own part, I never was before engaged in any study that so totally engrossed my attention and my time as this has lately done ; for what with making experiments when I can be alone, and repeating them to my friends and acquaintance, who from the novelty of the thing, come continually in crowds to see them, I have, during some months past, had little leisure for anything else."

It will be observed that he speaks of crowds coming to see the experiments, and this confirms what I have already shown of the strong interest in science which prevailed at that time in Pennsylvania, and which had evidently first aroused Franklin. In fact, a renewed interest in science had been recently stirred up all over the world, and people who had never before thought much of such things became investigators. Voltaire, who resembled Franklin in many ways, had turned aside from literature, and at forty-one, the same age at which Franklin began the study of electricity, had become a man of science, and for four years devoted himself to experiments.

Franklin was by no means alone in his studies. Besides the crowds who were interested from mere curiosity, there were three men—Ebenezer Kinnersley, Thomas Hopkinson, and Philip Syng—who experimented with him, and it was no mere amateurish work in which these men were engaged. Franklin was their spokesman and reported the results of his and their labor by means of letters to Mr. Peter Collinson. Within six months Hopkinson had observed the power of points to throw off electricity, or electrical fire, as he called it, and Franklin had discovered and described what is now known as positive and negative electricity. Within the same time Syng had invented an electrical machine, consisting of a sphere revolved on an axis with a handle, which was better adapted for producing the electrical spark than the tube-rubbing practised in Europe.

The experiments and the letters to Collinson describing them continued, and about this time we find Franklin writing a long and apparently the first intelligent explanation of the action of the Leyden jar. Then followed attempts to explain thunder and lightning as phenomena of electricity, and on July 29, 1750, Franklin sent to Collinson a paper announcing the invention of the lightning-rod, together with an explanation of its action.

In these papers he also suggested an experiment which would prove positively that lightning was a form of electricity. The two phenomena were alike as regarded light, color, crooked direction, noise, swift motion, being conducted by metals, subsisting in water or ice, rending bodies, killing animals, melting metals, and setting fire to various substances. It remained to demonstrate with absolute certainty that lightning resembled electricity in being attracted by points ; and for this purpose Franklin proposed that a man stand in a sort of sentry-box on the top of some high tower or steeple and with a pointed rod draw electricity from passing thunder-clouds.

This suggestion was successfully carried out in France, in the presence of the king, at the county-seat of the Duke D'Ayen ; and afterwards Buffon, D'Alibard, and Du Lor confirmed it by experiments of their own. But they did not use steeples ; they erected lofty iron rods, in one instance ninety-nine feet high. Nevertheless, it was in effect the same method that Franklin had suggested. The experiment was repeated in various forms in England, and the Philadelphia philosopher, postmaster, and author of " Poor Richard" became instantly famous as the discoverer of the identity of lightning with electricity.

Two years before these experiments were inaugurated he had retired from business for various reasons, chief among which was his strong desire to devote more time to science. His letters continue to be filled with closely reasoned details of all sorts of experiments. So earnest were these Philadelphia investigators, that when Kinnersley wrote complaining that in travelling to Boston he found difficulty in keeping up his experiments, Franklin, in reply, suggested a portable electrical apparatus which would not break on a journey.

In a letter written to Collinson on October 19, 1752, Franklin says he had heard of the success in

France of the experiment he had suggested for drawing the lightning from clouds by means of an elevated metal rod ; but in the mean time he had contrived another method for accomplishing the same result without the aid of a steeple or lofty iron rod. This was the kite experiment of which we have heard so much, and he goes on to describe it :

" Make a small cross of two light strips of cedar, the arms so long as to reach to the four corners of a large thin silk handkerchief when extended; tie the corners of the handkerchief to the extremities of the cross, so you have the body of a kite; which being properly accommodated with a tail, loop, and string, will rise in the air, like those made of paper; but this being of silk is fitter to bear the wet and wind of a thunder gust without tearing. To the top of the upright stick of the cross is to be fixed a very sharp pointed wire, rising a foot or more above the wood. To the end of the twine, next the hand, is to be tied a silk ribbon, and where the silk and twine join, a key may be fastened. This kite is to be raised when a thunder-gust appears to be coming on, and the person who holds the string must stand within a door or window, or under some cover, so that the silk ribbon may not be wet; and care must be taken that the twine does not touch the frame of the door or window. As soon as any of the thunder clouds come over the kite, the pointed wire will draw the electric fire from them, and the kite, with all the twine, will be electrified, and the loose filaments of the twine, will stand out every way, and be attracted by an approaching finger. And when the rain has wetted the kite and twine, so that it can conduct the electric fire freely, you will find it stream out plentifully from the key on the approach of your knuckle. At this key the phial may be charged : and from electric fire thus obtained, spirits may be kindled, and all the other electric experiments be performed, which are usually done by the help of a rubbed glass globe or tube, and thereby the sameness of the electric matter with that of lightning completely demonstrated."

This is the only description by Franklin of the experiment which added so much to his reputation. Franklin and the kite became a story for school-books; innumerable pictures of him and his son drawing the lightning down the string were made and reproduced for a century or more in every conceivable form, and even engraved on some of our national currency.

The experiment was made in June, 1752; in the following October the above letter was written, and the news it contained appears to have rushed over the world without any effort on his part to spread it. He never wrote anything more concerning this experiment than the very simple and unaffected letter to Mr. Collinson. But people, of course, asked him about it, and from the details which they professed to have obtained grand statements have been built up describing his conduct and emotions on that memorable June afternoon on the outskirts of Philadelphia, probably somewhere in the neighborhood of the present Vine Street, near Fourth; how his heart stood still with anxiety lest the trial should fail; how with trembling hand he applied his knuckles to the key, and the wild exultation with which he saw success crown his efforts.

But it is safe to say that there were none of these theatrical exhibitions, and that he made the experiment in that matter-of-fact and probably half-humorous way in which he did everything. Nothing important depended on it, for he had already proved conclusively, not only by reasoning but by his suggested experiments which had been tried in Europe, that thunder and lightning were phenomena of electricity. The kite was used because there were in Philadelphia no high steeples on which he could try the experiment that had proved his discovery in France.

But it was Franklin's good fortune on a number of occasions to be placed in picturesque and striking situations, which greatly increased his fame. He did not foresee that kite-flying would be one of these, and as it was not essential to his discovery of the nature of lightning, he was disinclined at first to think much of it, and did not even report it to Mr. Collinson until after several months had elapsed. But the world fixed upon it instantly as something easy to remember. To this day it is the popular way of illustrating Franklin's discovery, and is all that most people know of his contributions to science.

He went on steadily reporting his experiments to Collinson, and in 1753 was at work on the mistaken hypothesis of the sea being the grand source of lightning, but at the same time making the discovery of the negative and sometimes positive electricity of the clouds. He had a rod erected on his house to draw down into it the mystical fire of any passing clouds, with bells arranged to warn him when his apparatus was working ; and it was about this time that he was struck senseless and almost killed while trying the effect of an electrical shock on a turkey.

Collinson kept his letters, and in May, 1751, had them published in a pamphlet called " New Experiments and Observations in Electricity made at Philadelphia in America." It had immediately, like all of Franklin's writings, a vast success, at first in France, and afterwards in England and other countries. Franklin was, strange to say, always more popular in France than in either America or England. In England his experiments in electricity were at first laughed at, and the Royal Society refused to publish his letters in their proceedings. But after Collinson had secured their publication in a pamphlet, they were translated into German, Italian, and Latin, as well as into French, and were greatly admired not only for the discoveries and knowledge they revealed, but for their fascinating style and noble candor tinged occasionally with the most telling and homely humor.

It has been repeatedly charged that Franklin was indebted to his fellow-worker, Kinnersley, for his discoveries in electricity. The charge is so vaguely made that it is impossible to ascertain which of them are supposed to have been stolen. In Franklin's letters on electricity there are frequent foot-notes giving credit to Hopkinson and Syng for their original work, and there are also in his published works letters to and from Kinnersley. He and Kinnersley seem to have been always fast friends, and, so far as I can discover, the latter never accused Franklin of stealing from him.

After he had proved in such a brilliant manner that lightning was merely one of the forms or phenomena of that mysterious fire which appears when we rub a glass tube with buckskin, Franklin made no more discoveries in science ; but his interest and patience of research were unabated. He cannot be ranked among the great men of science, the Newtons and Keplers, or the Humboldts, Huxleys, or Darwins. He belongs rather in the second class, among the minor discoverers. But his discovery of the nature of lightning was so striking and so capable of arousing the wonder of the masses of mankind, and his invention of the lightning-rod was regarded as so universally valuable, that he has received more popular applause than men whose achievements were greater and more important.

During the rest of his life his work in science was principally in the way of encouraging its study. He was always observing, collecting facts, and writing out his conclusions. The public business in which he was soon constantly employed, and the long years of his diplomatic service in England and France, were serious interruptions, and during the last part of his life it was not often that he could steal time for that loving investigation of nature which after his thirtieth year became the great passion of his life.

His command of language had seldom been put to better use than in explaining the rather subtle ideas and conceptions in the early development of electricity. Even now after the lapse of one hundred and fifty years we seem to gain a fresher understanding of that subject by reading his homely and beautiful explanations; and modern students would have an easier time if Franklin were still here to write their text-books. His subsequent letters and essays were many of them even more happily expressed than the famous letters on electricity.

In old editions of his works all his writings on science were collected in one place, so that they could be read consecutively, which was rather better than the modern strictly chronological plan by which they are scattered throughout eight or ten large volumes. As we look over one of the old editions we feel almost compelled to begin original research at once,—it seems so easy and pretty. There are long investigations about water-spouts and whirlwinds,—whether a water-spout ever actually touches the surface of the sea, and whether its action is downward from the sky or upward from the water. He interviewed sea-captains and received letters from people in the West Indies to help him, and those who had once come within the circle of his fascination were never weary of giving aid.

He investigated what he called the light in sea-water, now called phosphorescence. The cause of the saltness of the sea and the existence of masses of salt or salt-mines in the earth he explained by the theory that all the water of the world had once been salt, for sea-shells and the bones of fishes were found, he said, on high land ; upheavals had isolated parts of the original water, which on evaporation had left the salt, and this being covered with earth, became a salt-mine. This explanation was given in a letter to his brother Peter, and is really a little essay on geology, which was then not known by that or any other name, but consisted merely of a few scattered observations.

Many of his most interesting explanations of phenomena appear in letters to the young women with whom he was on such friendly terms. Indeed, it has been said that he was never at his best except when writing to women. People believe, he tells

Miss Stevenson, that all rivers run into the sea, and he goes on to show in his most clever way that some rivers do not. The waters of the Delaware, for example, and the waters of the rivers that flow into Chesapeake Bay, probably never reach the ocean. The salt water backing up against them twice a day acts as a dam, and their fresh water is dissipated by evaporation. Only a few, like the Amazon and the Orinoco, are known to force their fresh water far out on the surface of the sea. In this same letter he describes the experiments he made to prove that dark colors absorb more of the sun's rays, and are therefore warmer than white.

While representing Pennsylvania in England, and living with Mrs. Stevenson, in Craven Street, London, he made an experiment to prove that vessels move faster in deep than in shallow water. This was generally believed by seafaring men ; but Franklin had a wooden trough made with a false bottom by which he could regulate the depth of water, and he put in it a little boat drawn by a string which ran over a pulley at the end of the trough, with a shilling attached for a weight. In this way he succeeded in demonstrating a natural law which, though known to practical men, had never been described in books of science.

He took much pains to collect information about the Gulf Stream. This wonderful river in the ocean has been long known, but the first people to observe it closely were the Nantucket whalemen, who found that their game was numerous on the edges of it, but was never seen within its warm waters. In consequence of their more exact knowledge they were able to make faster voyages than other seamen. Franklin learned about it from them, and on his numerous voyages made many observations, which he carefully recorded. He obtained a map of it from one of the whalemen, which he caused to be engraved for the general benefit of navigation on the old London chart then universally used by sailors. But the British captains slighted it, and this, like his other efforts in science, was first appreciated in France.

He has been called the discoverer of the temperature of the Gulf Stream ; but this statement is somewhat misleading. That the stream was warmer than the surrounding ocean seems to have been long known ; but Franklin was the first to take its temperature at different points with a thermometer. He did this most systematically on several of his voyages, even when suffering severely from sea-sickness, and thus suggested the use of the thermometer in investigating ocean currents. He first took these temperatures in 1775, and the next year Dr. Charles Blagden, of the British army, took them while on the voyage to America with troops to suppress the Revolution. He and Franklin are ranked together as the first to show the value of an instrument which is now universally used in ocean experiments as well as in the practical navigation of ships.*

In the same careful manner he collected all that was known of the effect of oil in stilling waves by

---

* Pillsbury's Gulf Stream, published by the U. S. government.

making the surface so smooth and slippery that the wind cannot act on it. So fascinated was he with this investigation that he had a cane made with a little receptacle for oil in the head of it, and when walking in the country in England experimented on every pond he passed. But it would be long to tell of all he wrote on light and heat, the *vis inertiæ* of matter, magnetism, rainfall, evaporation, and the aurora borealis.

One of the discomforts of colonial times, when large open fireplaces were so common, was a smoky chimney. Franklin's attention was drawn to this question about the time that he invented the Pennsylvania fireplaces, and he made an exhaustive study of the nature of smoke and heated air. He became very skilful in correcting defects in the chimneys of his friends' houses, and while he was in England noblemen and distinguished people often sought his aid. It was not, however, until 1785, near the close of his life, that he put his knowledge in writing in a letter to Dr. Ingenhausz, physician to the Emperor of Austria. The letter was published and extensively circulated as the best summary of all that was known on this important question. It is as fresh and interesting to-day as when it was written, and well worth reading, because it explains so charmingly the philosophy of some phenomena of common occurrence which modern books of science are not at much pains to make clear.

His enemies, of course, ridiculed him as a chimney doctor, and his friends have gone to the other extreme in implying that he was the only man in the world who understood the action of heat and smoke, and that, alone and unaided, he delivered mankind from a great destroyer of their domestic comfort. But his letter shows that most of his knowledge and remedies were drawn from the French and Germans. In this, as in many other similar services, he was merely an excellent collector of scattered material, which he summarized so well that it was more available than before. He was by no means the only person in the world who could doctor a chimney; but there were few, if any, who could describe in such beautiful language the way in which it was done.

He invented a stove that would consume its own smoke, taking the principle from a Frenchman who had shown how the flame of a burning substance could be made to draw downward through the fuel, so that the smoke was burnt with the fuel. But the way in which this invention is usually described would lead one to suppose that it was entirely original with Franklin.

He was much interested in agriculture, and was an earnest advocate of mineral manures, encouraged grape culture, and helped to introduce the basket willow and broom-corn into the United States. He at one time owned a farm of three hundred acres near Burlington, New Jersey, where he tried agricultural experiments. He dabbled in medicine, as has been shown, and also wasted time over that ancient delusion, phonetic spelling.

Knowing, as we do, Franklin's versatility, it is nevertheless somewhat of a surprise to find him venturing into the sphere of music. He is said to have been able to play on the harp, the guitar, and the violin, but probably only in a philosopher's way and not well on any of them. Some people in Eng- • land had succeeded in constructing a musical instrument made of glasses, the idea being taken from the pleasant sound produced by passing a wet finger round the brim of a drinking-glass. When in England Franklin was so delighted with these instruments that he set about improving them. He had glasses specially moulded of a bell-like shape and ground with great care until each had its proper note. They were placed in a frame in such a way that they could all be set revolving at once by means of a treadle worked by the foot, and as they revolved they were played by the wet fingers pressed on their brims. He gave the name "Armonica" to his instrument, and describes its tones as "incomparably sweet beyond those of any other." It is said to have been used in public concerts, and it was one of the curiosities at his famous Craven Street lodging-house in London, where he also had a fine electrical apparatus, and took pleasure in showing his English friends the American experiments of which they had heard so much.

He seems to have studied music with great care as a science, just as he studied the whirlwinds, the smoke, and the lightning ; but he was unalterably opposed to the so-called modern music then becoming fashionable, and which is still to a great extent the music of our time. The pleasure derived from it was, he said, not the natural pleasure caused by harmony of sounds, but rather that felt on seeing the surprising feats of tumblers and rope-dancers.

> "Many pieces of it are mere compositions of tricks. I have sometimes, at a concert, attended by a common audience, placed myself so as to see all their faces, and observed no signs of pleasure in them during the performance of a great part that was admired by the performers themselves; while a plain old Scotch tune, which they disdained, and could scarcely be prevailed upon to play, gave manifest and general delight."

In a letter to Lord Kames which has been often quoted he explained at length, and for the most part in very technical language, the reasons for the superiority of the Scotch tunes.

> "Farther, when we consider by whom these ancient tunes were composed and how they were first performed we shall see that such harmonical successions of sounds were natural and even necessary in their construction. They were composed by the minstrels of those days to be played on the harp accompanied by the voice. The harp was strung with wire, which gives a sound of long continuance and had no contrivance like that in the modern harpsichord, by which the sound of the preceding could be stopped the moment a succeeding note began. To avoid actual discord, it was therefore necessary that the succeeding emphatic note should be a chord with the preceding, as their sounds must exist at the same time. Hence arose that beauty in those tunes that has so long pleased, and will please forever, though men scarce know why."

Franklin's numerous voyages naturally turned his mind to problems of the sea. He pondered much on the question whether the daily motion of the earth from west to east would increase the speed of a ship sailing eastward and retard it on a westward passage. He was not quite sure that the earth's motion would have such an effect, but he thought it possible.

"I wish I had mathematics enough to satisfy myself whether the much shorter voyages made by ships bound hence to England, than by those from England hither, are not in some degree owing to the diurnal motion of the earth, and if so in what degree. It is a notion that has lately entered my mind; I know not if ever any other's." (Bigelow's Works of Franklin, vol. ii. p. 14.)

He referred to the subject again soon after, and finally a few years before his death,* but always as an unsettled question. The idea seems never to have got beyond the stage of investigation with him, but Parton has built up out of it a wonderful discovery.

"He conceived an idea still more practically useful, which has since given rise to a little library of nautical works, and conferred unmerited honor upon a naval charlatan—Maury. This idea was that by studying the form and motions of the earth and directing a ship's course so that it shall partake of the earth's diurnal motion a voyage may be materially shortened." (Parton's "Life of Franklin," vol. ii. p. 72.)

This is certainly a most extraordinary statement to be made by a writer like Parton, who has given the main facts of Franklin's life with considerable fidelity. He refers to it again in another passage, in which he says that this method of navigation is now used by all intelligent seamen. But there is no evidence that it was ever so used. He may have confused it with great circle sailing. The theory is an exploded one. There is no library of nautical works on the subject, and I think that the officers of the United States navy, the captains of the great ocean liners, and thousands of sailors all over the world

* Bigelow's Works of Franklin, vol. ii. p. 331; vol. ix. p. 185.

would be very much surprised to hear Maury called a charlatan.

Maury's wonderful investigations were not in the line of sailing a ship so as to take advantage of the earth's diurnal motion, and could not have been suggested by such an idea. He explored the physical geography of the sea, and particularly the currents, trade-winds, and zones of calm. It was he who first worked out the shortest routes from place to place, which are still used. Although he never made a picturesque and brilliant discovery about lightning, and had not Franklin's exquisite power of expression, he was a much more remarkable man of science.

In a long letter to Alphonsus Le Roy, of Paris, written in 1785, on his voyage home from France with Captain Truxton, Franklin summed up all his maritime observations, including what he knew of the Gulf Stream. This letter is full of most curious suggestions for the navigation of ships, and was accompanied by a plate of carefully drawn figures, which has been reproduced in most editions of his works.

So much attention had been given, he said, to shaping the hull of a vessel so as to offer the least resistance to the water, that it was time the sails were shaped so as to offer the least resistance to the air. He proposed to do this by making the sails smaller and increasing their number, and contrived a most curious rig (Fig. 4) which he thought would offer the least resistance both in sailing free and in beating to windward.

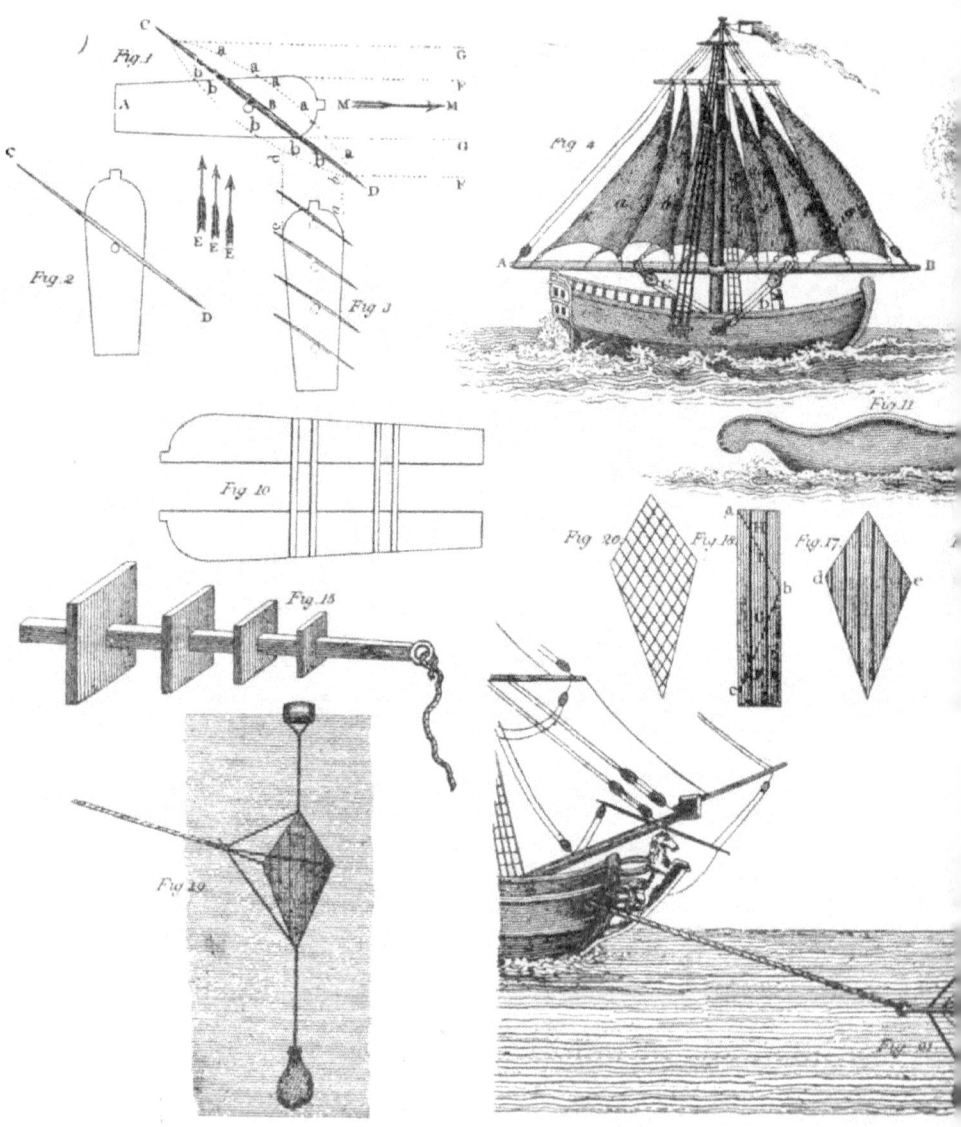

Fig.1

Fig.2

Fig 3

fig 4

Fig.11

Fig 10

Fig 20

Fig 18

Fig.17

Fig.15

Fig 19

Fig 21

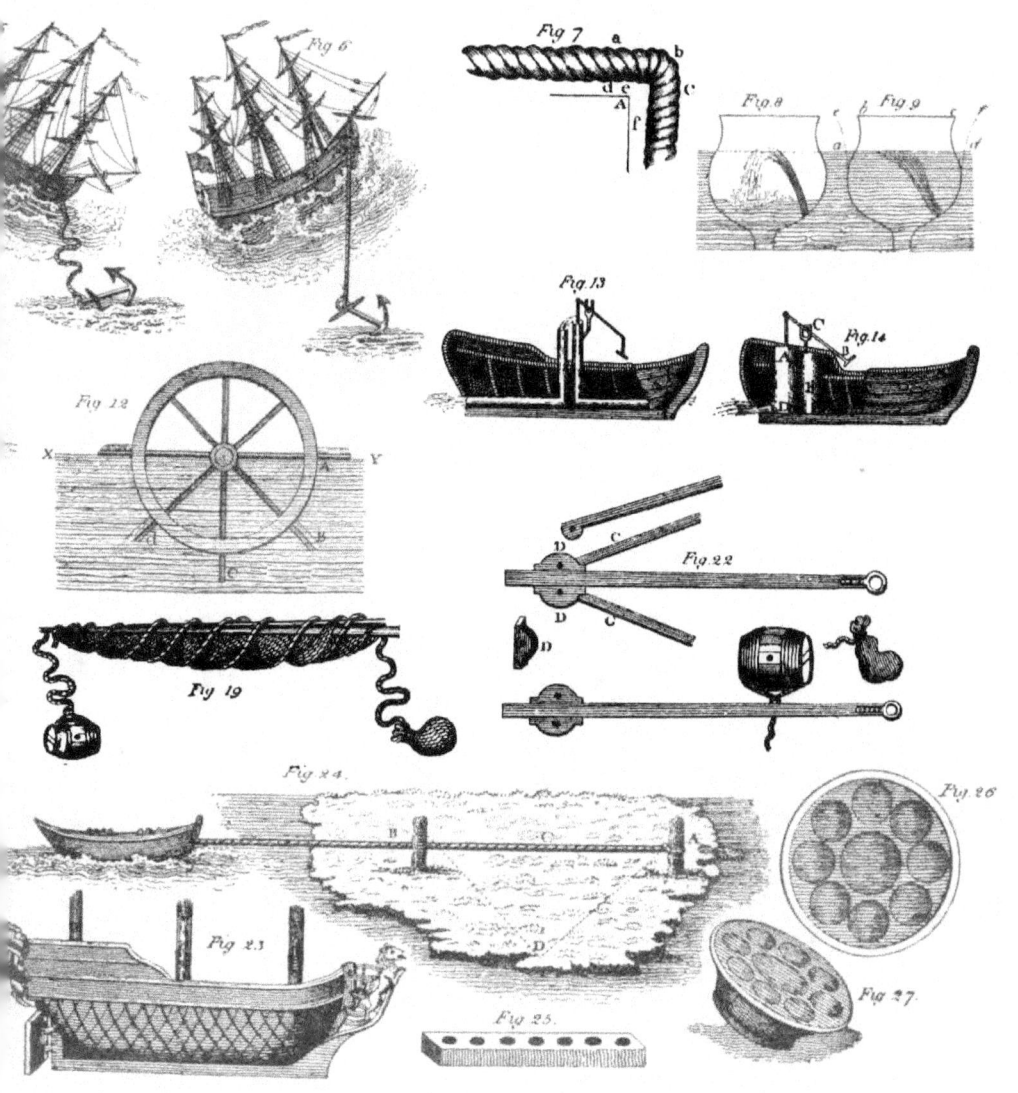

Fig 6

Fig 7

Fig. 8 Fig. 9

Fig. 13

Fig. 14

Fig 12

Fig. 22

Fig 19

Fig. 24

Fig. 26

Fig. 23

Fig. 25

Fig. 27

Figs. 5, 6, and 7 show why, in those days of rope cables, a ship was always breaking the cable where it bent at right angles just outside the hawse-hole. All the strain was on the outer strands of the rope at *a b c*, Fig. 7, and as they broke the others followed one by one. His remedy for this was to have a large wheel or pulley in the hawse-hole.

Figs. 8 and 9 show how a vessel with a leak at first fills very rapidly, so that the crew, finding they cannot gain on the water with the pumps, take to their boats. But if they would remain they would find after a while that the quantity entering would be less as the surfaces without and within became more nearly equal, and that the pumps would now be able to prevent it from rising higher. The water would also begin to reach light wooden work, empty chests, and water-casks, which would give buoyancy, and thus the ship could be kept afloat longer than the crew at first expected. In this connection he calls attention to the Chinese method of water-tight compartments which Mr. Le Roy had already adopted in his boat on the Seine.

Fig. 12 is intended to show the loss of power in a paddle-wheel because the stroke from A to B is downward and from D to X upward, and the only effective stroke is from B to D. A better method of propulsion, he thinks, is by pumping water out through the stern, as shown in Figs. 13 and 14.

Figs. 15, 16, 17, 18, 19, 20, 21, and 22 illustrate methods of making floating sea anchors by which to lay a vessel to in a gale. Fig. 24 shows how a heavy boat may be drawn ashore by bending the rope from

C to *D*. Fig. 23 represents a new way of planking ships to secure greater strength, and Figs. 26 and 27 are soup-dishes which will not spill in a heavy sea. But this delightful letter is published in all of the editions of his works, and should be read in order to render his ingenious contrivances intelligible.

Among the few of Franklin's writings on scientific subjects which are not in the form of letters is an essay, entitled "Peopling of Countries," supposed to have been written in 1751. It is in part intended to show that Great Britain was not injured by the immigration to America; the gap was soon filled up; and the colonies, by consuming British manufactures, increased the resources of the mother country. The essay is full of reflections on political economy, which had not then become a science, and the twenty-second section contains the statement that there is no bound to the productiveness of plants and animals other than that occasioned by their crowding and interfering with one another's means of subsistence. This statement supplied Malthus with the foundation for his famous theory that the population of the earth increased in a geometrical ratio, while the means of subsistence increased only in an arithmetical ratio, and some of those who opposed this theory devoted themselves to showing error in Franklin's twenty-second section rather than to disputing the conclusions of Malthus, which they believed would fall if Franklin could be shown to be in the wrong.

He investigated the new field of political economy with the same thoroughness as the other departments of science, and wrote on national wealth, the price of corn, free trade, the effects of luxury, idleness, and industry, the slave-trade, and peace and war. The humor and imagination in one of his letters to Dr. Priestley on war justify the quoting of a part of it:

"A young angel of distinction being sent down to this world on some business, for the first time, had an old courier-spirit assigned him as a guide. They arrived over the seas of Martinico, in the middle of the long day of obstinate fight between the fleets of Rodney and De Grasse. When through the clouds of smoke he saw the fire of the guns, the decks covered with mangled limbs and bodies dead and dying, or blown into the air, and the quantity of pain, misery, and destruction the crews yet alive were thus with so much eagerness dealing round to one another, he turned angrily to his guide and said, 'You blundering blockhead, you are ignorant of your business; you undertook to conduct me to the earth and you have brought me into hell!' "No, sir,' says the guide, 'I have made no mistake; this is really the earth, and these are men. Devils never treat one another in this cruel manner; they have more sense, and more of what men (vainly) call humanity.'" (Bigelow's Works of Franklin, vol. vii. p. 465.}

VI

THE PENNSYLVANIA POLITICIAN

WHILE Franklin kept his little stationery shop and printing-office, sent out his almanacs every year, read and studied, experimented in science, and hoped for an assured income which would give larger leisure for study and experiment, he was all the time drifting more and more into public life. In a certain sense he had been accustomed to dealing with living public questions from boyhood. When an apprentice in his teens, he had written articles for his brother's newspaper attacking the established religious and political system of Massachusetts, and during his brother's imprisonment the newspaper had been published in the apprentice's name. In Pennsylvania his own newspaper, the *Gazette*, which he established when he was but twenty-three years old, made him something of a public man; and his pamphlet in favor of paper money, which appeared at about the same period, showed how strongly his mind inclined towards the large questions of government.

When he reached manhood he also developed a strong inclination to assist in public improvements, in the encouragement of thrift and comfort, and in the relief of suffering, subjects which are now included under the heads of philanthropy and reform.

He had in full measure the social and public spirit of the Anglo-Saxon, the spirit which instinctively builds up the community while at the same time it is deeply devoted to its own concerns. The only one of his ancestors that had risen above humble conditions was of this sort, and had been a leader in the public affairs of a village.

His natural disposition towards benevolent enterprises was much stimulated, he tells us, by a book called "Essays to do Good," by the eminent Massachusetts divine, Cotton Mather, of witchcraft fame. He also read about the same time De Foe's "Essay upon Projects," a volume recommending asylums for the insane, technical schools, mutual benefit societies, improved roads, better banking, bankrupt laws, and other things which have now become the commonplace characteristics of our age.

His club, the Junto, was the first important fruit of this benevolent disposition. At first its members kept all their books at its rooms for the common benefit ; but some of the books having been injured, all were taken back by the owners, and this loss suggested to Franklin the idea of a circulating library supported by subscriptions. He drew up a plan and went about soliciting money in 1731, but it took him more than a year to collect forty-five pounds. James Logan, the secretary of the province, gave advice as to what books to buy, and the money was sent to London to be expended by Mr. Peter Collinson, to whom Franklin's famous letters on electricity were afterwards written.

Mr. Collinson was the literary and philosophic

agent of Pennsylvania in those days. To him John Bartram, the first American botanist, sent the plants that he collected in the New World, and Mr. Collinson obtained for him the money with which to pursue his studies. Collinson encouraged the new library in every way. For thirty years he made for it the annual purchase of books, always adding one or two volumes as a present, and it will be remembered that it was through him that Franklin obtained the electrical tube which started him on his remarkable discoveries.

The library began its existence at the Junto's rooms and grew steadily. Influential people gradually became interested in it and added their gifts. For half a century it occupied rooms in various buildings,—at one time in the State-House, and during the Revolution in Carpenters' Hall,—until in 1790, the year of Franklin's death, it erected a pretty building on Fifth Street, opposite Independence square. During the period from 1731 to 1790 similar libraries were established in the town, which it absorbed one by one: in 1769 the Union Library, in 1771 the Association Library Company and Amicable Library Company, and, finally, in 1790 the Loganian Library, which James Logan had established by his will. Before the Revolution the number of books increased but slowly, and in 1785 was only 5487. They now number 190,000.

Franklin says that it was the mother of subscription libraries in North America, and that in a few years the colonists became more of a reading people, and the common tradesmen and farmers were as intelligent as most gentlemen from other countries. This statement seems to be justified ; for within a few years libraries sprang up in New England and the South, and they may have been suggested by the Philadelphia Library which Franklin founded.

I have already shown how Franklin established the academy which soon became the College of Philadelphia, but this was some twenty years after he founded the library. Almost immediately after the academy was started Dr. Thomas Bond sought his assistance in establishing a hospital. Pennsylvania was receiving at that time great numbers of German immigrants, who arrived in crowded ships after a voyage of months, in a terrible state of dirt and disease. There was no proper place provided for them, and they were a source of danger to the rest of the people. A hospital was needed, and Dr. Bond, at first meeting with but little success, finally accomplished his object with the assistance of Franklin, who obtained for him a grant of two thousand pounds from the Assembly, and helped to stir up subscribers.

This was the first hospital in America, and it still fulfils its mission in the beautiful old colonial buildings which were originally erected for it. Additional buildings have been since added, fortunately, in the same style of architecture. For the corner-stone Franklin wrote an inscription matchless for its originality and appropriateness :

"In the year of CHRIST MDCCLV George the Second happily reigning (for he sought the happiness of his people), Philadelphia flourishing (for its inhabitants were public spirited), this building, by the bounty of the government, and of many private persons, was piously founded for the relief of the sick and miserable. May the GOD OF MERCIES bless the undertaking.''

In the same spirit Franklin secured by a little agitation the paving of the street round the market, and afterwards started subscriptions to keep this pavement clean. At that time the streets of Philadelphia, like those of most of the colonial towns, were merely earth roads, and it was not until some years after Franklin's first efforts at the market that there was any general paving done. He also secured a well-regulated night watch for the city in place of the disorderly, drunken heelers of the constables, who had long made a farce of the duty; and he established a volunteer fire company which was the foundation of the system that prevailed in Philadelphia until the paid department was introduced after the civil war.

The American Philosophical Society, which was also originated by him, might seem to be more entitled to mention in the chapter on science. But it was really a benevolent enterprise, intended to propagate useful knowledge, to encourage agriculture, trade, and the mechanic arts, and to multiply the conveniences and pleasures of life. He first suggested it in 1743, in which year he prepared a plan for a society for promoting useful knowledge, and one appears to have been organized which led a languishing existence until 1769, when it was joined by another organization, called "The American Society held at Philadelphia for Promoting Useful Knowledge," and from this union resulted the

American Philosophical Society, which still exists. Franklin was for a long time its president, and was succeeded by Rittenhouse. It was the first society in America devoted to science. Thomas Jefferson and other prominent persons throughout the colonies were members of it, and during the colonial period and long afterwards it held a very important position.

Franklin was by nature a public man ; but the beginning of his life as an office-holder may be said to have dated from his appointment as clerk of the Assembly. This took place in 1736, when he had been in business for himself for some years, and his newspaper and " Poor Richard" were well under way. It was a tiresome task to sit for hours listening to buncombe speeches, and drawing magic squares and circles to while away the time. But he valued the appointment because it gave him influence with the members and a hold on the public printing.

The second year his election to the office was opposed ; an influential member wanted the place for a friend, and Franklin had a chance to show a philosopher's skill in practical politics.

" Having heard that he had in his library a certain very scarce and curious book, I wrote a note to him, expressing my desire of perusing that book, and requesting he would do me the favour of lending it to me for a few days. He sent it immediately, and I return'd it in about a week with another note, expressing strongly my sense of the favour. When we next met, in the House, he spoke to me (which he had never done before), and with great civility; and he ever after manifested a readiness to serve me on all occasions, so that we became great friends and our friendship continued to his death. This is another instance of the truth of an old maxim I had learned, which says ' He that has once done you a kindness will be more ready to do you another, than he whom you yourself have obliged.' " (Bigelow's Franklin from his own Writings, vol. i. p. 260.)

Some people have professed to be very much shocked at this disingenuous trick, as they call it, although perhaps capable of far more discreditable ones themselves. It would be well if no worse could be said of modern practical politics.

Franklin held his clerkship nearly fifteen years. During this period he was also postmaster of Philadelphia, and these two offices, with the benevolent enterprises of the library, the hospital, the Philosophical Society, and the academy and college, made him very much of a public man in the best sense of the word long before he was engaged in regular politics.

In the year 1747 he performed an important public service by organizing the militia. War had been declared by England against both France and Spain, and the colonies were called upon to help the mother country. Great difficulty was experienced in recruiting troops in Quaker Pennsylvania, although the Quakers would indirectly consent to it when given a reasonable excuse. They would vote money for the king's use, and the king's officials might take the responsibility of using it for war; they would supply provisions to the army, for that was charity; and on one occasion they voted four thousand pounds for the purchase of beef, pork, flour, wheat, or *other grain ;* and as powder was grain, the money was used in supplying it.

But the actual recruiting of troops was more difficult, and it was to further this object that Franklin exerted himself. He wrote one of his clever pamphlets showing the danger of a French invasion, and supplied biblical texts in favor of defensive war. Then calling a mass-meeting in the large building afterwards used for the college, he urged the people to form an association for defence. Papers were distributed among them, and in a few minutes he had twelve hundred signatures. These citizen soldiers were called "Associators,"—a name used down to the time of the Revolution to describe the Pennsylvania militia. In a few days he had enrolled ten thousand volunteers, which shows how large the combatant portion of the population was in spite of Quaker doctrine.

In 1748 he retired from active business with the purpose of devoting himself to science. It was the custom at that time to give retired men of business the more important public offices; and in 1752, about the time of his discovery of the nature of lightning, he was elected to the Assembly as one of the members to represent Philadelphia. In the same year he was also elected a justice of the peace and a member of the City Councils.

At this time France and England were temporarily at peace. The treaty of Aix-la-Chapelle in 1748 had resulted in a sort of cessation of hostilities, which France was using to push more actively her advantages on the Ohio River and in the Mississippi Valley. She intended to get behind all the colonies and occupy the continent to the Pacific Ocean. The efforts of Great Britain to check these designs, including the expeditions of the youthful Washington to the Ohio, need not be given here.* England

---

* Pennsylvania: Colony and Commonwealth, p. 147.

broke the treaty of Aix-la-Chapelle, and what is known as the Seven Years' War began with the memorable defeat of Braddock.

Franklin was sent by the Pennsylvania Assembly to Braddock's head-quarters in Virginia to give any assistance he could and to prevent Braddock from making a raid into Pennsylvania to procure wagons, as he had threatened. The journey was made on horseback in company with the governors of New York and Massachusetts, and on the way Franklin had an opportunity to observe the action of a small whirlwind, which he reported in a pleasant letter to Mr. Collinson. It was while on this visit that Franklin appears in Thackeray's "Virginians," in which he is strangely described as a shrewd, bright little man who would drink only water.

He told Braddock that there were plenty of wagons in Pennsylvania, and he was accordingly commissioned to procure them. He returned to Philadelphia, and within two weeks had delivered one hundred and fifty wagons and two hundred and fifty pack-horses. He had received only eight hundred pounds from Braddock, and was obliged to advance two hundred pounds himself and give bond to indemnify the owners of such horses as should be lost in the service. Claims to the amount of twenty thousand pounds were afterwards made against him, and he would have been ruined if the government, after long delay, had not come to his rescue. Such disinterested service was not forgotten, and his popularity was greatly increased.

He had the year before been one of the repre-

sentatives of Pennsylvania in the convention at Albany, where he had offered a plan for the union of
all the colonies, which was generally approved, and
I shall consider this plan more fully in another chapter. It was intended, of course, primarily to enable
the colonies to make more effective resistance against
the French and Indians, and as an additional assistance he suggested that a new colony be planted on
the Ohio River. The establishment of this colony
was a favorite scheme with him, and he urged it
again many years afterwards while in England.

As a member of the Pennsylvania Assembly he
joined the Quaker majority in that body and became
one of its leaders. This majority was in continual
conflict with the governor appointed by William
Penn's sons, who were the proprietors of the province. The government of the colony was divided
in a curious way. The proprietors had the right to
appoint the governor, judges, and sheriffs, or, in
other words, had absolute control of the executive
offices, while the colonists controlled the Legislature,
or Assembly, as it was called, and in this Assembly
the Quakers exercised the strongest influence.

During the seventy years that the colony had been
founded the Assembly had built up by slow degrees
a body of popular rights. It paid the governor his
salary, and this gave it a vast control over him ; for
if he vetoed any favorite law it could retaliate by
cutting off his means of subsistence. This right to
withhold the governor's salary constituted the most
important principle of colonial constitutional law, and
by it not only Pennsylvania but the other colonies

maintained what liberty they possessed and saved themselves from the oppression of royal or proprietary governors.

Another right for which the Pennsylvania Assembly always strenuously contended was that any bill passed by it for raising money for the crown must be simply accepted or rejected by the governor. He was not to attempt to force its amendment by threats of rejection, or to interfere in any way with the manner of raising the money, and was to have no control over its disbursement. The king had a right to ask for aid, but the colony reserved the right to use its own methods in furnishing it.

These rights the proprietors were constantly trying to break down by instructing their governors to assent to money and other bills only on certain conditions, among which was the stipulation that they should not go into effect until the king's pleasure was known. They sent out their governors with secret instructions, and compelled them to give bonds for their faithful performance. When the governors declined to reveal these instructions, the Assembly thought it had another grievance, for it had always refused to be governed in this manner; and was now more determined than ever to maintain this point because several bills had been introduced in Parliament for the purpose of making royal instructions to governors binding on all the colonial assemblies without regard to their charters or constitutions.

These were all very serious designs on liberty, and the proprietors took advantage of the war necessities and Braddock's defeat to carry them out in the most extreme form. The home government was calling on all the colonies for war supplies, and Pennsylvania must comply not only to secure her own safety but under fear of displeasing the Parliament and king. If under such pressure she could be induced to pass some of the supply bills at the dictation of the governor, or with an admission of the validity of his secret instructions, a precedent would be established and the proprietary hold on the province greatly strengthened.

The Quakers, especially those comprising the majority in the Assembly, were not at heart opposed to war or to granting war supplies. As they expressed it in the preamble to one of their laws, they had no objection to others bearing arms, but were themselves principled against it. If the others wished to fight, or if it was necessary for the province to fight, they, as the governing body, would furnish the means. Franklin relates how, when he was organizing the Associators, it was proposed in the Union Fire Company that sixty pounds should be expended in buying tickets in a lottery, the object of which was to raise money for the purchase of cannon. There were twenty-two Quakers in the fire company and eight others; but the twenty-two, by purposely absenting themselves, allowed the proposition to be carried.

The Quaker Assembly voted money for war supplies as liberally and as loyally as the Assembly of any other colony; but at every step it was met by the designs of the governor to force upon it those conditions which would be equivalent to a surrender of the liberties of the colony. Thus, in 1754 it voted a war supply of twenty thousand pounds, which was the same amount as Virginia, the most active of the colonies against the French, had just subscribed, and was much more than other colonies gave. New York gave only five thousand pounds, Maryland six thousand pounds, and New Jersey nothing. But the governor refused his assent to the bill unless a clause was inserted suspending it until the approval of the king had been obtained, and this condition the Assembly felt bound to reject.

During the whole seven years of the war these contests with the governor continued; and the members of the Assembly, to show their zeal for the war, were obliged at times to raise the money on their own credit without submitting their bill to the governor for his approval. In these struggles Franklin bore a prominent part, drafting the replies which the Assembly made to the governor's messages, and acquiring a most thorough knowledge of all the principles of colonial liberty. At the same time he continued to enjoy jovial personal relations with the governors whom he resisted so vigorously in the Assembly, and was often invited to dine with them, when they would joke with him about his support of the Quakers.

The disputes were increased about the time of Braddock's defeat by a new subject of controversy. As the Assembly was passing bills for war supplies which had to be raised by taxation, it was thought to be no more than right that the proprietary estates should also bear their share of the tax. The proprietors owned vast tracts of land which they had not yet sold to the people, and as the war was being waged for the defence of these as well as all the other property of the country, the Assembly and the people in general were naturally very indignant when the governor refused his consent to any bill which did not expressly exempt these lands from taxation. The amount assessed on the proprietary land was trifling,—only five hundred pounds ; but both parties felt that they were contending for a principle, and when some gentlemen offered to pay the whole amount in order to stop the dispute, it was rejected.

The proprietors, through the governor, offered a sort of indirect bribe in the form of large gifts of land,—a thousand acres to every colonel, five hundred to every captain, and so on down to two hundred to each private,—which seemed very liberal, and was an attempt to put the Assembly in an unpatriotic position if it should refuse to exempt the estates after such a generous offer. But the Assembly was unmoved, and declined to vote any more money for the purposes of the war, if it involved a sacrifice of the liberties of the people or enabled the proprietors to escape taxation. "Those," said Franklin, "who would give up essential liberty for the sake of a little temporary safety, deserve neither liberty nor safety."

But the proprietors were determined to carry the point of exemption of their estates, and as a clamor was being raised against them in England for defeating, through their governor, the efforts of the Assembly to raise money for the war, they sent over word that they would subscribe five thousand pounds for the protection of the colony. Such munificence took the Assembly by surprise, and an appropriation bill was passed without taxing the proprietary estates. But popular resentment against the proprietors was raised to a high pitch when it was discovered that the five thousand pounds was to be collected out of the arrears of quit-rents due the proprietors. It was merely a clever trick on their part to saddle their bad debts on the province, have their estates exempted from taxation, and at the same time give themselves a reputation for generosity.

The defeat of Braddock in July, 1755, was followed in September and October by a terrible invasion of the Indians, who massacred the farmers almost as far east as Philadelphia. Evidently something more was necessary to protect the province than the mere loose organization of the Associators, and a militia law drafted by Franklin was passed by the Quaker Assembly. The law had a long preamble attached, which he had prepared with great ingenuity to satisfy Quaker scruples. It was made up largely of previous Quaker utterances on war, and declared that while it would be persecution, and therefore unlawful in Pennsylvania, to compel Quakers to bear arms against their consciences, so it would be wrong to prohibit from engaging in war those who thought it their duty. The Quaker Assembly, as representing all the people of the province, would accordingly furnish to those who wanted to fight the legal means for carrying out their wish ; and the law then went on to show how they should be organized as soldiers.

In his *Gazette* Franklin published a Dialogue written by himself, which was intended to answer criticisms on the law and especially the objections of those who were disgusted because the new law exempted the Quakers. Why, it was asked, should the combatant portion of the people fight for the lives and property of men who are too cowardly to fight for themselves? These objectors required as delicate handling as the Quakers, and Franklin approached them with his usual skill.

"Z. For my part I am no coward, but hang me if I will fight to save the Quakers.

"X. That is to say, you will not pump ship, because it will save the rats as well as yourself."

As a consequence of his success in writing in favor of war, the philosopher, electrician, and editor found himself elected colonel of the men he had persuaded, and was compelled to lead about five hundred of them to the Lehigh Valley, where the German village of Gnadenhutten had been burnt and its inhabitants massacred. He had no taste for such business, and would have avoided it if he could; for he never used a gun even for amusement, and would not keep a weapon of any kind in his house. But the province with its peace-loving Quakers and Germans had never before experienced actual war, nor even difficulties with the Indians, and Franklin was as much a military man as anybody.

So the philosopher of nearly fifty years, famous the world over for his discoveries in electricity and his " Poor Richard's Almanac," set forth in December, slept on the ground or in barns, arranged the order of scouting parties, and regulated the serving of grog to his men. He built a line of small forts in the Lehigh Valley, and during the two months that he was there no doubt checked the Indians who were watching him all the time from the hilltops, and who went no farther than to kill ten unfortunate farmers. He had no actual battle with them, and was perhaps fortunate in escaping a surprise ; but he was very wily in his movements, and in his shrewd common-sense way understood Indian tactics. He has left us a description in one of his letters how a force like his should, before stopping for the night, make a circuit backward and camp near their trail, setting a guard to watch the trail so that any Indians following it could be seen long before they reached the camp.

He, indeed, conducted his expedition in the most thorough and systematic manner, marching his men in perfect order with a semicircle of scouts in front, an advance-guard, then the main body, with scouts on each flank and spies on every hill, followed by a watchful rear-guard. He observed all the natural objects with his usual keen interest, noting the exact number of minutes required by his men to fell a tree for the palisaded forts he was building. After two months of roughing it he could not sleep in a bed on his return to Bethlehem. " It was so different," he says, " from my hard lodging on the floor of a hut at Gnadenhutten with only a blanket or two."

Very characteristic of him also was the suggestion

he made to his chaplain when the good man found it difficult to get the soldiers to attend prayers. "It is perhaps beneath the dignity of your profession," said Franklin, "to act as steward of the rum; but if you were only to distribute it after prayers you would have them all about you." The chaplain thought well of it, and "never," Franklin tells us, "were prayers more generally or more punctually attended."

On the return of the troops to Philadelphia after their two months' campaign they had a grand parade and review, saluting the houses of all their officers with discharges of cannon and small-arms; and the salute given before the door of their philosopher colonel broke several of the glasses of his electrical apparatus.

The next year, 1756, brought some relief to the colonists by Armstrong's successful expedition against the Indians at Kittanning. But the year 1757 was more gloomy than ever. Nothing was wanting but a few more soldiers to enable the French to press on down the Mississippi and secure their line to New Orleans, or to fall upon the rear of the colonies and conquer them. The proprietors of Pennsylvania took advantage of the situation to force the Assembly to abandon all its most cherished rights. The new governor came out with full instructions to assent to no tax bill unless it exempted the proprietary estates, to have the proprietary quit-rents paid in sterling instead of Pennsylvania currency, and to assent to no money bill unless the money to be raised was appropriated for some particular object or was to be at the disposal of the governor and Assembly jointly.

Their attack on the liberties of the province was well timed; for, the English forces having been everywhere defeated, the Assembly felt that it must assist in the prosecution of the war at all hazards. It therefore resolved to waive its rights for the present, and passed a bill for raising thirty thousand pounds to be expended under the joint supervision of the Assembly and the governor. So the proprietors gained one of their points, and they soon gained another. The Assembly was before long obliged to raise more money, and voted one hundred thousand pounds, the largest single appropriation ever made. It was to be raised by a general tax, and the tax was to include the proprietary estates. The governor objected, and the Assembly, influenced by the terrible necessities of the war, yielded and passed the bill in February, 1757, without taxing the estates.

But it was determined to carry on its contest with the governor in another way, and resolved to send two commissioners to England to lay before the king and Privy Council the conduct of the proprietors. The first avowed object of the commissioners was to secure the taxing of the proprietary estates, and the second was to suggest that the proprietorship be abolished and the province taken under the direct rule of the crown. Franklin and Isaac Norris, the Speaker of the Assembly, were appointed commissioners, but Norris being detained by ill health, Franklin started alone.

He set forth as a sort of minister plenipotentiary to London, where he had at one time worked as a journeyman printer. He had left London an obscure, impoverished boy; he was returning as a famous man of science, retired from worldly business on an assured income. He remained in England for five years, and so full of pleasure, interesting occupation, and fame were those years that it is remarkable that he was willing to come back to Pennsylvania.

He secured lodgings for himself and his son William at Mrs. Stevenson's, No. 7 Craven Street. Here he lived all of the five years and also during his subsequent ten years' residence in London. He had been recommended to her house by some Pennsylvania friends who had boarded there; but he soon ceased to be a mere lodger, and No. 7 Craven Street became his second home. He and Mrs. Stevenson became firm friends, and for her daughter Mary he formed a strong attachment, which continued all his life. His letters to her are among the most beautiful ever written by him, and he encouraged her to study science. "In all that time," he once wrote to her, referring to the happy years he had spent at her mother's house, "we never had among us the smallest misunderstanding; our friendship has been all clear sunshine, without the least cloud in its hemisphere."

Mrs. Stevenson took care of the small every-day affairs of his life, advised as to the presents he sent home to his wife, assisted in buying them, and when a child of one of his poor English relatives needed assistance, she took it into her house and cared for it with almost as tender an interest as if she had been its mother. Many years afterwards, in a letter to her written while he was in France, Franklin regrets "the want of that order and economy in my family which reigned in it when under your prudent direction." *

The familiar, pleasant life he led with her family is shown in a little essay written for their amusement, called "The Craven Street Gazette." It is a burlesque on the pompous court news of the English journals. Mrs. Stevenson figures as the queen and the rest of the family and their friends as courtiers and members of the nobility, and we get in this way pleasant glimpses of each one's peculiarities and habits, the way they lived, and their jokes on one another.

He had an excellent electrical machine and other apparatus for experiments in her house, and went on with the researches which so fascinated him in much the same way as he had done at home. It was at No. 7 Craven Street that he planned his musical instrument, the armonica, already described, and exhibited it to his friends who came to see his electrical experiments. He quickly became a member of all the learned societies, was given the degree of doctor of laws by the universities of St. Andrew's, Edinburgh, and Oxford, and soon knew all the celebrities in England. But he does not appear to have seen much of that burly and boisterous literary

---

* Bigelow's Works of Franklin, vol. vi. p. 300.

chieftain, Dr. Johnson. This was unfortunate, for Franklin's description of him would have been invaluable.

Peter Collinson, to whom his letters on electricity had been sent, of course welcomed him. He became intimate with Dr. Fothergill, the fashionable physician of London, who had assisted to make his electrical discoveries known. This was another of his life-long friendships : the two were always in perfect sympathy, investigating with the enthusiasm of old cronies everything of philosophic and human interest.

Priestley, the discoverer of oxygen and one of the foremost men of science of that time, became another bosom friend, and Franklin furnished him the material for his " History of Electricity." William Strahan, the prosperous publisher and friend of Dr. Johnson, also conceived a great liking for the Pennsylvania agent. Strahan afterwards became a member of Parliament, and was fond of saying to Franklin that they both had started life as printers, but no two printers had ever risen so high. He was a whole-souled, jovial man, wanted his son to marry Franklin's daughter, and wanted Mrs. Franklin to come over to England and settle there with her husband, who, he said, must never go back to America. He used to write letters to Mrs. Franklin trying to persuade her to overcome her aversion to the sea, and he made bets with Franklin that his persuasions would succeed.

We need not wonder that Franklin spent five years on his mission, when he was so comfortably settled with his own servant in addition to those of Mrs. Stevenson, his chariot to drive in like an ambassador, and his son William studying law at the inns of court. During his stay, and about the year 1760, William presented him with an illegitimate grandson, William Temple Franklin. This boy was brought up exclusively by his grandfather, and scarcely knew his father, who soon married a young lady from the West Indies. In his infancy Temple was not an inmate of the Craven Street house, but he lived there afterwards during his grandfather's second mission to England, and accompanied him to France.

The birth of Temple and his parentage were probably not generally known among Franklin's English friends during this first mission. It has been said also that William's illegitimacy was not known in London, but this is unlikely. It did not, however, interfere with the young man's advancement; for in 1762, just before Franklin returned to America, William was appointed by the crown governor of New Jersey. This honor, it is said, was entirely unsolicited by either father or son, and the explanation usually given is that it was intended to attach the father more securely to the royal interest in the disputes which were threatening between the colonies and the mother country.

William and his father were on very good terms at this time. Every summer they took a little tour together, and on one occasion travelled in Holland. On a visit they made to the University of Cambridge they were entertained by the heads of colleges, the chancellor, and the professors in the most distinguished manner, discussed new points of science with them, and with Professor Hadley experimented on what was then a great wonder, the production of cold by evaporation. They wandered also to the old village of Ecton, where the Franklins had lived poor and humble for countless generations, saw many of the old people, and copied inscriptions on tombstones and parish registers. But Scotland they enjoyed most of all. There they met Lord Kames, the author of the "Elements of Criticism," and the historians Hume and Robertson. It was an atmosphere of philosophy and intelligence which Franklin thoroughly enjoyed. "The time we spent there," he wrote to Lord Kames, "was six weeks of the *densest* happiness I have met with in any part of my life."

During his stay in England the war against the French and Indians, which was raging when he left America, came to a close, and Quebec and Canada were surrendered. It became a question in settling with France whether it would be most advantageous for Great Britain to retain Canada or the Guadeloupe sugar islands, and there were advocates on both sides. Franklin published an admirable argument in favor of retaining Canada, without which the American colonies would never be secure from the Indians instigated by the French, and the acquisition of Canada would also tend to a grander development of the British empire. It was an able appeal, but there is no evidence that it alone influenced the final decision of the ministry, as has been claimed, any more than there is evidence that Franklin suggested the policy of William Pitt which had brought the war to a successful close. There were many advocates of these opinions and suggestions, and Franklin was merely one of them, though unquestionably an able one.

He also published his essay on the "Peopling of Countries" and an article in favor of the vigorous prosecution of the war in Europe. These, with his pleasures and experiments in science, occupied most of the five years, and the work of his mission, though well done, was by no means absorbing.

When he arrived, in July, 1757, he had, under the advice of Dr. Fothergill, first sought redress from the proprietors themselves before appealing to the government; but meeting with no success, he tried the members of the Privy Council, and first of all William Pitt, the great minister who was then conducting the war against France and recreating England. But he could not even secure an interview with that busy minister, which is a commentary on the extravagant claims of those who say that Franklin suggested Pitt's policy.

Two years and more passed without his being able to accomplish anything except enlighten the general public concerning the facts of the situation. An article appeared in the *General Advertiser* abusing the Pennsylvania Assembly, and his son William replied to it. The reply being extensively copied by other newspapers, the son was set to work on a book now known as the "Historical Review of Pennsylvania," which went over the whole ground of the quarrels of the Assembly with the proprietors and their deputy governors. It was circulated quite widely, some copies being sold and others distributed free to important persons. But it is doubtful whether it had very much influence, for it was an extremely dull book, and valuable only for its quotations from the messages of the governors and the replies of the Assembly.

His opportunity to accomplish the main object of his mission came at last by accident. The Assembly in Pennsylvania were gradually starving the governor into submission by withholding his salary, and under pressure for want of money, he gave his assent to a bill taxing the proprietary estates. The bill being sent to England, the proprietors opposed it before the Privy Council as hostile to their rights, and obtained a decision in their favor in spite of the arguments of Franklin and his lawyers. But Franklin secured a reconsideration, and Lord Mansfield asked him if he really thought that no injury would be done the proprietary estates by the Assembly, for the proprietors had represented that the colonists intended to tax them out of existence. Franklin assured him that no injury would be done, and he was immediately asked if he would enter into an engagement to assure that point. On his agreeing to do this, the papers were drawn, the Assembly's bill taxing the estates was approved by the crown, and from that time the assaults of the proprietors on the liberties of the colony were decisively checked.

Franklin was now most furiously attacked and

hated by the proprietary party in Pennsylvania, but from the majority of the people, led by the Quakers, he received increased approbation and applause, and his willingness to risk his own personal engagement, as in the affair with Braddock, was regarded as an evidence of the highest public spirit.

He remained two years longer in England on one pretext or another, and no doubt excuses for continuing such a delightful life readily suggested themselves. He returned in the early autumn of 1762, receiving from the Assembly three thousand pounds for his services, and during the five years of his absence he had been annually elected to that body. For a few months he enjoyed comparative quiet, but the next year he was again in the turmoil of a most bitter political contest.

The war with France was over, and Canada and the Ohio Valley had been ceded to the English by the treaty of Paris, signed in February, 1763. But the Indians, having lost their French friends, determined to destroy the English, and, inspired by the genius of Pontiac, they took fort after fort and, rushing upon the whole colonial frontier of Pennsylvania, swept the people eastward to the Delaware with even worse devastation and slaughter than they had inflicted after Braddock's defeat. I cannot give here the full details of this war,* and must confine myself to one phase of it with which Franklin was particularly concerned.

The Scotch-Irish who occupied the frontier coun-

---

* Pennsylvania : Colony and Commonwealth, p. 221.

ties of Pennsylvania suffered most severely from these Indian raids, and believed that the proprietary and Quaker government at Philadelphia neglected the defence of the province. Their resentment was strongest against the Quakers. They held the Quaker religion in great contempt and viewed with scorn the attempts of the Quakers to pacify the Indians and befriend those of them who were willing to give up the war-path and adopt the white man's mode of life.

Some friendly Indians, descendants of the tribes that had welcomed William Penn, were living at Conestoga, near Lancaster, in a degenerate condition, having given up both war and hunting, and following the occupations of basket- and broommaking. They were the wards of the proprietary government, and were given presents and supplies from time to time. There were also at Bethlehem some other friendly Indians who had been converted to Christianity by the Moravians.

The Scotch-Irish believed that all of these so-called friendly Indians were in league with the hostile tribes, furnished them with information, and even participated in their murders. They asked the governor to remove them, and assured him that their removal would secure the safety of the frontier. Nothing being done by the governor, a party of Scotch-Irish rangers started to destroy the Moravian Indians, but were prevented by a rain-storm. The governor afterwards, through commissioners, investigated these Moravian Indians, and finding reason to suspect them, they were all brought down to Phila-

delphia and quartered in barracks. But the Conestoga Indians were attacked by a party of fifty-seven
Scotch-Irish, afterwards known as the "Paxton
Boys," who, finding only six of them in the village,—three men, two women, and a boy,—massacred them all, mangled their bodies, and burnt their
property. The remaining fourteen of the tribe were
collected by the sheriff and put for protection in the
Lancaster jail. The Paxtons hearing of it, immediately attacked the jail and cut the Indians to pieces
with hatchets.

We have grown so accustomed to lynch law that
this slaughter of the Conestogas would not now cause
much surprise, especially in some parts of the country; but it was a new thing to the colonists, who in
many respects were more orderly than are their descendants, and a large part of the community were
shocked, disgusted, and indignant. Franklin wrote
a pamphlet which had a wide circulation and assailed
the Scotch-Irish as inhuman, brutal cowards, worse
than Arabs and Turks; fifty-seven of them, armed
with rifles, knives, and hatchets, had actually succeeded, he said, in killing three old men, two women,
and a boy.

The Paxton lynchers, however, were fully supported by the people of the frontier. A large body
of frontiersmen marched on Philadelphia with the
full intention of revolutionizing the Quaker government, and they would have succeeded but for the
unusual preparations for defence. They were
finally, with some difficulty, persuaded to return
without using their rifles.

The governor was powerless to secure even the arrest of the men who had murdered the Indians in the jail, and the disorder was so flagrant and the weakness of the executive branch of the government so apparent that the Quakers and a majority of the people thought there was now good reason for openly petitioning the crown to abolish the proprietorship. While in England, Franklin had been advised not to raise this question, and he had accordingly confined his efforts to taxing the proprietary estates.

The arrangement he had made provided that the estates should be fairly taxed, but the governor and the Assembly differed in opinion as to what was fair. The governor claimed that the best wild lands of the proprietors should be taxed at the rate paid by the people for their worst, and he tried the old tactics of forcing this point by delaying a supply bill intended to defend the province against Pontiac and his Indians. The Assembly passed the bill to suit him, but immediately raised the question of the abolition of the proprietorship. Twenty-five resolutions were passed most abusive of the proprietors, and the Assembly then adjourned to let the people decide by a general election whether a petition should be sent to the king asking for direct royal government.

A most exciting political campaign followed in which Franklin took the side of the majority in favor of a petition, and wrote several of his most brilliant pamphlets. He particularly assailed Provost Smith, who, in a preface to a printed speech by John Dickinson defending the proprietary government, had eulogized William Penn in one of those laudatory epitaphs which were the fashion of the day :

"Utterly to confound the assembly, and show the excellence of proprietary government, the Prefacer has extracted from their own votes the praises they have from time to time bestowed on the first proprietor, in their addresses to his son. And, though addresses are not generally the best repositories of historical truth, we must not in this instance deny their authority.

"That these encomiums on the father, though sincere, have occurred so frequently, was owing, however, to two causes : first, a vain hope the assemblies entertained, that the father's example, and the honors done his character, might influence the conduct of the sons; secondly, for that, in attempting to compliment the sons upon their own merits, there was always found an extreme scarcity of matter. Hence, *the father, the honored and honorable father*, was so often repeated, that the sons themselves grew sick of it, and have been heard to say to each other with disgust, when told that A, B, and C, were come to wait upon them with addresses on some public occasion, ' *Then I suppose we shall hear more about our father.*' So that, let me tell the Prefacer, who perhaps was unacquainted with this anecdote, that if he hoped to curry more favor with the family, by the inscription he has framed for that great man's monument, he may find himself mistaken; for there is too much in it of *our father.*"

Franklin then goes on to say that he will give a sketch "in the lapidary way" which will do for a monument to the sons of William Penn.

"Be this a Memorial
Of T—— and R—— P ——
P—— of P——
Who with estates immense
Almost beyond computation
When their own province
And the whole British empire
Were engaged in a bloody & most expensive war
Begun for the defence of those estates
Could yet meanly desire
To have those very estates
Totally or partially
Exempted from taxation

While their fellow subjects all around them
Groaned
Under the universal burden.
To gain this point
They refused the necessary laws
For the defence of their people
And suffered their colony to welter in its blood
Rather than abate in the least
Of these their dishonest pretensions.
The privileges granted by their father
Wisely and benevolently
To encourage the first settlers of the province
They
Foolishly and cruelly,
Taking advantage of public distress,
Have extorted from the posterity of those settlers;
And are daily endeavoring to reduce them
To the most abject slavery;
Though to the virtue and industry of those people,
In improving their country
They owe all that they possess and enjoy.
A striking instance
Of human depravity and ingratitude;
And an irrefragable proof,
That wisdom and goodness
Do not descend with an inheritance;
But that ineffable meanness
May be connected with unbounded fortune."

Dickinson's followers, of course, assailed Franklin on all sides. Their pamphlets are very exciting reading, especially Hugh Williamson's "What is Sauce for a Goose is also Sauce for a Gander," which describes itself in its curious old-fashioned subtitle as

" Being a small Touch in the Lapidary Way, or Tit for Tat, in your own way. An Epitaph on a certain Great Man. Written by a Departed Spirit, and now most humbly inscribed to all his dutiful Sons and Children, who may hereafter choose to distinguish him by the Name of A Patriot. Dear Children, I send you here a little Book for you to look upon that you may see your Pappy's Face when he is dead and gone. Philadelphia, Printed in Arch Street 1764."

"Pappy" is then described for the benefit of his children in an epitaph :

> " An Epitaph &c
> To the much esteem'd Memory of
> B . . . F . . . Esq., LL.D.
>
> .   .   .   .
>
> Possessed of many lucrative
> Offices
> Procured to him by the Interest of Men
> Whom he infamously treated
> And receiving enormous sums
> from the Province
> For Services
> He never performed
> After betraying it to Party and Contention
> He lived, as to the Appearance of Wealth
> In moderate circumstances;
> His principal Estate, seeming to consist
> In his Hand Maid Barbara
> A most valuable Slave
> The Foster Mother
> of his last offspring
> Who did his dirty Work
> And in two Angelic Females
> Whom Barbara also served
> As Kitchen Wench and Gold Finder
> But alas the Loss!
> Providence for wise tho' secret ends
> Lately deprived him of the Mother
> of Excellency.
> His Fortune was not however impaired
> For he piously withheld from her
> Manes
> The pitiful stipend of Ten pounds per Annum
> On which he had cruelly suffered her
> To starve
> Then stole her to the Grave in Silence
> Without a Pall, the covering due to her dignity
> Without a tomb or even
> A Monumental Inscription."

Franklin was a more skilful "lapidary" than his enemies, and his pamphlets were expressed in better language, but there is now very little doubt that he and the majority of the people were in the wrong. The colony had valuable liberties and privileges which had been built up by the Assembly through the efforts of nearly a hundred years. In spite of all the aggressions of the proprietors these liberties remained unimpaired and were even stronger than ever. The appeal to the king to take the colony under his direct control might lead to disastrous results; for if the people once surrendered themselves to the crown and the proprietorship was abolished, the king and Parliament might also abolish the charter and destroy every popular right.* In fact, the ministry were at that very time contemplating the Stamp Act and other measures which brought on the Revolution. Franklin seemed incapable of appreciating this, and retained for ten years, and in the face of the most obvious facts, his strange confidence in the king.

But the petition was carried by an overwhelming majority, although Franklin failed to be re-elected to the Assembly. He never had been so fiercely assailed, and it is probable that the attacks on his morals and motives were far more bitter in ordinary conversation than in the pamphlets. This abuse may have had considerable effect in preventing his election. He was, however, appointed by the Assembly its agent to convey the petition to England and present it to the king. He set out in November, 1764,

---

* Pennsylvania: Colony and Commonwealth, chap. xix.

on this his second mission to England which resulted in a residence there of ten years. Fortunately, the petition was unsuccessful. He did not press it much, and the Assembly soon repented of its haste.

He settled down comfortably at No. 7 Craven Street, where Mrs. Stevenson and her daughter were delighted to have again their old friend. His scientific studies were renewed,—spots on the sun, smoky chimneys, the aurora borealis, the northwest passage, the effect of deep and shallow water on the speed of boats,—and he was appointed on committees to devise plans for putting lightning-rods on St. Paul's Cathedral and the government powder-magazines. The circle of his acquaintance was much enlarged. He associated familiarly with the noblemen he met at country houses, was dined and entertained by notables of every sort, became acquainted with Garrick, Mrs. Montague, and Adam Smith, and added another distinguished physician, Sir John Pringle, to the list of his very intimate friends. He dined out almost every day, was admitted to all sorts of clubs, and of course diligently attended the meetings of all the associations devoted to learning and science.

Although only an amateur in medicine, he was invited by the physicians to attend the meetings of their club, and it was of this club that he told the story that the question was once raised whether physicians had, on the whole, done more good than harm. After a long debate, Sir John Pringle, the president, was asked to give his opinion, and replied that if by physicians they meant to include old women, he thought they had done more good than harm; otherwise more harm than good.

During this his second mission to England he became more intimate than ever with the good Bishop of St. Asaph, spending part of every summer with him, and it was at his house that he wrote the first part of his Autobiography. In a letter to his wife, dated August 14, 1771, he describes the close of a three weeks' stay at the bishop's:

" The Bishop's lady knows what children and grandchildren I have and their ages; so, when I was to come away on Monday, the 12th, in the morning, she insisted on my staying that one day longer, that we might together keep my grandson's birthday. At dinner, among other nice things, we had a floating island, which they always particularly have on the birthdays of any of their own six children, who were all but one at table, where there was also a clergyman's widow, now above one hundred years old. The chief toast of the day was Master Benjamin Bache, which the venerable old lady began in a bumper of *mountain*. The Bishop's lady politely added ' and that he may be as good a man as his grandfather.' I said I hoped he would be *much better*. The Bishop, still more complaisant than his lady, said: ' We will compound the matter and be contented if he should not prove *quite so good.*' " (Bigelow's Works of Franklin, vol. vi. p. 71.)

The bishop's daughters were great friends of Franklin, and often exchanged with him letters which in many respects were almost equal to his own. Years afterwards, when he was in France during the Revolution, and it was rather imprudent to write to him, one of them, without the knowledge of her parents, sent him a most affectionate and charming girl's letter, which is too long to quote, but is well worth reading.

He had his wife send him from Pennsylvania a

number of live squirrels, which he gave to his friends. One which he presented to one of the bishop's daughters having escaped from its cage, and being killed by a dog, he wrote an epitaph on it rather different from his political epitaph:

> "Alas! poor MUNGO!
> Happy wert thou, hadst thou known
> Thy own felicity.
> Remote from the fierce bald eagle
> Tyrant of thy native woods,
> Thou hadst naught to fear from his piercing talons,
> Nor from the murdering gun
> Of the thoughtless sportsman.
> Safe in thy weird castle
> GRIMALKIN never could annoy thee.
> Daily wert thou fed with the choicest viands,
> By the fair hand of an indulgent mistress;
> But, discontented,
> Thou wouldst have more freedom.
> Too soon, alas! didst thou obtain it;
> And wandering
> Thou art fallen by the fangs of wanton cruel Ranger!
> Learn hence
> Ye who blindly seek more liberty,
> Whether subjects, sons, squirrels or daughters,
> That apparent restraint may be real protection
> Yielding peace and plenty
> With security."

Franklin's pleasures in England remind us of other distinguished Americans who, having gone to London to represent their country, have suddenly found themselves in congenial intercourse with all that was best in the nation and enjoying the happiest days of their lives. Lowell, when minister there, had the same experience as Franklin, and when we read their experiences together, the resemblance is very striking. Others, though perhaps in less degree, have felt the same touch of race. Blood is thicker than water. But I doubt if any of them—Lowell, Motley, or even Holmes in his famous three months' visit—had such a good time as Franklin.

He loved England and was no doubt delighted with the appointments that sent him there. If it is true, as his enemies have charged, that he schemed for public office, it is not surprising in view of the pleasure he derived from appointments such as these. Writing to Miss Stevenson on March 23, 1763, after he had returned to Pennsylvania from his first mission, he says,—

"Of all the enviable things England has, I envy it most its people. Why should that petty Island, which, compared to America, is but a stepping stone in a brook, scarce enough of it above water to keep one's shoes dry; why, I say should that little Island enjoy, in almost every neighborhood, more sensible, virtuous, and elegant minds than we can collect in ranging a hundred leagues of our vast forests?" (Bigelow's Works of Franklin, vol. iii. p. 233.)

In fact, he had resolved at one time, if he could prevail on Mrs. Franklin to accompany him, to settle permanently in England. His reason, he writes to Mr. Strahan, was for America, but his inclination for England. "You know which usually prevails. I shall probably make but this one vibration and settle here forever. Nothing will prevent it, if I can, as I hope I can, prevail with Mrs. F. to accompany me, especially if we have a peace." * This

* Bigelow's Works of Franklin, vol. iii. p. 212; vol. x. pp. 295, 302.

fondness for the old home no doubt helped to form that very conservative position which he took in the beginning of the Revolution, and which was so displeasing to some people in Massachusetts. His reason, though not his inclination, was, as he says, for America, but the ignorant and brutal course of the British ministry finally made reason and inclination one.

VII

DIFFICULTIES AND FAILURE IN ENGLAND

FRANKLIN'S diplomatic career was now to begin in earnest. Although the petition to change Pennsylvania into a royal province under the direct rule of the crown was, fortunately, not acted upon and not very seriously pressed, he, nevertheless, continued to believe that such a change would be beneficial and might some day be accomplished.

He looked upon the king as supreme ruler of the colonies, and retained this opinion until he heard of actual bloodshed in the battle of Lexington. The king and not Parliament had in the beginning given the colonies their charters ; the king and not Parliament had always been the power that ruled them ; wherefore the passage by Parliament of stamp acts and tea acts was a usurpation. This was one of the arguments in which many of the colonists had sought refuge, but few of them clung to it so long as Franklin.

Almost immediately after his arrival in London in December, 1764, the agitations about the proposed Stamp Act began, and within a few weeks he was deep in them. His previous residence of five years in London when he was trying to have the proprietary estates taxed had given him some knowledge of men and affairs in the great capital ; had given him, indeed, his first lessons in the diplomat's art; but he was now powerless against the Stamp Act. The ministry had determined on its passage, and they considered the protests of Franklin and the other colonial agents of little consequence.

The act passed, and Franklin wrote home on the subject one of his prettiest letters to Charles Thomson:

"Depend upon it, my good neighbor, I took every step in my power to prevent the passing of the Stamp Act. But the tide was too strong against us. . . . The nation was provoked by American claims of independence, and all parties joined in resolving by this act to settle the point. We might as well have hindered the sun's setting. That we could not do. But since it is down, my friend, and it may be long before it rises again, let us make as good a night of it as we can. We may still light candles. Frugality and industry will go a great way towards indemnifying us. Idleness and pride tax with a heavier hand than kings and parliaments. If we can get rid of the former we may easily bear the latter."

Grenville, in conformity with his assurance that the act would work satisfactorily even to the Americans, announced that stamp officers would not be sent from England, but that the kind mother would appoint colonists, and he asked the colonial agents to name to him honest and responsible men in their several colonies. Franklin recommended his old friend John Hughes, a respectable merchant of Philadelphia, never dreaming that by so doing he was getting the good man into trouble. But as soon as Hughes's commission arrived his house was threatened by the mob and he was forced to resign.

Franklin had no idea that the colonies would be so indignant and offer so much resistance. He supposed that they would quietly submit, buy the stamps, and paste them on all their documents. He bought a quantity of stamped paper and sent it over to his partner, David Hall, to sell in the little stationery shop which was still attached to their printing-office. When he heard of the mob violence and the positive determination not to pay the tax, he was surprised and disgusted. He wrote to John Hughes, expressing surprise at the indiscretion of the people and the rashness of the Virginia Assembly. "A firm loyalty to the crown," he said, "and a faithful adherence to the government of this nation, which it is the safety as well as honour of the colonies to be connected with, will always be the wisest course for you and I to take." *

His old opponents, the proprietary party, were not slow to take this opportunity to abuse him as faithless to his province and the American cause. A certain Samuel Smith went about telling the people that Franklin had planned the Stamp Act and intended to have the Test Act put in force in America. A caricature of the time represents the devil whispering in his ear, "Thee shall be agent, Ben, for all my dominions," and underneath was printed—

> "All his designs concentre in himself
> For building castles and amassing pelf.
> The public 'tis his wit to sell for gain,
> Whom private property did ne'er maintain."

The mob even threatened his house, much to the alarm of his wife, who, however, sturdily remained

---

* Pennsylvania : Colony and Commonwealth, p. 314.

and refused to seek safety in flight. This and other events, together with the information that he received from America during the next few months, compelled him to change his ground. He saw that there was to be substantial resistance to the act, and he joined earnestly in the agitation for its repeal. This agitation was carried on during the autumn of 1765 and a very strong case made for the colonies, the most telling part of which was the refusal of the colonists to buy English manufactured goods, which had already lost the British merchants millions of pounds sterling.

In December Parliament met and the whole question was gone into with thoroughness. For six weeks testimony was taken before the House sitting as committee of the whole, and merchants, manufacturers, colonial agents, and every one who was supposed to be able to throw light on the subject were examined. It was during the course of this investigation that Franklin was called and gave those famous answers which enhanced his reputation more than any other one act of his life, except, perhaps, his experiment with the kite.

For a long time before the examination he had been very busy interviewing all sorts of persons, going over the whole ground of the controversy and trying to impress members of Parliament with the information and arguments that had come to him from the colonies. His answers in the examination were not given so entirely on the spur of the moment as has sometimes been supposed, for he had gone over the subject again and again in conversation, and was well prepared. But his replies are truly wonderful in their exquisite shrewdness, the delicate turns of phrase, and the subtle but perfectly clear meaning given to words. The severe training in analyzing and rewriting the essays of the *Spectator* stood him in good stead that day, and we realize more fully what he himself said, that it was to his mastery of language that he owed his great reputation.

They asked him, for example, "Are you acquainted with Newfoundland?" He could not tell to what they might be leading him, and some people would have replied no, or yes; but the wily old philosopher contented himself with saying, "I never was there."

They drove him into an awkward corner at one point of the examination. He had been showing that the colonies had no objection to voting of their own free will supplies to the British crown, and had frequently done so in the French and Indian wars.

"But," said his questioner, "suppose one of the colonial assemblies should refuse to raise supplies for its own local government, would it not then be right, in order to preserve order and carry on the government in that locality, that Parliament should tax that colony, inasmuch as it would not tax itself for its own support?"

Franklin parried the question by saying that such a case could not happen, and if it did, it would cure itself by the disorder and confusion that would arise.

"But," insisted his tormentor, "just suppose that

it did happen; should not Parliament have the right to remedy such an evil state of affairs?"

The philosopher yielded a little to this last question, and said that there might be such a right if it were used only for the good of the people of the colony. This was exactly what they had wanted him to say, so they put the next question which would clinch the nail.

"But who is to judge of that, Britain or the colonies?"

This was difficult to answer; but with inimitable sagacity their victim replied,—

"Those that feel can best judge."

It was a narrow escape, but he was safely out of the trap. Then they badgered him about the difference between external taxes, such as customs duties and taxes on commerce, which he said the colonists had always been willing to pay, and internal taxes, like the Stamp Tax, which they would never pay and could not be made to pay. He was very positive on this point; so a member asked him whether it was not likely, since the colonists were so opposed to internal taxes, that they would in time assume the same rebellious attitude towards external taxes. Franklin's reply was very subtle in showing how Great Britain was driving the colonies more and more into rebellion:

"They never have hitherto. Many arguments have been lately used here to show them that there is no difference, and that if you have no right to tax them internally, you have none to tax them externally, or make any other law to bind them. At present they do not reason so; but in time they may possibly be convinced by these arguments."

They reminded him of the clause in the charter of Pennsylvania which expressly allowed Parliament to tax that colony. How, then, they said, can the Pennsylvanians assert that the Stamp Act is an infringement of their rights? This was a poser; but Franklin was equal to the occasion.

"They understand it thus: by the same charter and otherwise they are entitled to all the privileges and liberties of Englishmen. They find in the Great Charters and the Petition and Declaration of Rights that one of the privileges of English subjects is, that they are not to be taxed but by their common consent. They have therefore relied upon it, from the first settlement of the province, that the Parliament never would, nor could, by color of that clause in the charter, assume a right of taxing them till it had qualified itself to exercise such right by admitting representatives from the people to be taxed, who ought to make a part of that common consent."

But to print all the brilliant passages of this examination would require too much space. It should be read entire; for in its wonderful display of human intelligence we see Franklin at his best. He never did anything else quite equal to it, and he never again had such an opportunity. It was an ordeal that would have crushed or appalled ordinary men, and would have been too much for some very able men. They would have evaded the severe questions, given commonplace answers, or sought refuge in obscurity, eloquence, or sentiment. But Franklin, with perfect composure, ease, and almost indifference, met every question squarely as it was asked. Many other persons were examined during the long weeks of that investigation, but who now knows who they were? They may have been as well informed as

Franklin, and doubtless many of them were ; but they were submerged in the situation which he made a stepping-stone to greatness.

In nothing that he said can there be discovered the slightest trace of hurry, surprise, or disturbed temper ; everything is unruffled and smooth. He guards without effort the beauty and perfection of his language as carefully as its substance. Each reply is complete. Nothing can be added to it, and it would be impossible to abbreviate it. It was his superb physical constitution that enabled him to bear himself thus. No prize-fighter could have been more self-possessed.

As is well known, he could seldom speak long, especially at this time of his life, without jesting or telling stories ; but there is no trace of this in the examination, and the slightest touch of anything of the kind would have marred its wonderful merit. In his previous conversations with members he had been humorous enough. On one occasion a Tory asked him, as he would not agree to the act, to at least help them to amend it. He said he could easily do that by the change of a single word. The act read that it was to be enforced on a certain day in the year one thousand seven hundred and sixty-five. Just change one to two, he said, and America will have little or no objection to it. During his examination members who favored the repeal asked him questions calculated to bring out his favorite arguments, and one of them, remembering this jest, asked him a question which would lead to it. It seems to have been the only question he evaded ;

for, as he has told us, he considered such a jest too light and ridiculous for the occasion.

The Stamp Act was repealed principally through the efforts of the merchants and tradespeople who thronged the lobbies of the House of Commons and clamorously demanded that the Americans should be restored to a condition in which they would be willing to buy British goods ; but there is no question that Franklin's efforts and examination greatly assisted, and members of the opposition party thanked him for the aid he had given them in carrying the repeal. Pennsylvania reappointed him her agent, and he continued his life in London as a sort of colonial ambassador. In 1768 Georgia made him her agent, and during the next two years he was appointed agent for both New Jersey and Massachusetts ; so that he was in a sense representing at London the interests of America.

His appointment as the agent of Massachusetts had been opposed by many of the leaders of the liberty party in Boston ; for his opinions were rather too moderate to suit them. He still retained his confidence in George III. as a safe ruler for America, and he did all he could to soften and accommodate the differences existing between the colonies and the mother country.

His motives were, of course, attacked and his moderation ascribed to his love of office. He was at that time Postmaster of North America, and as his income of a thousand pounds a year from his partnership with David Hall in the printing business ceased in 1766, he was naturally desirous to retain his postmaster's salary. His zeal for the American cause was inclining Lord Sandwich, the Postmaster-General, to remove him, while the Duke of Grafton was disposed to give him a better office in England, in order to identify him with the mother country and bring him into close relations with the government.

There is no evidence that he was unduly influenced by love of office. His confidence in the king was merely a mistake which many other people made, and his moderation and attempt to settle all difficulties amicably were measures which a man of his temperament and in his position would naturally take.

He tried to give the English correct opinions about America, and to disclose the true interest and the true relations which should subsist between the mother and her daughters. To this end he wrote articles for the newspapers, and reprinted Dickinson's "Farmer's Letters" with a preface written by himself. There was a large party led by Burke, Barré, Onslow, Lord Chatham, and others who were favorable to America, and it seemed as if this party might be made larger. At any rate, Franklin felt bound to take sides with them, and assist them as far as possible. His articles were humorous, and necessarily anonymous; for he feared they would lose half of the slight effect they had if the name of the American agent were signed to them.

His two famous articles were published in the early autumn of 1773. One, called "Rules for Reducing a Great Empire to a Small One," was an admirable satire on the conduct of the British government. A great empire is like a cake, most easily diminished at the edges. Take care that colonies never enjoy the same rights as the mother country. Forget all benefits conferred by colonies ; treat them as if they were always inclined to revolt ; send prodigals, broken gamesters, and stock-jobbers to rule over them ; punish them for petitioning against injustice ; despise their voluntary grants of money, and harass them with novel taxes ; threaten that you have the right to tax them without limit ; take away from them trial by jury and *habeas corpus*, and those who are suspected of crimes bring to the mother country for trial ; send the most insolent officials to collect the taxes ; apply the proceeds of the taxes to increasing salaries and pensions ; keep adjourning the colonial assemblies until they pass the laws you want ; redress no grievances ; and send a standing army among them commanded by a general with unlimited power.

The popularity of this piece was so great that all the newspapers copied it and new editions had to be issued. The other article was a short squib, called "An Edict of the King of Prussia," and professes to be a formal announcement by Frederick the Great that, inasmuch as the British isles were originally Saxon colonies and have now reached a flourishing condition, it is just and expedient that a revenue be raised from them ; and he goes on to declare the measures he had decided to put in force, which are most clever burlesques on the measures adopted by England for America.

This edict also had a great run of popularity, and of course its authorship became known. Many of the slow-witted English at first thought it real, and Franklin in a letter to his son gives an interesting account of its reception, and at the same time allows us a glimpse of his life at English country houses :

"I was down at Lord le Despencer's, when the post brought that day's papers. Mr. Whitehead was there, too, (Paul Whitehead, the author of 'Manners,') who runs early through all the papers, and tells the company what he finds remarkable. He had them in another room, and we were chatting in the breakfast parlor, when he came running in to us out of breath, with the paper in his hand. 'Here,' says he, 'here's news for ye ! Here's the King of Prussia claiming a right to this kingdom !' All stared, and I as much as anybody ; and he went on to read it. When he had read two or three paragraphs, a gentleman present said, 'Damn his impudence ; I dare say we shall hear by next post that he is upon his march with one hundred thousand men to back this.' Whitehead, who is very shrewd, soon after began to smoke it, and looking in my face, said, 'I'll be hanged if this is not some of your American jokes upon us.' The reading went on, and ended with abundance of laughing, and a general verdict that it was a fair hit ; and the piece was cut out of the paper and preserved in my Lord's collection."

This was all very pleasant for Franklin, and increased his fame, especially among the Whigs, who were already on the side of America. But the Tories, whom it was necessary to win, were so indignant and so deeply disgusted that these brilliant essays may be said to have done more harm than good.

It is not usual for an ambassador in a foreign country to discuss in the public prints the questions at issue between that country and his own. It would generally be regarded as serious misconduct, and the rule which prohibits it seems to be founded on good reasons. The ambassador is not there for the purpose of instructing or influencing the general public. He is not in any way concerned with them, but is concerned only with the heads of the government, with whom alone he carries on the business of his mission. In order that he may fulfil his part successfully he must be acceptable, or at least not offensive, to the persons in control of the government. But how can he be acceptable to them if he is openly or in secret appealing to the people of the country against them? Will they not regard him very much as if he were a spy or an enemy in disguise in their midst?

This was precisely the difficulty into which Franklin got himself. He was not called an ambassador, and he would not have been willing to admit that he was in a foreign country. But in effect he was in that position, being the duly accredited agent of colonies that had a serious quarrel with the mother country which every one knew might terminate in war. When he began to write anonymous articles full of sarcasm and severity against the ministry of the party in power he was doing what, under ordinary diplomatic circumstances, might have caused his dismissal. It was distinctly a step downward. It was not different in essentials from that of an ambassador joining one of the political parties of the country to which he is accredited and making stump speeches for it. His arguments were approved only by people among the English liberals who were already convinced, while they made him bitter enemies among the Tory governing class at a time when he had every reason to mollify them, and when he was doing his utmost to accommodate amicably the differences between the mother and her daughters. They had now a handle against him, something that would offset the charm of his conversation, his learning, and his discoveries in science which gave him such influence among notable people. They soon had the opportunity they wanted in the famous episode of the Hutchinson letters.

In order to carry out his purpose of accommodating all disputes, he was in the habit of saying wherever he went in England that the colonies were most loyal and loving; that there was no necessity for the severe measures against Boston,— quartering troops on her, and other oppressions. Such severities created the impression among the Americans that the whole English nation was against them ; they did not stop to think that it was merely the ministry and the party in power. Accordingly there were riots and tumults among some of the disorderly classes in America which in their turn created a wrong impression in England, where such disturbances were falsely supposed to be representative of the colonists at large. In this way the misunderstanding was continually aggravated because the true state of things was unknown.

Many people in England were disposed to smile at this pretty delusion of peace and affection, but they thought it best to let the colonial agents continue under its influence and not acquaint them

with the means they had of knowing the contrary.
At last, however, in the year 1772, one of them let
the cat out of the bag. Franklin was talking in
his usual strain to a Whig member of Parliament
who was disposed to be very friendly to America,
when that member frankly told him that he must
be mistaken. The disorders in America were much
worse than he supposed. The severe measures complained of were not the mere suggestion of the party
in power in England, but had been asked for by
people in Boston as the only means of restoring
order and pacifying the country, which was really
in a most rebellious and dangerous state.

When Franklin expressed surprise and doubt, the
member said he would soon satisfy him, and a few
days after placed in his hands a packet of letters
which had been written by Thomas Hutchinson, the
Governor of Massachusetts, Andrew Oliver, the
Lieutenant-Governor, and some other officials to
Mr. William Whately, a man who had held some
subordinate offices and had been an important political worker in the Grenville party.

The letters described the situation in Massachusetts in the year 1768 ; the riotous proceedings when
John Hancock's sloop was seized for violating the
revenue laws ; how the customs officers were in-
sulted, beaten, the windows of their houses broken,
and they obliged to take refuge on the " Romney"
man-of-war. These and other proceedings the
writers of the letters intimated were approved by
the majority of the people, and they recommended
that these turbulent colonists should, for their own

good, be restrained by force, and the liberty they were misusing curtailed. "There must be an abridgment," said one of Hutchinson's letters, "of what are called English liberties."

Hutchinson, as well as some of the other writers of the letters, were natives of New England; and Hutchinson, before he became governor, had had a long public career in Massachusetts in which he had distinguished himself as a most conservative, prudent, and able man who had conferred many benefits on the colony. The letters by him and the other officials had been handed about among prominent people in London, who regarded them as better evidence of the real situation in America than the benevolent talk of the colonial agent or his brilliant and anonymous sallies in the newspapers.

The condition which the member of Parliament annexed to his loan of the letters to Franklin was that they should not be printed or copied, and after having been read by the leaders of the patriot movement in Massachusetts, they were to be returned to London. He must have had very little knowledge of the world, and Franklin must have smiled at the condition. Of course, in transmitting the letters to Massachusetts Franklin mentioned the condition. This relieved him from responsibility, and John Adams and John Hancock could do what they thought right under the circumstances.

What might have been expected soon followed. The leaders in Boston read the letters and were furious. Here were their own governors and officials secretly furnishing the British government with information that would bring punishment on the colony, and actually recommending that the punishment should be inflicted. One of Hutchinson's letters distinctly stated that the information furnished by him in a previous letter had brought the troops to Boston ; and, as is well known, it was the collision of some of these troops with a mob which led to what has been called the " Boston massacre."

John Adams showed the letters to his aunt ; others showed them to relatives and friends, no doubt, with the most positive instructions that they were not to be copied or printed, and were to be exhibited only to certain people. The Assembly met, and John Hancock, with a mysterious air, announced that a most important matter would in a few days be submitted to that body for consideration ; but most of the members knew about it already ; and when the day arrived the public was refused admittance and the letters read to the Assembly in secret session. As for publishing them, they were soon in print in London as well as in the colonies ; and when the originals could be of no further use, John Adams put them in an envelope and sent them back to London, as the condition required.

The Assembly resolved to ask the crown to remove both Hutchinson and Oliver, and prepared a petition to that effect, basing the request on the ground that these two men had plotted to encourage and intensify the quarrel of the colonies with the mother country. By their false representations they had caused a fleet and an army to be brought to

Massachusetts, and were therefore the cause of the confusion and bloodshed which had resulted. This petition reached the king in the summer of 1773.

Franklin thought that the whole affair would have a good effect. The resentment of the colonies against the mother country would be transferred to Hutchinson and the other individuals who had caused it; the ministry would see that the colonists were sincerely desirous of a good understanding with the British government and that Hutchinson and Oliver were evil persons bent on fomenting trouble and responsible for all the recent difficulties in Massachusetts. This was a pleasant theory, but it turned out to be utterly unsound and useless. The effect of the letters was just the opposite of what was expected. Instead of modifying the feelings of the colonists and the ministry, they increased the resentment of both.

The king and his Privy Council were not inclined to pay any attention to the petition, and it might have slept harmlessly like other petitions from America at that time. But when the letters were printed in London, people began to wonder how they had reached the colonists. They were in a sense secret information, and had been intrusted to persons who were supposed to understand that they were for government circles alone. William Whately, to whom they had been written, was dead, and as it began to be suspected that his brother and executor, Thomas Whately, might have put them into circulation, he felt bound to defend himself.

As a matter of fact, they seem to have passed out

of William Whately's hands before his death, and were never in the possession of the executor. But the executor had given permission to John Temple to look over the deceased Whately's papers and to take from them certain letters which Temple and his brother had written to him. Accordingly, Thomas Whately went to see Temple, who gave the most positive assurances that he had taken only his own and his brother's letters, and he repeated these assurances twice afterwards. But the suspicion against him getting into the newspapers, he demanded from Whately a public statement exonerating him. Whately published a statement which merely gave the facts and exonerated him no more than to say that Temple had assured him he did not take the Hutchinson letters. Such a statement left an unpleasant implication against Temple, for the executor seemed studiously to avoid saying that he believed Temple's assurances.

So Temple challenged Whately, and the challenge was carried by Ralph Izard, of South Carolina. They fought a queer sort of duel which would have amused Frenchmen, and half a century later would have amused Carolinians. Whately declined to be bothered with a second, so Temple could not have one. They met in Hyde Park at four in the morning, Whately with a sword and Temple with both sword and pistols. Seeing that Whately had only a sword, he supposed that he must be particularly expert with it, and he therefore suggested that they fight with pistols. They emptied their weapons without effect, and then took to their blades.

Temple, who was something of a swordsman, soon discovered that Whately knew nothing of the art, and he chivalrously tried to wound him slightly, so as to end the encounter. But Whately slashed and cut in a bungling way that was extremely dangerous; and Temple, finding that he was risking his life by his magnanimity, aimed a thrust which would have killed Whately if he had not seized the blade in his left hand. As it was, it wounded him severely in the side, and he suggested that the fight end. But his opponent in this extraordinary duel was deaf, and, recovering his sword, as Whately slipped forward he wounded him in the back of the shoulder.

Izard and Arthur Lee, of Virginia, now arrived on the scene and separated the combatants. One result of not fighting in the regular manner with witnesses was that some people believed, from the wound on Whately's back, that Temple had attempted to stab him when he was down. Meantime Franklin, who had been out of town on one of his pleasant excursions, returned to London and, hearing that another duel between the two was imminent, published a letter in the newspapers announcing that he was the person who had obtained and sent the letters to Massachusetts, and that they had never been in the possession of the executor and consequently could not have been stolen from him by Temple.

He supposed that he had ended the difficulty most handsomely, and he continued to hope for good results from making the letters public. But the ministry and the Tories had now the opportunity they wanted. They saw a way to deprive him of his office of postmaster and attack his character. He had admitted sending the letters to Massachusetts. But how had he obtained them? How did he get possession of the private letters of a deceased member of the government; letters, too, that every one had been warned not to allow to get into a colonial agent's hands? If the distinguished man of science whose fascinating manner and conversation were the delight of London drawing-rooms and noblemen's country-seats had stepped down from the heights of philosophy to do this sort of work, why, then, his great reputation and popularity need no longer be considered as protecting him.

It was unfortunate that Franklin sent these letters to Massachusetts in the way that has been described. At the same time it is rather too much to expect that he should have foreseen all the results. But after more than a hundred years have passed we can perhaps review the position of the Tory government a little more calmly than has been usual.

Let us suppose that the Spanish minister in the United States should get possession of letters sent from Spain by our minister there to the Secretary of State at Washington; and we will assume also that these letters relate to a matter of serious controversy between our country and Spain, and are the private communications from our minister to the Secretary of State. If the Spanish minister should send these letters to his government, and that government should publish them in its own and our newspapers, would there not be considerable indignation in America? Would it not be said that the Spanish minister was here to conduct diplomatic negotiations in the usual way and not for the purpose of securing possession of the private documents of our government? Would it not be assumed at once that he must have bribed some one to give him the letters, or got them in some other clandestine way? and would not his country in all probability be asked to recall him?

Then, too, we must remember that Franklin's argument that the colonies were all loyal and needed only a little kind treatment was in the eyes of the Tories a pious sham; and they were somewhat justified in thinking so. It is true, indeed, that outside of Massachusetts the people were very loyal, and determined not to break with Great Britain unless they were forced to it. But in Massachusetts Samuel Adams was laboring night and day to force a breach. He had as much contempt as the Tories for Franklin's peace and love policy, and thought it ridiculous that such a man should be the agent for Massachusetts. He was convinced that there never would be peace, that it was not desirable, and that the sooner there were war and independence the better.

The Tory government knew all this; it knew of the committees of correspondence that the Boston patriots were inaugurating to inflame the whole country; it knew all these things, from the reports of the royal governors and other officials in the colonies, and it was probably better acquainted with the real situation than was Franklin. There may still be read among the documents of the British government the affidavits of the persons who followed Samuel Adams about and took down his words when he was secretly inciting the lower classes of the people in Boston to open rebellion.* About the time that Whately and Temple fought their duel, in December, 1773, the tea was thrown overboard in Boston harbor, and it is now generally believed that Samuel Adams inspired and encouraged this act as one which would most surely lead to a breach with the mother country.

The school-book story of the "Boston Tea Party" has been so deeply impressed upon our minds as one of the glorious deeds of patriotism that its true bearings are obscured. There were many patriots at the time who did not consider it a wise act. Besides Boston, the tea was sent by the East India Company to Charleston, Philadelphia, and New York, and in these cities the people prevented its being landed and sold; but they did not destroy it. They considered that they had a right to prevent its landing and sale; that in doing this they were acting in a legal and constitutional manner to protect their rights; but to destroy it would have been both a riotous act and an attack on private property.

The Tory ministry, while having no serious objection to the method adopted in Charleston, Philadelphia, and New York, considered the Boston method decidedly riotous, and from its point of view such a conclusion was natural. It seemed to be of a piece with all the other occurrences which Hutchinson

---

* Hosmer's Life of Samuel Adams, p. 117.

and Oliver had described in their letters, and it confirmed most strongly all the statements and recommendations in those letters. It was decided to punish Boston in a way that she would remember, and in the following March, after careful deliberation, Parliament passed the Boston Port Bill, which locked up the harbor of that town, destroyed for the time her commerce, and soon brought on the actual bloodshed of the Revolution.

Meantime the ministry also attended to Franklin's case. The Privy Council sent word to Franklin that it was ready to take up the petition of the Massachusetts Assembly asking for the removal of Governor Hutchinson, and required his presence as the colony's agent. He found that Hutchinson and Oliver had secured as counsel Alexander Wedderburn, a Scotch barrister, afterwards most successful in securing political preferment, and ending his career as Lord Rosslyn. Franklin had no counsel, and asked for a postponement of three weeks to obtain legal aid and prepare his case, which was granted.

The day fixed for the hearing aroused great expectations. An unprecedented number of the members of the Privy Council attended. The Archbishop of Canterbury, Burke, Dr. Priestley, Izard, Lee, and many other distinguished persons, friends or opponents of Franklin, crowded into the chamber. The members of the Privy Council sat at a long table, and every one else had to stand as a mark of respect. The room was one of those apartments which tourists are often shown in palaces in Europe, somewhat like a large drawing-room with an open fireplace at one end. The fireplace projected into the room, and in one of the recesses at the side of it Franklin stood, not far behind Lord Gower, president of the Council, who had his back to the fireplace.

Franklin's astute counsel, John Dunning, a famous barrister, afterwards Lord Ashburton, told him that his peace and love theory was not a very good ground to rest his case on before the Council. It would be well not to use the Hutchinson letters at all, or refer to them as little as possible ; for the Privy Council believed every word in them to be true, and the passages in them which had most inflamed the colonists were the very ones which were most acceptable to the Council.

So Dunning made a speech in which he said that no crime or offence was charged against Hutchinson and Oliver ; they were in no way attacked or accused ; the colonists were simply asking a favor of His Majesty, which was that the governor and the lieutenant-governor had become so distasteful to the people that it would be good policy and tend to peace and quiet to remove them.

It was a ridiculous attempt, of course, and none knew better than Dunning that there was not the slightest hope of success. The Privy Council would never have taken up the petition, it would have slept in the dust of its pigeon-hole, if the council had not seen in it a way of attacking Franklin. Wedderburn's speech was the event awaited, and to it the Tories looked forward as to a cock-fight or a bull-baiting.

A little volume published in England and to be found in some of the libraries in America contains an account of the proceedings and gives a large part of Wedderburn's speech. He has been most abundantly abused in America and by Whigs in England as an unprincipled office-seeker and a shallow orator, with no other talent than that of invective. That he was successful in obtaining office and rising to high distinction as an ardent Tory cannot be denied, and in this respect he did not differ materially from others or from the Whigs themselves when they had their innings. As to the charge of shallowness, it is not borne out by his speech on this occasion. Once concede his point of view as a Tory, and the speech is a very clever one.

He began by a history of Hutchinson's useful public career in Massachusetts; and there is no question that Hutchinson had been a most valuable official; even the Massachusetts people themselves conceded that. The difficulty with Hutchinson was the same as with Wedderburn,—his point of view was not ours. Having reviewed Hutchinson, he went on to show how ridiculous it was to suppose that he alone had been the cause of sending the troops to Boston, and in this he was again probably right. The home government, as he well said, had abundant other means of information from General Gage, Sir Francis Bernard, and its officials all through the colonies; and he concluded this part of his speech with the point that Hutchinson, by the admission of Massachusetts herself, had never done anything wrong except write these letters, and would it not be ridiculous to dismiss a man for giving information which had been furnished by a host of others?

Then he turned his attention to Franklin. How had he obtained those letters? And here it must be confessed that Franklin was in a scrape, and from the Tory point of view was fair game. He could not disclose the name of the member of Parliament who gave them to him, for he had promised not to do so, and even without this promise it would have been wanton cruelty to have subjected the man to the ruin and disgrace that would have instantly fallen upon him. Nothing could drag this secret from Franklin. He refused to answer questions on the subject, and it is a secret to this day, as it is also still a secret who was the mother of his son. Ingenious persons have written about one as about the other, and supposed and guessed and piled up probabilities to no purpose. Franklin told the world more private matters than is usual with men in his position; but in the two matters on which he had determined to withhold knowledge the world has sought for it in vain.

Praiseworthy as his conduct may have been in this respect, it gave his opponents an advantage which we must admit they were entitled to take. If, as Wedderburn put it, he refused to tell from whom he received the letters, they were at liberty to suppose the worst, and the worst was that he had obtained them by improper means and fraud.

For a time which must have seemed like years to Franklin, Wedderburn drew out and played on this

point with most exasperating skill. Gentlemen respect private correspondence. They do not usually
steal people's letters and print them. Even a foreign
ambassador on the outbreak of war would hardly be
justified in stealing documents. Must he not have
known as soon as the letters were handed to him
that honorable permission to use them could be obtained only from the family of Whately? Why had
he chosen to bring that family into painful notoriety
and one of them within a step of being murdered?
He had sent the letters to Massachusetts with the
address removed from them, and he was here supporting the petition with nothing but copies of the
letters. He would, forsooth, have removed from
office a governor in the midst of a long career of
usefulness on the ground of letters the originals of
which he could not produce and which he dared
not tell how he had obtained.

The orator went on to cite some of Franklin's letters to the people in Massachusetts encouraging
them in their opposition. He read the resolutions
of New England town meetings, and gave what,
indeed, was a truthful description, from his point of
view, of the measures taken for resistance in America. Franklin was aspiring to be Governor of Massachusetts in the place of Hutchinson, that was the
secret of the whole affair, he said; and as for that
beautiful argument that Hutchinson and Oliver had
incensed the mother country against the colonies,
what absurdity!

We are perpetually told, he said, of men's in-
censing the mother country against the colonies,

but we hear nothing of the vast variety of acts which have been made use of to incense the colonies against the mother country, setting at defiance the king's authority, treating Parliament as usurpers, pulling down the houses of royal officials and attacking their persons, burning His Majesty's ships of war, and denying the supreme jurisdiction of the British empire; and yet these people pretend a great concern about these letters as having a tendency to incense the parent state against the colonies, and would have a governor turned out because he reports their doings. "Was it to confute or prevent the pernicious effect of these letters that the good men of Boston have lately held their meetings, appointed their committees, and with their usual moderation destroyed the cargo of three British ships?"

While this ferocious attack was being delivered,— and it is said to have been delivered in thundering tones, emphasized by terrible blows of the orator's fist on a cushion before him on the table,—Franklin stood with head erect, unmoved, and without the slightest change upon his face from the beginning to the end. When all was over he went out, silent, dignified, without a word or sign to any one except that, as he passed Dr. Priestley, he secretly pressed his hand. His superb nerves and physique again raised him far above the occasion.

It was one of the most remarkable traits of his wonderful personality that in all the great trials of his life he could give a dramatic interest and force to the situation which in the end turned everything in his favor. Burke said that his examination before Parliament reminded him of a master examined by a parcel of school-boys; and Whitefield said that every answer he gave made the questioner appear insignificant. In his much severer test before Wedderburn and the Privy Council he was defeated; but his supreme and serene manner was never forgotten by the spectators, and will live forever as a dramatic incident. Pictures have been painted of it, for it lends itself irresistibly to the purposes of the artist. In these pictures Franklin is the hero, for it is impossible, from an artistic point of view, to make any one else the hero in that scene.

The petition of the Massachusetts Assembly was, of course, rejected with contempt; Franklin was immediately deprived of his office of postmaster of the colonies, and his usefulness as a colonial agent or as a diplomatist was at an end. He could no longer go to court or even be on friendly terms with the Tory party which controlled the government; and from this time on he was compelled to associate almost exclusively with the opposition, who still continued to be his friends. In other words, from being a colonial representative he had become a mere party man or party politician in England, and his own acts had brought him to this condition. While in a position which was essentially diplomatic, he had chosen to write anonymous newspaper articles against the very men with whom he was compelled to carry on his diplomatic negotiations. They naturally watched their opportunity to destroy him; and his conduct with regard to the Hutchinson letters gave it to them.

He fully realized his situation, and made preparations to return to Philadelphia. He was, in fact, in danger of arrest ; and the government had sent to America for the originals of some of his letters on which to base a prosecution for treason. But when it became known that the first Continental Congress was called to meet in September, he was persuaded to remain, as the Congress might have business for him to transact. He still believed that all difficulties would be finally settled. He did not think that there would be war ; and this belief may have been caused partly by his conviction of the utter folly of such a war and partly because it was impossible for him to get full and accurate information of the real state of mind of the people in America. He had great faith in a change of ministry. If the Americans refused for another year to buy British goods, there would be such a clamor from the merchants and manufacturers that the Whigs would ride into power and colonial rights be safe.

He remained until the following spring, without being able to accomplish anything, but he caught at several straws. Lord Chatham, who, as William Pitt, had conquered Canada in the French and Indian wars and laid the foundations of the modern British empire, was thoroughly disgusted at the conduct of the administration towards America. An old man, living at his country-seat within a couple of hours' drive from London, and suffering severely at times from the gout, he nevertheless aroused himself to reopen the subject in the House of Lords. He sent for Franklin, who has left us a most graphic

account of the great man, so magnificent, eloquent,
and gracious in his declining years.

Franklin went over the whole ground with him;
but the aged nobleman who had been such a con-
queror of nations was fond of having everything his
own way, and Franklin confesses that he was so
charmed in watching the wonderful powers of his
mind that he cared but little about criticising his
plans. His lordship raised the question in the
House of Lords in a grand oration, parts of which
are still spoken by our school-boys, and he followed it by other speeches. He was for withdraw-
ing all the troops from the colonies and restoring
peace; but his oratory had no more effect on
Parliament than Franklin's jokes.

At the same time Lord Howe, brother of the
General Howe who was afterwards prominent in the
war against the colonies, attempted a plan of paci-
fication which was to be accomplished through
Franklin's aid. The Howes were favorably inclined
towards America. Their brother, General Viscount
Howe, had been very popular in the colonies, was
killed at Ticonderoga in 1758 in the French and
Indian war, and Massachusetts had erected a monument to his memory in Westminster Abbey.

Lord Howe's object was to secure some basis of
compromise which both Franklin and the ministry
could agree upon, an essential part of which was
that his lordship was to be sent over to the colonies
as a special commissioner to arrange final terms.
The negotiations began by Franklin being asked to
play chess with Lord Howe's sister, and he was also

approached by a prominent Quaker, David Barclay, and by his old friend, Dr. Fothergill. There were numerous interviews, and Franklin prepared several papers containing conditions to which he thought the colonies would agree. Lord Howe promised him high rewards in case of success, and even offered, as an assurance of the good things to come, to pay him at once the arrears of his salary as agent of Massachusetts.

Whether this was a sincere attempt at accommodation on the part of some of the more moderate of the Tories, or a scheme of Lord Howe's private ambition, or a mere trap for Franklin, has never been made clear. Franklin, however, rejected all the bribes and stood on the safe ground of terms which he knew would be acceptable in America ; so this attempt also came to naught.

After reading the long account Franklin has given of these negotiations, and the innumerable letters and proposals that were exchanged, one may see many causes of the break with the colonies,—ignorance, blindness, the infatuation of the king or of North or of Townsend,—but the primary cause of all is the one given at the end by Franklin,—corruption. The whole British government of that time was penetrated through and through with a vast system of bribery. Statesmen and politicians cared for nothing and would do nothing that did not give them offices to distribute. That was one of the objects of Lord Howe's scheme. Dr. Fothergill was intimate with all the governing class, and he said to Franklin, "Whatever specious pretences are offered, they are hollow; to get a larger field on which to fatten a herd of worthless parasites is all that is regarded." England lost her colonies by corruption, and she could not have built up her present vast colonial empire unless corruption had been abolished.

At the end of April Franklin set out on his return to Philadelphia, and there was some question whether he would not be arrested before he could start. He used some precautions in getting away as quietly as possible, and sailed from Portsmouth unmolested.

He still believed that there would be no war, and fully expected to return in October with instructions from the Continental Congress that would end the controversy. His ground for this belief seems to have been the old one that the hostility in England towards America was purely a ministerial or party question, and would be overthrown by the refusal of the colonists to buy British goods. But on his arrival in Philadelphia on the 5th of May he heard of the battle of Lexington, and never after that entertained much hope of a peaceful accommodation.

VIII

AT HOME AGAIN

FRANKLIN's wife had died while he was in England, and his daughter, Mrs. Sarah Bache, was now mistress of his new house, which had been built during his absence. The day after his arrival the Assembly made him one of its deputies in the Continental Congress which was soon to meet in Philadelphia. For the next eighteen months (from his arrival on the 5th of May, 1775, until October 26, 1776, when he sailed for France) every hour of his time seems to have been occupied with labors which would have been enough for a man in his prime, but for one seventy years old were a heavy burden.

He was made Postmaster-General of the united colonies, and prepared a plan for a line of posts from Maine to Georgia. He dropped all his conservatism and became very earnest for the war, but was humorous and easy-going about everything. He had, of course, the privilege of franking his own letters; but instead of the usual form, "Free. B. Franklin," he would mark them "B free Franklin." He prepared a plan or constitution for the union of the colonies, which will be considered hereafter. Besides his work in Congress, he was soon made a member of the Pennsylvania Legislature, and was on the Committee of Safety which was preparing the defences of the province, and was, in effect, the executive government in place of the proprietary governor. From six to nine in the morning he was with this committee, and from nine till four in the afternoon he attended the session of Congress. He assisted in devising plans for obstructing the channel of the Delaware River, and the *chevaux-de-frise*, as they were called, which were placed in the water were largely of his design.

It was extremely difficult for the Congress to obtain gunpowder for the army. The colonists had always relied on Europe for their supply, and were unaccustomed to manufacturing it. Franklin suggested that they should return to the use of bows and arrows :

"These were good weapons not wisely laid aside : 1st. Because a man may shoot as truly with a bow as with a common musket. 2dly. He can discharge four arrows in the time of charging and discharging one bullet. 3dly. His object is not taken from his view by the smoke of his own side. 4thly. A flight of arrows seen coming upon them, terrifies and disturbs the enemies' attention to their business. 5thly. An arrow striking any part of a man puts him *hors de combat* till it is extracted. 6thly. Bows and arrows are more easily provided everywhere than muskets and ammunition."

This suggestion seems less strange when we remember that the musket of that time was a smooth-bore and comparatively harmless at three hundred yards.

His letters to his old friends in England were full of resentment against the atrocities of the British fleet and army, especially the burning of the town of Portland, Maine. It was at this time that he

FRANKLIN'S LETTER TO STRAHAN

wrote his famous letter to his old London friend, Mr. Strahan, a reproduction of which, taken from the copy at the State Department, Washington, is given in this volume. It is a most curiously worded, half-humorous letter, and the most popular one he ever wrote. It has been reprinted again and again, and *fac-similes* of it have appeared for a hundred years, some of them in school-books.

He could have desired nothing better than its appearance in school-books. One of his pet projects was that all American school-children should be taught how shockingly unjust and cruel Great Britain had been to her colonies ; they must learn, he said, to hate her ; and while he was in France he prepared a long list of the British outrages which he considered contrary to all the rules of civilized warfare. He intended to have a picture of each one prepared by French artists and sent to America, that the lesson of undying hatred might be burnt into the youthful mind.

In the autumn of 1775 he went with two other commissioners to Washington's army before Boston to arrange for supplies and prepare general plans for the conduct of the war. In the following March he was sent to Canada with Samuel Chase and Charles Carroll, of Maryland, to win over the Canadians to the side of the revolted colonies. Charles Carroll's brother John, a Roman Catholic priest, accompanied them at the request of the members of Congress, who hoped that he would be able to influence the French Canadian clergy.

It was a terrible journey for Franklin, now an old

man ; for as they advanced north they found the
ground covered with snow and the lakes filled with
floating ice. They spent five days beating up the
Hudson in a little sloop to Albany, and two weeks
after they had started they reached Lake George.
General Schuyler, who lived near Albany, accompanied them after they had rested at his house, and
assisted in obtaining wagons and boats. Franklin
was ill with what he afterwards thought was an in-
cipient attack of the gout which his constitution
wanted strength to develop completely. At Sara-
toga he made up his mind that he would never see
his home again, and wrote several letters of farewell.

But by the care and assistance of John Carroll, the
priest, with whom he contracted a life-long friendship,
he was able to press on, and they reached the southern end of Lake George, where they embarked on a
large flat-bottomed boat without a cabin, and sailed
the whole length of the lake through the floating ice
in about a day. Their boat was hauled by oxen
across the land to Lake Champlain, and after a delay
of five days they embarked again amidst the floating
ice. Sailing and rowing, sleeping under a canvas
cover at night, and going ashore to cook their meals,
they made the upper end of the lake in about four
days, and another day in wagons brought them to
Montreal.

Their mission was fruitless. The army under
General Montgomery which had invaded the country had been unsuccessful against the British, had
contracted large debts with the Canadians which it
was unable to pay, and the Canadians would not

join in the Revolution. So Franklin and the commissioners had to make their toilsome journey back again without having accomplished anything; and many years afterwards Franklin mentioned this journey, which nearly destroyed his life, as one of the reasons why Congress should vote him extra pay for his services in the Revolution.

In June, 1776, Franklin was made a member of the convention which framed a new constitution for Pennsylvania to supply the place of the old colonial charter of William Penn, and he was engaged in this work during the summer, when his other duties permitted; but of this more hereafter. At the same time he was laboring in the Congress on the question of declaring independence. He was in favor of an immediate declaration, and his name is signed to the famous instrument.

During this same summer he also had another conference with Lord Howe, who had arrived in New York harbor in command of the British fleet, and again wanted to patch up a peace. He failed, of course, for he had authority from his government only to receive the submission of the colonies; and he was plainly told by Franklin and the other commissioners who met him that the colonies would make no treaty with England except one that acknowledged them as an independent nation.

IX

THE EMBASSY TO FRANCE AND ITS SCANDALS

FRANKLIN'S most important duties in the Continental Congress were connected with his membership of the "Secret Committee," afterwards known as the "Committee of Correspondence." It was really a committee on foreign relations, and had been formed for the purpose of corresponding with the friends of the revolted colonies in Europe and securing from them advice and assistance. From appointing agents to serve this committee in France or England, Franklin was soon promoted to be himself one of the agents and to represent in France the united colonies which had just declared their independence.

On September 26, 1776, he was given this important mission, not by the mere appointment of his own committee, but by vote of Congress. He was to be one of three commissioners of equal powers, who would have more importance and weight than the mere agents hitherto sent to Europe. The news received of the friendly disposition of France was very encouraging, and it was necessary that envoys should be sent with full authority to take advantage of it. Silas Deane, who had already gone to France as a secret agent, and Thomas Jefferson were elected as Franklin's fellow-commissioners. The ill health of

Jefferson's wife compelled him to decline, and Arthur Lee, already acting as an agent for the colonies in Europe, was elected in his place.

When the result of the first ballot taken in Congress showed that Franklin was elected, he is said to have turned to Dr. Rush, sitting near him, and remarked, "I am old and good for nothing; but as the storekeepers say of their remnants of cloth, I am but a fag end, you may have me for what you please."

There was, however, fourteen more years of labor in the "fag end," as he called himself; and the jest was one of those appropriately modest remarks which he knew so well how to make. He probably looked forward with not a little satisfaction to the prospect of renewing again those pleasures of intercourse with the learned and great which he was so capable of enjoying and which could be found only in Europe. His reputation was already greater in France than in England. He would be able to see the evidences of it as well as increase it in this new and delightful field. But the British newspapers, of course, said that he had secured this appointment as a clever way of escaping from the collapse of the rebellion which he shrewdly foresaw was inevitable.

On October 26, 1776, he left Philadelphia very quietly and, accompanied by his two grandsons, William Temple Franklin and Benjamin Franklin Bache, drove some fifteen miles down the river to Marcus Hook, where the "Reprisal," a swift war-vessel of the revolted colonies, awaited him. She set sail immediately and got out of the river into the ocean as quickly as possible, for the British desired nothing better than to capture this distinguished envoy to the court of France. Wickes, the captain, afterwards famous for the prizes he took from the British, knew that he must run the gauntlet of the cruisers, and he drove his little vessel with all sail through the November gales, making Quiberon Bay, on the coast of France, in thirty-three days.

It was a rough, dangerous, exciting voyage ; the venerable philosopher of seventy years was confined to a little, cramped cabin, more sick and distressed than he had ever been before on the ocean ; and yet he insisted on taking the temperature of the water every day to test again his theory of the Gulf Stream. They were chased by cruisers, but the fleet "Reprisal" could always turn them into fading specks on the horizon's verge ; and as she neared the coast of France she fell in with some good luck,— two British vessels loaded with lumber, wine, brandy, and flaxseed, which were duly brought to and carried into a French port to be sold. The "Reprisal" had on board a small cargo of indigo, which, with the prizes, was to go towards paying the expense of the mission to France. In this simple and homely way were the colonies beginning their diplomatic relations.

The French people received Franklin with an outburst of enthusiasm which has never been given by them to any other American. So weak from the sickness of the voyage that he could scarcely stand, the old man was overwhelmed with attention,—a grand dinner at Nantes, an invitation to a country house where he expected to find rest, but had none from the ceaseless throng of visitors. The unexpected and romantic manner of his arrival, dodging the cruisers and coming in with two great merchantmen as prizes, aroused the greatest interest and delight. It was like a brilliant stroke in a play or a tale from the "Arabian Nights," worthy of French imagination ; and here this wonderful American from the woods had made it an accomplished fact.

The enthusiasm of this reception never abated, but, on the contrary, soon became extravagant worship, which continued during the nine years of his residence in France. Even on his arrival they were exaggerating everything about him, adding four years to his age to make his adventures seem more wonderful ; and Paris waited in as much restless expectation for his arrival as if he had been a king.

Beneath all this lay, of course, the supreme satisfaction with which the French contemplated the revolt of the colonies and the inevitable weakening of their much-hated enemy and rival, Great Britain ; and they had made up their minds to assist in this dismemberment to the utmost of their ability. They were already familiar with Franklin ; his name was a household word in France ; his brilliant discovery of the nature of lightning appealed strongly to every imagination ; " Poor Richard" had been translated for them, and its shrewd economy and homely wisdom had been their delight for years. Its author was the synonyme and personification of liberty,— that liberty which they were just beginning to rave about, for their own revolution was not twenty years away.

It interested them all the more that the man who represented all this for them, and whose name seemed to be really a French one, came from the horrible wilderness of America, the home of interminable dark forests, filled with savage beasts and still more savage men.

France at that time was the gay, pleasure- and sensation-loving France which had just been living under the reign of Louis XIV. Sated with luxury and magnificence, with much intelligence and culture even among the middle classes, there was no novelty that pleased Frenchmen more than something which seemed to be close to nature ; and when they discovered that this exceedingly natural man from the woods had also the severe and serene philosophy of Cato, Phocion, Socrates, and the other sages of antiquity, combined with a conversation full of wit, point, and raillery like their own, it is not surprising that they made a perpetual joy and feast over him. It was so delightful for a lady to pay him a pretty compliment about having drawn down the fire from heaven, and have him instantly reply in some most apt phrase of an old man's gallantry ; and then he never failed ; there seemed to be no end to his resources.

Amidst these brilliant surroundings he wore for a time that shocking old fur cap which appears in one of his portraits ; and although his biographers earnestly protest that he was incapable of such affectation, there is every reason to believe that he found

FRANKLIN CANNOT DIE

(From a French engraving)

that it intensified the character the French people had already formed of him. Several writers of the time speak of his very rustic dress, his firm but free and direct manner which seemed to be the simplicity of a past age. But if he was willing to encourage their laudation by a little clever acting, he never carried it too far; and there is no evidence that his head was ever turned by all this extravagant worship. He was altogether too shrewd to make such a fatal mistake. He knew the meaning and real value of it, and nursed it so carefully that he kept it living and fresh for nine years.

So he went to live in Paris, while the people began to make portraits, medals, and busts of him, until there were some two hundred different kinds to be set in rings, watches, snuff-boxes, bracelets, looking-glasses, and other articles. Within a few days after his arrival it was the fashion for every one to have a picture of him on their mantel-piece. He selected for his residence the little village of Passy, about two miles from the heart of Paris, and not too far from the court at Versailles. There for nine years his famous letters were dated, and Franklin at Passy, with his friends, their gardens and their wit, was a subject of interest and delight to a whole generation of the civilized world.

M. Ray de Chaumont had there a large establishment called the Hôtel de Valentinois. In part of it he lived himself, and, to show his devotion to the cause of America, he insisted that Franklin should occupy the rest of it as his home and for the business of the embassy free of rent. This arrangement

Franklin accepted in his easy way, and nothing more was thought of it until precise John Adams arrived from Massachusetts and was greatly shocked to find an envoy of the United States living in a Frenchman's house without paying board.

Pleasantly situated, with charming neighbors who never wearied of him, enjoying the visits and improving conversation of the great men of the learned and scientific worlds, caressed at court, exchanging repartees and flirtations with clever women, oppressed at times with terrible anxiety for his country, but slowly winning success, and dining out six nights of nearly every week when he was not disabled by the gout, the old Philadelphia printer cannot be said to have fallen upon very evil days.

His position was just the reverse of what it had been in England, where his task had been almost an impossible one. In France everything was in his favor. There were no Wedderburns or Tory ministers, no powerful political party opposed to his purposes, and no liberal party with which he might be tempted to take sides. The whole nation—king, nobles, and people—was with him. He had only to suggest what was wanted ; and, indeed, a great deal was done without even his suggestion.

This condition of affairs precluded the possibility of his accomplishing any great feat in diplomacy. The tide being all in his favor, he had only to take advantage of it and abstain from anything that would check its flow. Instead of the aggressive course he had seen fit to follow in England, he must avoid everything which in the least resembled aggression. He must be complaisant, popular, and encourage the universal feeling instead of opposing it, and this part he certainly played to perfection.

He was by no means the sole representative of his country in France, and considerable work had been accomplished before he arrived. In fact, the French were ready to do the work themselves without waiting for a representative. When Franklin was leaving London in 1775 the French ambassador called upon him and gave him to understand in no doubtful terms that France would be on the side of the colonies.

It is a mistake to suppose, as has sometimes been done, that some one person suggested to the French government, or that Franklin himself suggested or urged, the idea of weakening England by assisting America. It was a policy the wisdom of which was obvious to every one. As early as the time of the Stamp Act, Louis XV. sent De Kalb to America to watch the progress of the rebellion, and to foment it. The English themselves foresaw and dreaded a French alliance with the colonies. Lord Howe referred to it in his last interview with Franklin ; Beaumarchais argued about it in long letters to the king ; it was favored by the Count d'Artois, the Duke of Orléans, and the Count de Broglie, not to mention young Lafayette ; and the colonists themselves thought of it as soon as they thought of resistance. The French king, Louis XVI., who, as an absolute monarch, disliked rebellion, hesitated for a time ; but he was won over by Vergennes and Beaumarchais.

France had just come out of a long war with England in which she had lost Canada and valuable possessions in the East and West Indies. England held the port of Dunkirk, on French soil, and searched French ships whenever she pleased. France was humiliated and full of resentment. She had failed to conquer the English colonies ; but it would be almost as good and some slight revenge if she deprived England of them by helping them to secure their own independence. It would cripple English commerce, which was rapidly driving that of France from the ocean. England had in 1768 helped the Corsican rebels against France, and that was a good precedent for France helping the American rebels against England.

In the autumn of 1775 the Secret Committee of Congress had sent Thomas Story to London, Holland, and France to consult with persons friendly to the colonies. He was also to deliver a letter to Arthur Lee, who had taken Franklin's place as agent of Massachusetts in London, and this letter instructed Lee to learn the disposition of foreign powers. A similar letter was to be delivered to Mr. Dumas in Holland, and soon after Story's departure M. Penet, a French merchant of Nantes, was sent to France to buy ammunition, arms, and clothing.

A few months afterwards, in the beginning of 1776, the committee sent to Paris Silas Deane, of Connecticut, who had served in the Congress. He was more of a diplomatic representative than any of the others, and was instructed to procure, if possible, an audience with Vergennes, the French Minister of

Foreign Affairs, suggest the establishment of friendly relations, the need of arms and ammunition, and finally lead up to the question whether, if the colonies declared their independence, they might look upon France as an ally.

Meantime that strange character, Beaumarchais, the author of "The Barber of Seville" and "The Marriage of Figaro," and still a distinguished light of French literature, fired by the general enthusiasm for the Americans, constituted himself their agent and ambassador, and was by no means an unimportant one. He was the son of a respectable watchmaker, and when a mere youth had distinguished himself by the invention of an improvement in escapements, which was stolen by another watchmaker, who announced it as his own. Beaumarchais appealed to the Academy of Sciences in a most cleverly written petition, and it decided in his favor. Great attention had been drawn to him by the contest; he appeared at court, and was soon making wonderful little watches for the king and queen; he became a favorite, the familiar friend of the king's daughters, and his career as an adventurer, courtier, and speculator began. A most wonderful genius, typical in many ways of his century, few men have ever lived who could play so many parts, and his excellent biographer, Loménie, has summed up the occupations in which he excelled:

"Watch-maker, musician, song writer, dramatist, comic writer, man of fashion, courtier, man of business, financier, manufacturer, publisher, ship-owner, contractor, secret agent, negotiator, pamphleteer, orator on certain occasions, a peaceful man by taste, and yet always at law, engaging, like Figaro, in every occupation, Beaumarchais was concerned in most of the events, great or small, which preceded the Revolution."

He traded all over the world, and made three or four fortunes and lost them ; he had at times forty vessels of his own on the ocean, and his private man-of-war assisted the French navy at the battle of Grenada. In fact, he was like his great contemporary, Voltaire, who, besides being a dramatist, a philosopher, a man of letters, and a reformer, was one of the ablest business men of France, a shipowner, contractor, and millionaire.

The resemblance of Franklin to these two men is striking. He showed the same versatility of talents, though perhaps in less degree. He had the same strange ability to excel at the same time in both literary and practical affairs, he had very much the same opinion on religion, and his morals, like Voltaire's, were somewhat irregular. When we connect with this his wonderful reputation in France, the adoration of the people, and the strange way in which during his residence in Paris he became part of the French nation, we are almost led to believe that through some hidden process the causes which produced Franklin must have been largely of French origin. He is, indeed, more French than English, and seems to belong with Beaumarchais and Voltaire rather than with Chatham, Burke, or Priestley.

But to return to Beaumarchais and the Revolution. He was carried away by the importance of the rebellion in America, and devoted his whole soul to bringing France to the assistance of the colonies. He argued with the court and the king, visited London repeatedly in the secret service of his government, and became more than ever convinced of the weakness of Great Britain.

The plan which the French ministry now adopted was to aid the colonies in secret and avoid for the present an open breach with England. Arms were to be sent to one of the French West India islands, where the governor would find means of delivering them to the Americans. Soon, however, this method was changed as too dangerous, and in place of it Beaumarchais established in Paris a business house, which he personally conducted under the name of Roderique Hortalez & Company. He did this at the request of the government, and his biographer, De Loménie, has given us a statement of the arrangement in language which he assumes Vergennes must have used in giving instructions to Beaumarchais :

"The operation must essentially in the eyes of the English government, and even in the eyes of the Americans, have the appearance of an individual speculation, to which the French ministers are strangers. That it may be so in appearance, it must also be so, to a certain point, in reality. We will give a million secretly, we will try to induce the court of Spain to unite with us in this affair, and supply you on its side with an equal sum; with these two millions and the co-operation of individuals who will be willing to take part in your enterprise you will be able to found a large house of commerce, and at your own risk can supply America with arms, ammunition, articles of equipment, and all other articles necessary for keeping up the war. Our arsenals will give you arms and ammunition, but you shall replace them or shall pay for them. You shall ask for no money from the Americans, as they have none; but you shall ask them for returns in products of their soil, and we will help you to get rid of them in this country, while you shall grant them, on your side, every facility possible. In a word, the operation, after being secretly supported by us at the commencement, must afterwards feed and support itself; but, on the other side, as we reserve to ourselves the right of favoring or discouraging it, according to the requirements of our policy, you shall render us an account of your profits and your losses, and we will judge whether we are to accord you fresh assistance, or give you an acquittal for the sums previously granted." (De Loménie's Beaumarchais, p. 273.)

It was in June, 1776, that Beaumarchais started his extraordinary enterprise in the Rue Vieille du Temple, in a large building called the Hôtel de Hollande, which had formerly been used as the residence of the Dutch ambassador. The million francs was paid to him by the French government, another million by Spain in September, and still another million by France in the following year. So with the greatest hopefulness and delight he began shipping uniforms, arms, ammunition, and all sorts of supplies to America. He had at times great difficulty in getting his laden ships out of port. The French government was perfectly willing that they should go, and always affected to know nothing about them. But Lord Stormont, the British ambassador, would often discover their destination and protest in most vigorous and threatening language. Then the French ministry would appear greatly surprised and stop the ships. This process was repeated during two years,—a curious triangular, half-masked contest between Beaumarchais, Lord Stormont, and the ministry.

"If government caused my vessels to be unloaded in one port, I sent them secretly to reload at a distance in the roads. Were they stopped under their proper names, I changed them immediately, or made pretended sales, and put them anew under fictitious commissions. Were obligations in writing exacted from my captains to go nowhere but to the West India Islands, powerful gratifications on my part made them yield again to my wishes. Were they sent to prison on their return for disobedience, I then doubled their gratifications to keep their zeal from cooling, and consoled them with gold for the rigor of our government."

In this way he sent to the colonies within a year eight vessels with supplies worth six million francs. Sometimes, in spite of all efforts, one of his vessels with a valuable cargo was obliged to sail direct to the West Indies, and could go nowhere else. In one instance of this sort he wrote to his agent Francy, in America, to have several American privateers sent to the West Indies to seize the vessel.

" My captain will protest violently, and will draw up a written statement threatening to make his complaint to the Congress. The vessel will be taken where you are. The Congress will loudly disavow the action of the brutal privateer, and will set the vessel at liberty with polite apologies to the French flag ; during this time you will land the cargo, fill the ship with tobacco, and send it back to me as quickly as possible, with all you may happen to have ready to accompany it."

Imagination is sometimes a very valuable quality in practical affairs, and this neat description by the man of letters was actually carried out in every detail and with complete success by his agent in America. He was certainly a valuable ambassador of the colonies, this wonderful Beaumarchais ; but he suffered severely for his devotion. Under his agreement with his government, the government's outlay was to be paid back gradually by American produce ; but Congress would not send the produce, or sent it so slowly that Beaumarchais was threatened with ruin, and suffered the torturing anxiety which comes with the conviction that those for whom you are making the greatest sacrifices are indifferent and incapable of gratitude.

It was in vain that he appealed to Congress ; for Arthur Lee was continually informing that body that he was a fraud and his claims groundless, because the French government intended that all the supplies sent through Hortalez & Co. should be a free gift to the revolted colonies. Lee may have sincerely believed this ; but it was very unfortunate, because more than two years elapsed before Congress became convinced that the supplies were not entirely a present, and voted Beaumarchais its thanks and some of the money he claimed. A large part of his claims were never paid. For fifty years there was a controversy about "the lost million," and for its romantic history the reader is referred to De Loménie, Durand's "New Material for the History of the American Revolution," and Dr. Stillé's "Beaumarchais and the Lost Million."

But he was not the only person who suffered. The truth is that the whole arrangement made by Congress for conducting the business in France was ridiculously inefficient, not to say cruel and inhuman. That we got most important aid from France was due to the eagerness and efforts of the French themselves, and not to anything done by Congress.

Franklin and his two fellow-commissioners, Silas Deane and Arthur Lee, had equal powers. They had to conduct a large and complicated business involving the expenditure of millions of dollars without knowing exactly where the millions were to come from, and with no regular system of accounts or means of auditing and investigating ; their arrangements had to be largely kept secret ; they expended money in lump sums without always knowing what use was made of it ; they were obliged to rely on the assistance of all sorts of people,—naval agents, commercial agents, and others for whose occupation there was no exact name ; and they had no previous experience or precedents to guide them. On their arrival at Paris, the three commissioners found a fourth person, Beaumarchais, well advanced in his work, and accomplishing in a practical way rather more than any of them could hope to do. Moreover, Beaumarchais's arrangement was necessarily so secret that though they knew in a general way, as did Lord Stormont and all Paris, what he was doing, yet only one of them, Deane, was ever fully admitted into the secret, and it is probable that the other two died without having fully grasped the real nature and conditions of his service.

That three joint commissioners of equal powers should conduct such an enormous business of expenditure and credit for a series of years without becoming entangled in the most terrible suspicions and bitter quarrels was in the nature of things impossible. The result was that the history of their horrible disputes and accusations against one another is more voluminous than the history of their services. Deane, who did more actual work than any one except

Beaumarchais, was thoroughly and irretrievably ruined. Arthur Lee, who accomplished very little besides manufacturing suspicions and charges, has left behind him a reputation for malevolence which no one will envy; Beaumarchais suffered tortures which he considered almost equivalent to ruin, and his reputation was not entirely rescued until nearly half a century after his death; and Franklin came nearer than ever before in his life to sinking his great fame in an infamy of corruption, for the attacks made upon him by Arthur Lee were a hundred times worse than those of Wedderburn.

It was a terrible ordeal for the four men,—those two years before France made an open alliance with the colonies,—and I will add a few other circumstances which contributed variety to their situation. Ralph Izard, of South Carolina, a very passionate man, was appointed by the wise Congress an envoy to the Grand Duke of Tuscany. He never went to Tuscany for the simple reason that the duke could not receive him without becoming embroiled with Great Britain; so he was obliged to remain in Paris, where he assisted Lee in villifying Deane, Franklin, and Beaumarchais, and his letters home were full of attacks on their characters.

He was not a member of the commission which had charge of French affairs, and yet, in the loose way in which all the foreign business of the colonies was being managed, it was perhaps natural that, as an energetic and able man and an American, he should wish to be consulted occasionally by Franklin and Deane. In a certain way he was directly connected with them, for he had to obtain money from them for some of his expenses incurred in attempting to go to Tuscany, and on this subject he quarrelled with Franklin, who thought that he had used too much. He was also obliged to apply to Franklin for certain papers to enable him to make a commercial treaty with Tuscany, and these, he said, Franklin had delayed supplying. He complained further of Franklin's neglect to answer his letters and obstructing his means of sending information to America.

Franklin afterwards admitted that he might have saved himself from Izard's enmity by showing him a little attention ; his letters to both Izard and Lee were very stinging ; in fact, they were the severest that he ever wrote ; and Izard's charge that he delayed answering letters was probably true, for we know from other sources that he was never orderly in business matters. At any rate, the result of his neglect of Izard was that that gentleman's hatred for him steadily increased to the end of his life, and years after Izard had left Paris he is described as unable to contain himself at the mention of Franklin's name, bursting out into passionate denunciation of him like the virtuous old ladies we are told of in Philadelphia.

Then there was William Lee, brother of Arthur Lee, appointed envoy to Berlin and Vienna, which places he could not reach for the same reason that prevented Izard from going to Tuscany. So he also stayed in Paris, assisted his brother Arthur, became a commercial agent, and had no love for either

Franklin or Deane. There was also Dr. Edward Bancroft, who had no regular appointment, but flitted back and forth between London and Paris. He was intimate with Franklin, assisted Deane, knew the secrets of the American business in Paris, which knowledge Lee tells us he used for the purpose of speculating in London, and Bancroft the historian says that he was really a British spy. Thomas Morris, a younger brother of Robert Morris, was a commercial agent at Nantes, wrecked himself with drink, and started what came near being a serious dispute between Robert Morris and Franklin ; and Franklin himself had his own nephew, Jonathan Williams, employed as naval agent, which gave Lee a magnificent opportunity to charge that the nephew was in league with the uncle and with Deane to steal the public money and share with them the proceeds of the sale of prizes.

It is impossible to go fully into all these details ; but we are obliged to say, in order to make the situation plain, that Deane, being taken into the full confidence of Beaumarchais, conducted with him an immense amount of business through the firm of Hortalez & Co. On several occasions Franklin testified in the warmest manner to Deane's efficiency and usefulness, and this testimony is the stronger because Franklin was never taken into the confidence of Beaumarchais, had no intercourse with him, and might be supposed to be piqued, as Lee was, by this neglect. But the greatest secrecy was necessary, and Deane could not reveal his exact relationship with the French contractor and dramatist. So letter after letter was received by Congress from Lee, describing what dreadful fraud and corruption the wicked pair, Deane and Beaumarchais, were guilty of every day. Deane, he said, was making a fortune for himself by his relations with Beaumarchais, and was speculating in London. Deane also urged that Beaumarchais should be paid for the supplies, which were not, he said, a present from the king, and this Lee, of course, thought was another evidence of his villany.

Some of Lee's accusations are on their face rather far-fetched. On the charge, however, that Deane and Franklin's nephew, Jonathan Williams, were speculating on their own account in the sale of prizes, he quotes a letter from Williams to Deane which is rather strong :

" I have been on board the prize brig. Mr. Ross tells me he has written to you on the subject and the matter rests whether according to his letter you will undertake or not; if we take her on private account she must be passed but 13,000 livres."

This, it must be confessed, looked very suspicious, for Williams was in charge of the prizes, and by this letter he seemed prepared to act as both seller and purchaser and to share with Deane.

The charge that Deane had assumed to himself the whole management of affairs and ignored Lee was undoubtedly true, and no one has ever denied it. Franklin also ignored him, for he was an unbearable man with whom no one could live at peace.

Lee kept on with his accusations, declaring that Deane's accounts were in confusion. A packet of despatches sent to Congress was found on its arrival to contain nothing but blank paper. It had evidently been opened and robbed. Lee promptly insinuated that Deane must have been the thief, and that Franklin probably assisted.

In a letter to Samuel Adams, Lee said,—

" It is impossible to describe to you to what a degree this kind of intrigue has disgraced, confounded, and injured our affairs here. The observation of this at head-quarters has encouraged and produced through the whole a spirit of neglect, abuse, plunder, and intrigue in the public business which it has been impossible for me to prevent or correct."

So the evidence, or rather suspicions, piled up against Deane, and he was ordered home. Supposing that Congress wanted him merely for information about the state of France, he returned after the treaty of alliance was signed, coming over, as he thought, in triumph with Admiral D'Estaing and the fleet that was to assist the Americans.

He expected to be welcomed with gratitude, but Congress would not notice him ; and when at last he was allowed to tell his story, the members of that body did not believe a word of it. He made public statements in the newspapers, fought Lee with paper and ink, and the curious may still read his and Lee's recriminations, calling one another traitors, and become more confused than ever over the controversy. His arguments only served to injure his case. He made the mistake of attacking Lee instead of merely defending himself, and he talked so openly about our affairs in France, revealing, among other things, the dissensions among the members of the commission, that he was generally regarded as having injured our standing among the governments of Europe.

He struggled with Congress, and returned to Paris to have his accounts audited ; but it was all useless ; he was ruined ; and, in despair and fury at the injustice done him, he went over to the British, like Arnold, and died in poverty and obscurity.

In America both he and Beaumarchais seem to have been considered rascals until far into the next century, when the publication of Beamarchais's life and the discovery of some papers by a member of the Connecticut Historical Society put a different face upon their history. Congress voted Deane's heirs thirty-eight thousand dollars as a recompense for the claims which the Continental Congress had refused to pay their ancestor. Indeed, the poverty in which Deane died was not consistent with Lee's story that he had been making millions by his arrangement with Beaumarchais. Franklin always stood by him, and publicly declared that in all his dealings with him he had never had any occasion to suspect that he lacked integrity.

Lee was a Virginian, a member of the famous family of that name, and a younger brother of Richard Henry Lee, who was a member of the Continental Congress. Though born in Virginia, he was educated in England at Eton and also at Edinburgh, where he took the degree of doctor of medicine. The easy-going methods by which Franklin and Deane handled millions of dollars, sold hundreds of prizes brought in by Paul Jones and other

American captains, and shipped cargoes of arms, ammunition, and clothing to America were extremely shocking to him. Or perhaps he was extremely shocked because he was not allowed a hand in it. But it was necessary to be prompt in giving assistance to the revolted colonies, and Franklin and Deane pushed the business along as best they could.

If Congress had made a less stupid arrangement the embassy might have been organized on a business-like system in which everything would move by distinct, definite orders, everybody's sphere be defined, with a regular method of accounts in which every item should have its voucher. But, as Franklin himself confessed, he never could learn to be orderly ; and now, when he was past seventy, infirm, often laid up with violent attacks of the gout, with a huge literary and philosophic reputation to support, tormented by Lee and Izard, the whole French nation insane with admiration for him, and dining out almost every day, it was difficult for him to do otherwise than as he did.

Although the others had equal power with him, he was necessarily the head of the embassy, for his reputation was so great in France that everything gravitated towards him. Most people scarcely knew that there were two other commissioners, and the little they knew of Lee they did not like. Lee was absent part of the time on journeys to Spain, Berlin, and Vienna, and as Deane had started the business of sending supplies before either Franklin or Lee arrived, the conduct of affairs naturally drifted away from Lee. It afforded a good excuse for ignoring

him. He was insanely suspicious, and charged John
Jay, Reed, Duane, and other prominent Americans
with treason, apparently without the slightest foundation.

Finding himself ignored and in an awkward and
useless position, he should have resigned, giving his
reasons. But he chose to stay and send private
letters to members of Congress attacking the characters of his fellow-commissioners and intriguing to
have himself appointed the sole envoy to France.
Among his letters are to be found three on this
subject, two to his brother in Congress and one to
Samuel Adams.

"There is but one way of redressing this and remedying the public evil; that is the plan I before sent you of appointing the Dr.
honoris causa to Vienna, Mr. Deane to Holland, Mr. Jennings to
Madrid, and leaving me here." (Life of Arthur Lee, vol. ii. p. 127.)

His attack on Franklin and his nephew, Jonathan
Williams, was a very serious one, and was published
in a phamphlet, entitled "Observations on Certain
Commercial Transactions in France Laid Before
Congress." Williams was one of Franklin's Boston
nephews who turned up in Paris poor and without employment. Franklin was always taking care
of his relatives with government positions, and he
gave this one the position of naval agent at Nantes.
He had charge of the purchase of supplies for American men-of-war, sold the prizes that were brought in,
and also bought and shipped arms and ammunition.
It was a large business involving the handling of
enormous sums of money, and there is no doubt that

there were .opportunities in it for making a fortune. Under the modern spoils system it would be regarded as a precious plum which a political party would be justified in making almost any sacrifices to secure.

Franklin and Deane seem to have let Williams manage this department pretty much as he pleased, and, as has been already shown, Lee had some ground for suspecting that Deane was privately interested with Williams in the sale of prizes. Williams certainly expended large sums on Deane's orders alone, and he was continually calling for more money from the commissioners' bankers. Lee demanded that there should be no more orders signed by Deane alone, and that Williams should send in his accounts; and, notwithstanding Lee's naturally captious and suspicious disposition, he was perfectly right in this.

Deane and Williams kept demanding more money, and Lee asked Franklin to stop it, which he not only refused to do, but wrote a letter to his nephew justifying him in everything :

"PASSY, Dec. 22, 1777.

"DEAR NEPHEW:

"I received yours of the 16th and am concerned as well as you at the difference between Messrs. Deane and Lee, but cannot help it. You need, however, be under no concern as to your orders being only from Mr. Deane. As you have always acted uprightly and ably for the public service, you would be justified if you had no orders at all. But as he generally consulted with me and had my approbation in the orders he gave, and I know they were for the best and aimed at the public good, I hereby certify you that I approve and join in those you received from him and desire you to proceed in the execution of the same."

Williams at last sent in his accounts, and Lee went over them, marking some items "manifestly unjust," others "plainly exorbitant," and others "altogether unsatisfactory for want of names, dates, or receipts." He refused to approve the accounts, sent them to Congress, and asked Williams to produce his vouchers. The vouchers, Lee tells us, were never produced. He asked for them again and again, but there was always some excuse, and he charges that Williams had in his possession a hundred thousand livres more than was accounted for. Finally, John Adams, who had come out to supersede Deane, joined with Franklin in giving Williams an order on the bankers for the balance claimed by him ; but the order expressly stated that it was not to be understood as an approval of his accounts, for which he must be responsible to Congress. Franklin appointed certain persons to audit the accounts, but at a time, Lee says, when they were on the point of sailing for America, and therefore could not act. Adams seems to have been convinced that Williams was not all that could be desired, and he and Franklin soon dismissed him from his office, again reminding him that this was not to be considered as an approval of his accounts.

Lee's charge against Franklin was that he had connived at the acts of his nephew and done everything possible to shield him and enable him to get possession of the balance of money he claimed. Readers must draw their own conclusions, for the matter was never officially investigated. It would have been unwise for Congress to inaugurate a public scandal at a time when the country was struggling for existence, needed all the moral and financial support it could obtain from Europe, and as yet saw no end to the Revolution.

One more point must be noticed. Lee commented with much sarcasm on the sudden prosperity of Jonathan Williams. He had been clerk to a sugar-baker in England, and was supposed to be without means ; but as naval agent he soon began to call himself a merchant, and when waiting on the commissioners charged five Louis d'ors a day for the loss of his time. Lee, according to some of his letters, had been trying for some time to have a certain John Lloyd, of South Carolina, appointed in the place of Williams ; and I shall quote part of one of these letters, which shows why Lee wanted Williams's place for one of his friends.

"My brother and myself have conceived that as the public allowance to the commercial agent is very liberal and the situation necessarily must recommend considerable business, the person appointed might with the most fair and conscientious discharge of his duty to the public make his own fortune." (Life of Arthur Lee, vol. ii. p. 144.)

He did not succeed in having Lloyd appointed, but he and his brother William secured the position for a friend of theirs called Schweighauser, on the dismissal of Williams, and this Schweighauser appointed a nephew of the Lees as one of his assistants.

It should be said that although Lee and Izard were constantly hinting at evil practices by Franklin, and sometimes directly stigmatized him as the "father of corruption" and deeply involved in the most disreputable schemes, they never produced any proof that he had enriched himself or was directly engaged in anything discreditable. There seems to be no doubt that certain people were making money under cover of the loose way in which affairs were managed. Franklin must have known of this, as well as Adams and the other commissioners, but neither he nor they were enriched by it. Lee's pamphlet goes no farther than to say that Franklin had shielded his nephew. John Adams, it may be observed, assisted in this shielding, if it can with justice be so called, for he signed with Franklin the order allowing the money to be paid to Williams on condition that it should not be considered an approval of his accounts. Adams afterwards described very concisely the situation, and how he, with the others, was compelled to connive at peculations under the absurd system.

"I knew it to be impossible to give any kind of satisfaction to our constituents, that is to Congress, or their constituents, while we consented or connived at such irregular transactions, such arbitrary proceedings, and such contemptible peculations as had been practised in Mr. Deane's time, not only while he was in France, alone, without any public character, but even while he was associated with Dr. Franklin and Mr. Arthur Lee in a real commission ; and which were continued in some degree while I was combined in the commission with Franklin and Lee, in spite of all the opposition and remonstrance that Lee and I could make." (Adams's Works, vol. i. p. 657.)

Franklin said and wrote very little on the subject. He sent no letters to members of Congress undermining the characters of his fellow-commissioners ;

the few statements that he made were exceedingly mild and temperate, and were usually to the effect that there were differences and disputes which he regretted. He usually invited his fellow-commissioners to dine with him every Sunday, and on these occasions they appeared very friendly, though at heart cherishing vindictive feelings towards one another.

In truth, Lee and Izard wrote so much and so violently that they dug the graves of their own reputations. It was Dr. Johnson who said that no man was ever written down except by himself, and Franklin once shrewdly remarked, "spots of dirt thrown upon my character I suffered while fresh to remain ; I did not choose to spread by endeavoring to remove them, but relied on the vulgar adage that they would all rub off when they were dry."

General public opinion was then and has remained in favor of Franklin, and the prominent men of France were, without exception, on his side. They all in the end detested Lee, whose conduct showed a vindictive disposition, and who evidently had purposes of his own to serve. One of his pet suspicions was that Paul Jones was a rascal in league with the other rascal, Franklin, and he protests in a letter to a member of Congress against Jones being "kept upon a cruising job of Chaumont and Dr. Franklin." Jones, he predicted, would not return from this cruise, but would go over to the enemy.

Franklin's service in France may be divided into four periods. First, from his arrival in December, 1776, until February, 1778, during which two years he and Deane conducted the business as best they could and quarrelled with Lee and Izard. Second, the year from February, 1778, until February, 1779, during which John Adams was in Paris in the place of Silas Deane. Third, some of the remaining months of 1779, during which, although Franklin was sole plenipotentiary to France, Lee, Izard, and others still retained their appointments to other countries, and remained in Paris, continuing the quarrels more viciously than ever. They were recalled towards the close of 1779, and from that time dates the fourth period, during which Franklin enjoyed the sole control, unassailed by the swarm of hornets which had made his life a burden.

I have already described most of the first period as briefly as possible ; its full treatment would require a volume. All that remains is to describe the act with which it closed,—the signing of the treaty of alliance. This treaty, which secured the success of our Revolution by giving us the assistance of a French army and fleet, was the result of unforeseen events, and was not obtained by the labors of Franklin or those of any of the commissioners.

France had been anxious to ally herself with us during the first two years of the Revolution, but dared not, because there was apparently no prospect that we would be successful. In fact, all the indications pointed to failure. Washington was everywhere defeated ; had been driven from New York, lost the battle of the Brandywine, lost Philadelphia, and then the news arrived in Europe that Burgoyne was moving from Canada down the Hudson, and would be joined by Howe from New York. This would cut the colonies in half; separate New England, the home of the Revolution, from the Middle and Southern Colonies and result in our total subjugation.

The situation of the commissioners in Paris was dismal enough at this time. They had been successful at first, with the aid of Beaumarchais; but now Beaumarchais was in despair at the ingratitude of Congress and its failure to pay him; no more prizes were coming in, for the British fleets had combined against the American war vessels and driven them from the ocean; the commissioners had spent all their money, and Franklin proposed that they should sell what clothing and arms they had been unable to ship and pay their debts as far as possible with the proceeds. At any moment they might hear that they had neither country nor flag, that the Revolution had collapsed, and that they must spend the rest of their lives in France as pensioners on the royal bounty, daring to go neither to America nor to England, where they would be hung as ringleaders of the rebels.

In their dire extremity they forgot their animosities, and one is reminded of those pictures of the most irreconcilable wild animals—foxes and hares, or wolves and wild-cats—seeking refuge together from a flood on a floating log. In public they kept a bold front, in spite of the sneers of the English residents in Paris and the shrugging shoulders of the Frenchmen.

"Well, doctor," said an Englishman to Franklin, "Howe has taken Philadelphia."

"I beg your pardon, sir; Philadelphia has taken Howe."

But in his heart Franklin was bowed down with anxiety and apprehension. We all know what happened. Burgoyne and Howe failed to connect, and Burgoyne surrendered his army to the American general, Gates. That was the turning-point of the Revolution, and there was now no doubt in France of the final issue. A young man, Jonathan Austin, of Massachusetts, was sent on a swift ship to carry the news to Paris. The day his carriage rolled into the court-yard of Chaumont's house at Passy, Franklin, Deane, both the Lees, Izard, Beaumarchais,—in fact, all the snarling and quarrelling agents,—were there, debating, no doubt, where they would drag out the remains of their miserable lives.

They all rushed out to see Austin, and Franklin addressed to him one sad question which they all wanted answered, whether Philadelphia really was taken.

"Yes, sir," said Austin.

The old philosopher clasped his hands and was stumbling back into the house.

"But, sir, I have greater news than that. General Burgoyne and his whole army are prisoners of war."

Beaumarchais drove his carriage back to Paris so fast that it was overturned and his arm dislocated. Austin relates that for a long time afterwards Franklin would often sit musing and dreaming and then break out, "Oh, Mr. Austin, you brought us glorious news."

Austin had arrived on December 3, 1777. On the

6th of the same month the French government requested the commissioners to renew their proposals
for an alliance.   Eleven days after that they were
told that the treaty would be made, and within two
months,—namely, on February 6, 1778,—after full
discussion of all the details, it was signed.   This was
certainly very prompt action on the part of France
and shows her eagerness.

On the day that he signed the treaty, Franklin, it
is said, wore the same suit of Manchester velvet in
which he had been dressed when Wedderburn made
his attack upon him before the Privy Council in London, and after the signing it was never worn again.
When asked if there had not been some special
meaning attached to the wearing of these clothes at
the signing, he would make no other reply than a
smile.   It was really beautiful philosophic ven-
geance, and adds point to Walpole's epigram on
the scene before the Council :

"Sarcastic Sawney, swol'n with spite and prate,
    On silent Franklin poured his venal hate.
    The calm philosopher, without reply,
    Withdrew, and gave his country liberty."

There was much discussion among the three
envoys over the terms of the treaty, and their love
for one another was not increased.   The principal
part of Izard's bitterness against Franklin is supposed to have begun at this time.   Lee made a
point on the question of molasses.   In the first
draft of the treaty it was agreed that France should
never lay an export duty on any molasses taken

from her West India islands by Americans. Vergennes objected that this was not fair, as the Americans bound themselves to no equivalent restriction on their own exports. Franklin suggested a clause that, in consideration of France agreeing to lay no export duty on molasses, the United States should agree to lay no export duty on any article taken by Frenchmen from America, and this was accepted by Vergennes.

Lee, however, objected that we were binding ourselves on every article of export, while France bound herself on only one. In this he was entirely right, and it was not an officious interference, as Franklin's biographers have maintained. He pressed his point so hard that it was finally agreed with the French government that Congress might accept or reject the whole arrangement on this question, if it saw fit. Congress supported Lee and rejected it.

The signing of the treaty of course rendered Beaumarchais's secret work through Hortalez & Co. of less importance. France was now the open ally of the United States ; the French government need no longer smuggle arms and clothing into America, but was preparing to send a fleet and an army to assist the insurgents, as they were still called in Paris. All this rendered the labors of the embassy lighter and less complicated.

In April, 1778, a few months after the signing of the treaty, John Adams, after a most dangerous and adventurous voyage across the Atlantic, arrived to take the place of Silas Deane. He has left us a very full account of the condition of affairs and his efforts at reform. Franklin's biographers have been sorely puzzled to know what to do with these criticisms; but any one who will take the trouble to read impartially all that Adams has said, and not merely extracts from it, will easily be convinced of his fairness. He makes no mistake about Lee; speaks of him as a man very difficult to get on with, and describes Izard in the same way. There is not the slightest evidence that these two men poisoned his mind against Franklin. He does not side with them entirely; but, on the contrary, in the changes he undertook to make was sometimes on their side and sometimes against them. He held the scales very evenly.

Lee wanted all the papers of the embassy brought to his own house, and Adams wrote him a letter which certainly shows that Adams had not gone over to the Lee party, and is also an example of the efforts he was making to improve the situation.

" I have not asked Dr. Franklin's opinion concerning your proposal of a room in your house for the papers, and an hour to meet there, because I know it would be in vain; for I think it must appear to him more unequal still. It cannot be expected, that two should go to one, when it is as easy again for one to go to two; not to mention Dr. Franklin's age, his rank in the country, or his character in the world; nor that nine-tenths of the public letters are constantly brought to this house, and will ever be carried where Dr. Franklin is. I will venture to make a proposition in my turn, in which I am very sincere; it is that you would join families with us. There is room enough in this house to accommodate us all. You shall take the apartments which belong to me at present, and I will content myself with the library room and the next to it. Appoint a room for business, any that you please, mine or another, a person to keep the papers, and certain hours to do business. This arrangement will save a large sum of money to the public, and, as it would give us a thousand opportunities of conversing together, which now we have not, and, by having but one place for our countrymen and others to go to, who have occasion to visit us, would greatly facilitate the public business. It would remove the reproach we lie under, of which I confess myself very much ashamed, of not being able to agree together, and would make the commission more respectable, if not in itself, yet in the estimation of the English, the French, and the American nations; and, I am sure, if we judge by the letters we receive, it wants to be made more respectable, at least in the eyes of many persons of this country." (Bigelow's Franklin from His Own Writings, vol. ii. p. 424.)

Adams had none of the rancor of Lee and Izard, but he tells us candidly that he found the public business in great confusion. It had never been methodically conducted. "There never was before I came a minute book, a letter book, or an account book; and it is not possible to obtain a clear idea of our affairs." Of Deane he says that he "lived expensively, and seems not to have had much order in his business, public or private; but he was active, diligent, subtle, and successful, having accomplished the great purpose of his mission to advantage."

Adams procured blank books and devoted himself to assorting the papers of the office at Passy, where Franklin had allowed everything to lie about in the greatest confusion. He found that too many people had been making money out of the embassy, and of these Jonathan Williams appears to have been one. He united with Lee in demanding Williams's accounts, and compelled Franklin to join in dismissing him. A man named Ross was another delinquent who was preying on the embassy, and the arrangement by which he was allowed to do it is described by Adams as "more irregular, more inconsistent with the arrangement of Congress and every way more unjustifiable than even the case of Mr. Williams."

He gives us many glimpses of Franklin's life,—his gayety, the bright stories he told, and his wonderful reputation among the French. An interesting young lady, Mademoiselle de Passy, was a great favorite with Franklin, who used to call her his flame and his love. She married a man whose name translated into English would be "Marquis of Thunder." The next time Madame de Chaumont met Franklin, she cried out, "Alas! all the conductors of Mr. Franklin could not prevent the thunder from falling on Mademoiselle de Passy."

Adams was at the Academy of Sciences when Franklin and Voltaire were present, and a general cry arose among the sensation-loving people that these two wonderful men should be introduced to each other. They accordingly bowed and spoke. But this was not enough, and the two philosophers could not understand what more was wanted. They took each other by the hand ; but still the clamor continued. Finally it was explained to them that "they must embrace in French fashion." The two old men immediately began hugging and kissing each other, which satisfied the company, and the cry spread through the whole country, "How beautiful it was to see Solon and Sophocles embrace !"

Some of Adams's criticisms and estimates of Franklin, though not satisfactory to his eulogists, are, on the whole, exceedingly just.

"That he was a great genius, a great wit, a great humorist, a great satirist, and a great politician is certain. That he was a great philosopher, a great moralist, and a great statesman is more questionable." (Adams's Works, vol. iii. p. 139.)

This brief statement will bear the test of very close investigation. Full credit, it will be observed, is given to his qualities as a humorous and satirical writer, and even as a politician. The word politician is used very advisedly, for up to that time Franklin had done nothing that would raise him beyond that class into statesmanship.

He had had a long career in Pennsylvania politics, where his abilities were confined to one province, and in the attempt to change the colony into a royal government he had been decidedly in the wrong. While representing Pennsylvania, Massachusetts, and Georgia in England from the time of the Stamp Act until the outbreak of the Revolution, he had accomplished nothing, except that his examination before Parliament had encouraged the colonists to persist in their opposition; he had got himself into a very bad scrape about the Hutchinson letters; and his plan of reconciliation with the mother country had broken down. In France, the government being already very favorable to the colonies, there was but little for the embassy to do except to conduct the business of sending supplies and selling prizes, and in this Deane and Beaumarchais did most of the work, while Franklin had kept no accounts, had allowed his papers to get into confusion, was utterly unable to keep the envoys in harmony, and had not made any effective appeal to Congress to change the absurd system which permitted the sending to a foreign country of three commissioners with equal powers. In the last years of his mission in France he did work which was more valuable ; but it was not until some years afterwards, when he was past eighty and on the verge of the grave, that he accomplished in the Constitutional Convention of 1787 the one act of his life which may be called a brilliant stroke of statesmanship.

His qualities as a moralist have been discussed in a previous chapter which fully justifies Adams's assertion. As a philosopher, by which Adams meant what we now call a man of science, Franklin was distinguished, but not great. It could not be said that he deserved to be ranked with Kepler or Newton. His discovery of the nature of lightning was picturesque and striking, and had given him popular renown, but it could not put him in the front rank of discoverers.

In a later passage in his Diary Adams attempts to combat the French idea that Franklin was the American legislator.

" ' Yes,' said M. Marbois, ' he is celebrated as the great philosopher and the great legislator of America.' ' He is,' said I, ' a great philosopher, but as a legislator of America he has done very little. It is universally believed in France, England, and all Europe, that his electric wand has accomplished all this revolution. But nothing is more groundless. He has done very little. It is believed that he made all the American constitutions and their confederation ; but he made neither. He did not even make the constitution of Pennsylvania, bad as it is.' . . .

" I said that Mr. Franklin had great merit as a philosopher. His discoveries in electricity were very grand, and he certainly was a

AMERICA SET FREE BY FRANKLIN

(From a French engraving)

great genius, and had great merit in our American affairs. But he had no title to the 'legislator of America.' M. Marbois said he had wit and irony; but these were not the faculties of statesmen. His Essay upon the true means of bringing a great Empire to be a small one was very pretty. I said he had wrote many things which had great merit, and infinite wit and ingenuity. His Bonhomme Richard was a very ingenious ti.'ng, which had been so much celebrated in France, gone through so many editions, and been recommended by curates and bishops to so many parishes and dioceses.

"M. Marbois asked, 'Are natural children admitted in America to all privileges like children born in wedlock?' . . . M. Marbois said this, no doubt, in allusion to Mr. F.'s natural son, and natural son of a natural son. I let myself thus freely into this conversation, being led on naturally by the Chr 'alier and M. Marbois on purpose, because I am sure it cannot be my duty, nor the interest of my country, that I should conceal any of my sentiments of this man, at the same time that I do justice to his merits. It would be worse than folly to conceal my opinion of his great faults." (Adams's Works, vol. iii. p. 220.)

The French always believed that Franklin was the originator of the Revolution, and that he was a sort of Solon who had prepared laws for all the revolted colonies, directed their movements, and revised all their state papers and public documents. It was under the influence of this notion that they worshipped him as the personification of liberty. It must have been extremely irritating to Adams and others to find the French people assuming that the old patriarch in his fur cap had emancipated in the American woods a rude and strange people who without him could not have taken care of themselves. But, protest as they might, they never could persuade the French to give up their ideal, and this was undoubtedly the foundation of a great deal of the hostility to Franklin which showed itself in Congress.

THE TRUE BENJAMIN FRANKLIN

In 1811, long after Franklin's death, Adams wrote a newspaper article defending himself against some complaints that Franklin had made, of which I shall have more to say hereafter. It is a most vigorous piece of writing, and, in spite of some unfounded suspicions which it contains and the bluster and egotism so characteristic of its author, is by far the most searching and fairest criticism of Franklin that was ever written :

> " His reputation was more universal than that of Leibnitz or Newton, Frederick or Voltaire, and his character more beloved and esteemed than any or all of them. . . . His name was familiar to government and people, to kings and courtiers, nobility, clergy and philosophers, as well as plebeians, to such a degree that there was scarcely a peasant or a citizen, a *valet de chambre*, coachman or footman, a lady's chambermaid or a scullion in a kitchen who was not familiar with it, and who did not consider him as a friend to human kind." (Adams's Works, vol. i. p. 660.)

A large part of this reputation rested, Adams thought, on great talents and qualities, but the rest was artificial, the result of peculiar circumstances which had exaggerated the importance of Franklin's opinions and actions. The whole tribe of printers and newspaper editors in Europe and America had become enamoured and proud of him as a member of their body. Every day in the year they filled the magazines, journals, pamphlets, and all the gazettes of Europe " with incessant praise of Monsieur Franklin." From these gazettes could be collected " a greater number of panegyrical paragraphs upon ' *le grand* Franklin' than upon any other man that ever lived." He had become a member of two of the most powerful democratic and liberal bodies in

Europe, the Encyclopedists and the Society of Economists, and thus effectually secured their devotion and praise. All the people of that time who were rousing discontent in Europe and preparing the way for the French Revolution counted Franklin as one of themselves. When he took part in the American Revolution their admiration knew no bounds. He was "the magician who had excited the ignorant Americans to resistance," and he would soon "abolish monarchy, aristocracy, and hierarchy throughout the world." But most important of all in building up his reputation was the lightning-rod.

"Nothing," says Adams, "perhaps, that ever occurred upon the earth was so well calculated to give any man an extensive and universal a celebrity as the discovery of the efficacy of iron points and the invention of lightning-rods. The idea was one of the most sublime that ever entered a human imagination, that a mortal should disarm the clouds of heaven, and almost 'snatch from his hand the sceptre and the rod.' The ancients would have enrolled him with Bacchus and Ceres, Hercules and Minerva. His paratonnerres erected their heads in all parts of the world, on temples and palaces no less than on cottages of peasants and the habitations of ordinary citizens. These visible objects reminded all men of the name and character of their inventor; and in the course of time have not only tranquillized the minds and dissipated the fears of the tender sex and their timorous children, but have almost annihilated that panic, terror, and superstitious horror which was once almost universal in violent storms of thunder and lightning." (Adams's Works, vol. I. p. 661.)

The Latin motto universally applied to Franklin at this time, *Eripuit cœlo fulmen septrumque tyrannis*, has usually been attributed to Turgot, the French Minister of Finance; but Adams believed that Sir William Jones was the author of it. Turgot made an alteration in it. As usually understood, the last

half referred to the American colonies delivered
from the oppression of Great Britain ; but as Franklin grew to be more and more the favorite of that
large class of people in Europe who were opposed
to monarchy, and who believed that he would soon
be instrumental in destroying or dethroning all kings
and abolishing all monarchical government, Turgot
suggested that the motto should read, *Eripuit cœlo
fulmen ; mox septra tyrannis*, which may be freely
translated, " He has torn the lightning from the sky ;
soon he will tear their sceptres from the kings."

At first Adams took the quarrelling lightly, trying
to ignore and keep clear of it ; but in a little while he
confesses that " the uncandor, the prejudices, the rage
among several persons here make me sick as death."
After about a month he was so disgusted with the
service, so fully convinced that the public business
was being delayed and neglected on account of the
disputes, that he determined to try to effect a change.
He therefore wrote to Samuel Adams, then in Congress, declaring that the affairs of the embassy were
in confusion, prodigious sums of money expended,
large sums yet due, but no account-books or documents ; the commissioners lived expensively, each
one at the rate of from three to six thousand pounds
a year ; this would necessarily continue as long as
their salaries were not definitely fixed, and it would
be impossible to get an account of the expenditure
of the public money. Equally ridiculous was the
arrangement which made the envoys half ambassa-
dors and half commercial agents. Instead of all
this he suggested that Congress separate the offices

FRANKLIN TEARS THE LIGHTNING FROM THE SKY AND THE SCEPTRE
FROM THE TYRANTS

(From a French engraving)

of public ministers from those of commercial agents, recall all the envoys except one, define with precision the salary he should receive, and see that he got no more.

This is what Lee should have done long before. Franklin had indeed recommended a change in one of his letters, but not with such force as to cause its adoption. Now that Adams had set the example, they all wrote letters in the succeeding months begging for reform. The wisdom of Adams's plan was so apparent that when the facts were laid before Congress it was quickly adopted and Franklin made sole plenipotentiary.

But Lee and Izard retained their missions to other countries and remained in Paris, renewing their discussions and attacks on Franklin until the subject was again brought before Congress, and it was proposed to order all of them back to America and send others in their stead. Franklin had a narrow escape. The large committee which had the question before it was at one time within a couple of votes of recalling him and sending Arthur Lee in his place, which, whatever were the failings of Franklin, would have been a terrible misfortune. The French minister to the United States, M. Gérard, came to the rescue. He disclosed the extreme favor with which the French government regarded Franklin and its detestation of Lee. Franklin's wonderful reputation in Europe saved him, for it would have been folly to recall under a cloud the one man whom our allies took such delight in honoring.

X

PLEASURES AND DIPLOMACY IN FRANCE

CONGRESS not only refused to recall Franklin, but relieved him entirely of the presence of Lee and Izard, so that the remaining six years of his service were peaceful and can be very briefly described. The improvement in the management of the embassy which immediately followed shows what a serious mistake the previous arrangement had been. Left entirely to his own devices, and master of the situation, he began the necessary reforms of his own accord, had complete books of account prepared, and managed the business without difficulty.

It is curious to read of the diverse functions the old man of seventy-four had to perform in this infancy of our diplomatic service. He was a merchant, banker, judge of admiralty, consul, director of the navy, ambassador to France, and negotiator with England for the exchange of prisoners and for peace, in addition to attending to any other little matter, personal or otherwise, which our representatives to other countries or the individual States of the Union might ask of him. The crudeness of the situation is revealed when we remember that not only was Congress obtaining loans of money and supplies of arms in Europe, but several of the States were doing the same thing, and it was often rather difficult for

Franklin to assist them all without discrimination or injustice.

Paul Jones and the other captains of our navy who were cruising against British commerce on that side of the Atlantic made their head-quarters in French ports, and were necessarily under the direction of Franklin because the great distance made it impossible to communicate with Congress without months of delay. That they were lively sailors we may judge from the exploits of the "Black Prince," which in three months on the English coast took thirty-seven prizes, and brought in seventy-five within a year. Franklin had to act as a court of admiralty in the matter of prizes and their cargoes, settle disputes between the officers and men, quiet discontent about their pay by advancing money, decide what was to be done with mutineers, and see that ships were refitted and repaired. A couple of quotations from one of his letters to Congress will give some idea of his duties :

"In the mean time, I may just mention some particulars of our disbursements. Great quantities of clothing, arms, ammunition, and naval stores, sent from time to time ; payment of bills from Mr. Bingham, one hundred thousand livres ; Congress bills in favor of Haywood & Co., above two hundred thousand ; advanced to Mr. Ross, about twenty thousand pounds sterling ; paid Congress drafts in favor of returned officers, ninety-three thousand and eighty livres ; to our prisoners in England, and after their escape to help them home, and to other Americans here in distress, a great sum, I cannot at present say how much ; supplies to Mr. Hodge for fitting out Captain Conyngham, very considerable ; for the freight of ships to carry over the supplies, great sums ; to Mr. William Lee and Mr. Izard, five thousand five hundred pounds sterling ; and for fitting the frigates *Raleigh, Alfred, Boston, Providence, Alliance, Ranger,* &c., I imagine not less than sixty or seventy thousand livres each, taken one with another; and for the maintenance of the English prisoners, I believe, when I get in all the accounts, I shall find one hundred thousand livres not sufficient, having already paid above sixty-five thousand on that article. And now, the drafts of the treasurer of the loans coming very fast upon me, the anxiety I have suffered, and the distress of mind lest I should not be able to pay them, have for a long time been very great indeed."

.   .   .   .

"With regard to the fitting out of ships, receiving and disposing of cargoes, and purchasing of supplies, I beg leave to mention, that, besides my being wholly unacquainted with such business, the distance I am from the ports renders my having anything to do with it extremely inconvenient. Commercial agents have indeed been appointed by Mr. William Lee; but they and the captains are continually writing for my opinion or orders, or leave to do this or that, by which much time is lost to them, and much of mine taken up to little purpose, from my ignorance. I see clearly, however, that many of the captains are exorbitant in their demands, and in some cases I think those demands are too easily complied with by the agents, perhaps because the commissions are in proportion to the expense. I wish, therefore, the Congress would appoint the consuls they have a right to appoint by the treaty, and put into their hands all that sort of employment. I have in my desk, I suppose, not less than fifty applications from different ports, praying the appointment, and offering to serve gratis for the honor of it, and the advantage it gives in trade; but I imagine, that, if consuls are appointed, they will be of our own people from America, who, if they should make fortunes abroad, might return with them to their country."

He was, in fact, deciding questions and assuming responsibilities which with other nations and afterwards with our own belonged to the home government. He had great discretionary power, an instance of which may be given in connection with the subject which was then agitating European countries, of "free ships, free goods." He wrote to Congress, telling that body how the matter stood:

"Whatever may formerly have been the law of nations, all the neutral powers at the instance of Russia seem at present disposed to change it, and to enforce the rule that *free ships shall make free goods*, except in the case of contraband. Denmark, Sweden, and Holland have already acceded to the proposition, and Portugal is expected to follow. France and Spain, in their answers, have also expressed their approbation of it. I have, therefore, instructed our privateers to bring in no more neutral ships, as such prizes occasion much litigation, and create ill blood."

He did not know whether Congress would approve of this new rule of law, but he took his chances. He was not the first person to suggest the principle of "free ships, free goods," nor was he a prominent advocate of it, as has sometimes been implied ; for his letter shows that Russia had suggested this improvement in the rules of international law, and that other nations were accepting it. He, however, urged on a number of occasions that war should be confined exclusively to regularly organized armies and fleets, that privateering should be abolished, that merchant vessels should be free from capture even by men-of-war, and that fishermen, farmers, and all who were engaged in supplying the necessaries of life should be allowed to pursue their avocations unmolested. The world has not yet caught up with this suggestion.

The great difficulty during the last two or three years of the Revolution was the want of money. The supplies sent out by Beaumarchais and Deane in the early part of the struggle merely served to start it. In the long run expenses increased enormously, the resources of the country were drained, the paper money depreciated with terrible rapidity, and we were compelled to continue borrowing from France or Holland. We borrowed principal and then borrowed more to pay the interest on the principal, and a large part of this business passed through Franklin's hands.

He persuaded the French government to lend, and then to lend again to pay interest. He was regarded as the source from which all the money was to come. Congress drew on him, John Jay in Spain drew on him, he had to pay salaries and the innumerable expenses appertaining to the fitting out and repairing of ships and the exchange of prisoners. These calls upon him were made often from a long distance, with a sort of blind confidence that he would in some way manage to meet them. A captain in the West Indies would run his ship into a port to be careened, refitted, and supplied, and coolly draw on him for the expense. It was extremely dangerous sometimes to refuse to accept a bill presented to him, and, as he said to Congress, if a single draft for interest on a loan went to protest there would be "dreadful consequences of ruin to our public credit both in America and Europe."

He suffered enough anxiety and strain to have destroyed some men. When Jay went to Spain in 1780, Congress was so sure he would obtain money from that monarchy that it drew on him. But as Jay could not get a cent, he forwarded the drafts to Franklin, who in reply wrote, "the storm of bills which I found coming upon us both has terrified and vexed me to such a degree that I have been deprived of sleep, and so much indisposed by continual anxiety as to be rendered almost incapable of writing." He would have gone under in this storm if he had not persuaded the French government to come to his rescue.

He was also from time to time receiving all sorts of proposals of peace from emissaries or agents of the British government; and he had a long correspondence on this subject with David Hartley, who helped him to arrange the exchange of prisoners in England. Nearly all these proposals contained a trap of some kind, as that we should break our alliance with France and then England would treat with us, or that there should be a peace without a definite recognition of independence; and some of them may have been intended to entrap Franklin himself. It was, in any event, most dangerous and delicate work, for it was corresponding with the public enemy. Most men in Franklin's position would have been compelled to drop it entirely, for fear of becoming involved in some serious difficulty; for it was suspected, if not actually proved, that persons connected with our own embassy in France were using their official knowledge to speculate in stocks in England. But Franklin came through it all unscathed.

He was much annoyed by numerous applications from people who wished to serve in the American army. Most of them had proved failures in France and were burdens on their relations. In the early years of the embassy many were sent out who gave endless trouble and embarrassment to Washington and Congress. Out of the whole horde, only about three—Lafayette, Steuben, and De Kalb—were ever anything more than a nuisance. But, to avoid giving offence to the French people, Franklin was often obliged to give these applicants some sort of letter of recommendation, and he drew up a form which he sometimes used in extreme cases :

"The bearer of this, who is going to America, presses me to give him a letter of recommendation, though I know nothing of him, not even his name. This may seem extraordinary, but I assure you it is not uncommon here. Sometimes, indeed, one unknown person brings another equally unknown, to recommend him ; and sometimes they recommend one another ! As to this gentleman, I must refer you to himself for his character and merits, with which he is certainly better acquainted than I can possibly be. I recommend him, however, to those civilities, which every stranger, of whom one knows no harm, has a right to ; and I request you will do him all the good offices, and show him all the favor, that, on further acquaintance, you shall find him to deserve. I have the honor to be, &c."

The old man's sense of humor carried him through many a difficulty ; and it is hardly necessary to say that the management of all this multifarious business, the exercise of such large authority and discretion, and the weight of such responsibility required a nervous force, patience, tact, knowledge of men and affairs, mental equipoise, broad, cool judgment, and strength of character which comparatively few men in America possessed. Indeed, it is difficult to name another who could have filled the position. John Adams could not have done it. He would have lost his temper and blazed out at some point, or have committed some huge indiscretion that would have wrecked everything. That Lee, Izard, or even Deane could have held the post would be ridiculous to suppose.

Adams appeared again in Paris in the beginning of the year 1780, having been sent by Congress to await England's expected willingness to treat for peace. He was authorized to receive overtures for a general peace, and also, if possible, to negotiate a special commercial treaty with England. He had nothing to do but wait, and was in no way connected with our embassy in France. But being presented at court and asked by Vergennes to furnish information, he must needs try to make an impression. He assailed Vergennes, the Minister of Foreign Affairs, with numerous reasons why he should at once disclose to the court at London his readiness to make a commercial treaty. He argued about the question of the Continental currency and how it should be redeemed. He urged the sending of a large naval force to the United States ; and when told that the force had already been sent without solicitation, he attempted to prove in the most tactless and injudicious manner that it was not without solicitation, but, on the contrary, the king had been repeatedly asked for it, and had yielded at last to importunity.

This conduct was so offensive to Vergennes that he complained of it to Franklin, who was obliged to rebuke Adams ; and Congress, when the matter came before it, administered another rebuke. Adams never forgave Franklin for this, and afterwards publicly declared that Franklin and Vergennes had conspired to destroy his influence and ruin him. At the time, however, he had the good sense to take his rebuff in silence, and went off grumbling to Holland to see if something could not be done to render the United States less dependent on France.

Adams represented a large party, composed principally of New-Englanders, who did not like the alliance with France and were opposed to Franklin's policy of extreme conciliation and friendliness with the French court. It was as one of this party that Adams had attempted to give Vergennes a lesson and show him that America was not a suppliant and a pauper. Like the rest of his party, he harbored the bitter thought that France intended to lord it over the United States, send a general over there who would control all the military operations, get all the glory, and give the French ever after a preponderating influence. He thought America had been too free in expressions of gratitude to France, that a little more stoutness, a greater air of independence and boldness in our demands, would procure sufficient assistance and at the same time save us from the calamity of passing into the hands of a tyrant who would be worse than Great Britain had been.

His attempt at stoutness, however, was at once checked by Vergennes, who refused to answer any more of his letters; and there is no doubt that if Adams's plan had been adopted by the United States government, our alliance with France would have been jeopardized. It is not pleasant to think that without the aid of France the Revolution would have failed and we would have again been brought under subjection to England; but it is unquestionably true, and as Washington had no hesitation in frankly admitting it, we need have none.

At the time of Adams's attempted interference with Franklin's policy our fortunes were at a very low ebb. The resources of the country were exhausted and the army could no longer be maintained on them. The soldiers were starving and naked, and the generals could not show themselves without being assailed with piteous demands for food and clothes. France had much to gain by assisting us against England, and she never pretended that she had not; but in all the documents and correspondence that have been brought to light there is no evidence that she intended to take advantage of our situation or that her ministers had designs on our liberties. Indeed, when we read the whole story of her assistance, including the secret correspondence, it will be found almost unequalled for its worthiness of purpose and for the honorable means employed.

Franklin had spent several years at the court, knew everybody, and thoroughly understood the situation.

"The king, a young and virtuous prince, has, I am persuaded, a pleasure in reflecting on the generous benevolence of the action in assisting an oppressed people, and proposes it as a part of the glory of his reign. I think it right to increase this pleasure by our thankful acknowledgments, and that such an expression of gratitude is not only our duty, but our interest. A different conduct seems to me what is not only improper and unbecoming, but what may be hurtful to us. . . . It is my intention while I stay here to procure what advantages I can for our country by endeavoring to please this court; and I wish I could prevei anything being said by any of our countrymen here that may have a contrary effect, and increase an opinion lately showing itself in Paris, that we seek a difference, and with a view of reconciling ourselves in England."

Please the court, as well as the whole French nation, he most certainly did. His communications with Vergennes, even when he was asking for money or some other valuable thing, were not only free from offence, but so adroit, so beautifully and happily expressed, that they charmed the exquisite taste of Frenchmen. There is not space in this volume to give expression to all that the people of the court thought of his way of managing the business intrusted to him by America, but one sentence from a letter of Vergennes to the French minister in America may be given :

"If you are questioned respecting our opinion of Dr. Franklin, you may without hesitation say that we esteem him as much on account of the patriotism as the wisdom of his conduct, and it has been owing in a great part to this cause, and to the confidence we put in the veracity of Dr. Franklin, that we have determined to relieve the pecuniary embarrassments in which he has been placed by Congress."

It is not likely that Gouverneur Morris, Jefferson, or any other American of that time possessed the qualifications necessary to give them such a hold on the French court as Franklin had. We were colonists, very British in our manners, of strong energy and intelligence, but quite crude in many things, and capable of appearing in a very ridiculous light in French society, which was in effect the society of Louis XIV., very exacting, and by no means so republican as it has since become.

As a matter of fact, the French disliked everybody we sent to them at that time except Franklin. Deane they tolerated, Izard they laughed at, Adams they snubbed, and Lee they despised as a stupid blunderer who knew no better than to abuse French manners in the presence of his servants, who spread the tale all over Paris. But dear, delightful, philosophic, shrewd, economical, naughty, flirtatious, and anecdote-telling Franklin seemed like one of themselves. He still remains the only American that the French have thoroughly known and liked. The more we read of him the more confidence we are inclined to place in the supposition that three or four centuries back he must have had a French ancestor who migrated to England, and some of whose characteristics were reproduced in his famous descendant. The little fables and allegories he wrote to please them read like translations from the most subtle literary men of France. Fancy any other American or Englishman writing to Madame Brillon the letter which was really a little essay afterwards known as the "Ephemera," and very popular in France.

"You may remember, my dear friend, that when we lately spent that happy day in the delightful garden and sweet society of the Moulin Joly, I stopped a little in one of our walks, and stayed some time behind the company. We had been shown numberless skeletons of a kind of little fly, called an ephemera, whose successive generations, we were told, were bred and expired within the day. I happened to see a living company of them on a leaf, who appeared to be engaged in conversation. You know I understand all the inferior animal tongues. My too great application to the study of them is the best excuse I can give for the little progress I have made in your charming language. I listened through curiosity to the discourse of these little creatures ; but as they, in their natural vivacity, spoke three or four together, I could make but little of their conversation. I found, however, by some broken expressions that I heard now and then, they were disputing warmly on the merit of two foreign musicians, one a *cousin*, the other a *moscheto ;* in which dispute they spent their time, seemingly as regardless of the shortness of life as if they had been sure of living a month. Happy people ! thought I ; you are certainly under a wise, just, and mild government, since you have no public grievances to complain of, nor any subject of contention but the perfections and imperfections of foreign music. I turned my head from them to an old grey-headed one, who was single on another leaf, and talking to himself. Being amused with his soliloquy, I put it down in writing, in hopes it will likewise amuse her to whom I am so much indebted for the most pleasing of all amusements, her delicious company and heavenly harmony." . . .

The letter is too long to quote entire ; but some of the fine touches in the passage given should be observed. He refers to the little progress he had made in French, and he certainly spoke that language badly, although he read it with ease. He probably had a large vocabulary ; but he trampled all over the grammar, as Adams tells us. He managed, however, by means of a little humor to make this defect endear him still more to the people. The musical dispute of the insects is a hit at a similar dispute among the Parisians over two musicians, Gluck and Picini. But what a depth of subtlety is shown in the suggestion which follows, that the French were under such a wise government and such a good king that they could afford to waste their time in disputing about trifles ! No wonder that all the notable people and the rulers loved him.

This single delicately veiled point was alone almost sufficient to make his fortune in the peculiar society of that time. It was in such perfect taste, so French, such a rebuke to the fanatics who were laying the foundations of the Reign of Terror ; and yet, at the same time, Franklin, as the apostle of liberty, was regarded by many of those fanatics as one of themselves. In this way he carried with him all France.

But suppose that John Adams had been given the opportunity to write such a letter to a French lady; what would he have done? The straightforward fellow would probably have thought it his religious, moral, and patriotic duty to tell her that the government she lived under was wasteful and extravagant, and was plotting to destroy the liberties of America.

Madame Brillon, for whom the "Ephemera" was written, was a charming woman and more domestic than French ladies are supposed to be. For her amusement were written some of Franklin's most famous essays,—"The Morals of Chess," "The Dialogue between Franklin and the Gout," "The Story of the Whistle," "The Handsome and Deformed Leg," and "The Petition of the Left Hand." In a letter telling how the "Ephemera" happened to be written he has described the intimacy he and his grandson enjoyed at her house :

"The person to whom it was addressed is Madame Brillon, a lady of most respectable character and pleasing conversation ; mistress of an amiable family in this neighborhood, with which I spend an evening twice every week. She has, among other elegant accomplishments, that of an excellent musician ; and with her daughter who sings prettily, and some friends who play, she kindly entertains me and my grandson with little concerts, a cup of tea, and a game of chess. I call this *my Opera*, for I rarely go to the Opera at Paris."

Madame Helvetius, a still more intimate friend, was a very different sort of woman. She was the widow of a literary man of some celebrity, and she and Franklin were always carrying on an absurd sort of flirtation. They hugged and kissed each other in public, and exchanged extravagant notes which were sometimes mock proposals of marriage, although some have supposed them to have been real ones. He wrote a sort of essay addressed to her, in which he imagines himself in the other world, where he meets her husband, and, after the exchange of many clever remarks with him about madame, he discovers that Helvetius is married to his own deceased wife, Mrs. Franklin, who declares herself rather better pleased with him than she had been with the Philadelphia printer.

"Indignant at this refusal of my Eurydice, I immediately resolved to quit those ungrateful shades, and return to this good world again, to behold the sun and you! Here I am: let us *avenge ourselves!*"

Such sport over deceased wives and husbands would not be in good taste in America or England, but it was correct enough in France. One of his short notes to Madame Helvetius has also been preserved :

"Mr. Franklin never forgets any party at which Madame Helvetius is expected. He even believes that if he were engaged to go to Paradise this morning, he would pray for permission to remain on earth until half-past one, to receive the embrace promised him at the Turgots'."

Mrs. Adams has left a description of Madame Helvetius which admirers of Franklin have in vain attempted to explain away by saying that all French women were like her, and that she was, after all, a really noble person :

"She entered the room with a careless, jaunty air ; upon seeing ladies who were strangers to her, she bawled out, ' Ah ! mon Dieu, where is Franklin? Why did you not tell me there were ladies here ?' You must suppose her speaking all this in French. ' How I look !' said she, taking hold of a chemise made of tiffany, which she had on over a blue lute-string, and which looked as much upon the decay as her beauty, for she was once a handsome woman ; her hair was frizzled ; over it she had a small straw hat, with a dirty gauze half-handkerchief round it, and a bit of dirtier gauze than ever my maids wore was bowed on behind. She had a black gauze scarf thrown over her shoulders. She ran out of the room ; when she returned, the Doctor entered at one door, she at the other ; upon which she ran forward to him, caught him by the hand, ' Hélas ! Franklin ;' then gave him a double kiss, one upon each cheek, and another upon his forehead. When we went into the room to dine, she was placed between the Doctor and Mr. Adams. She carried on the chief of the conversation at dinner, frequently locking her hand into the Doctor's, and sometimes spreading her arms upon the backs of both the gentlemen's chairs, then throwing her arm carelessly upon the Doctor's neck.

" I should have been greatly astonished at this conduct, if the good Doctor had not told me that in this lady I should see a genuine Frenchwoman, wholly free from affectation or stiffness of behavior, and one of the best women in the world. For this I must take the Doctor's word ; but I should have set her down for a very bad one, although sixty years of age, and a widow. I own I was highly disgusted, and never wish for an acquaintance with any ladies of this cast. After dinner she threw herself upon a settee, where she showed more than her feet. She had a little lap-dog, who was, next to the Doctor, her favorite. This she kissed, and when he wet the floor she wiped it up with her chemise. This is one of the Doctor's most intimate friends, with whom he dines once every week, and she with him. She is rich, and is my near neighbor ; but I have not yet visited her. Thus you see, my dear, that manners differ exceedingly in different countries. I hope, however, to find amongst the French ladies manners more consistent with my ideas of decency, or I shall be a mere recluse." (Letters of Mrs. John Adams, p. 252.)

It is not likely that Franklin had the respect for Madame Helvetius that he had for Madame Brillon. She was, strange to say, an illiterate woman, as one of her letters to him plainly shows. Some of his letters to her read as if he were purposely feeding her inordinate vanity. He tells her in one that her most striking quality is her artless simplicity; that statesmen, philosophers, and poets flock to her; that he and his friends find in her "sweet society that charming benevolence, that amiable attention to oblige, that disposition to please and to be pleased which we do not always find in the society of one another." She lived at Auteuil, and he and the Abbé Morellet and others called her "Our Lady of Auteuil." They boasted much of their love for her, and enjoyed many wonderful conversations on literature and philosophy, and much gayety at her house, which they called "The Academy."

After Franklin had returned to America the Abbé Morellet, who was an active and able man in his way, wrote him many amusing letters about their lady and her friends.

"I shall never forget the happiness I have enjoyed in knowing you and seeing you intimately. I write to you from Auteuil, seated in your arm chair, on which I have engraved *Benjamin Franklin hic sedebat*, and having by my side the little bureau, which you bequeathed to me at parting with a drawerful of nails to gratify the love of nailing and hammering, which I possess in common with you. But, believe me, I have no need of all these helps to cherish your endeared remembrance and to love you.

"'Dum memor ipse mei, dum spiritus hos reget artus.'"

One of the cleverest letters Franklin wrote while in France was addressed to an old English friend,

FRANKLIN RELICS IN THE POSSESSION OF THE HISTORICAL SOCIETY OF PENNSYLVANIA

Mrs. Thompson, who had called him a rebel. "You are too early, *hussy*," he says, "as well as too saucy, in calling me *rebel;* you should wait for the event, which will determine whether it is a *rebellion* or only a *revolution.* Here the ladies are more civil; they call us *les insurgens*, a character that usually pleases them." He continues chaffing her, and describes himself as wearing his own hair in France, where every one else had on a great powdered wig. If they would only dismiss their *friseurs* and give him half the money they pay to them, "I could then enlist these *friseurs*, who are at least one hundred thousand, and with the money I would maintain them, make a visit with them to England, and dress the heads of your ministers and privy councillors, which I conceive at present to be *un peu dérangées.* Adieu, madcap; and believe me ever, your affectionate friend and humble servant."

In the large house of M. de Chaumont, which he occupied, he, of course, had his electrical apparatus, and played doctor by giving electricity to paralytic people who were brought to him. On one occasion he made the wrong contact, and fell to the floor senseless. He had, also, a small printing-press with type made in the house by his own servants, and he used it to print the little essays with which he amused his friends.

His friendships in France seem to have been mostly among elderly people. There are only a few traces of his fondness for young girls, and we find none of those pleasant intimacies such as he enjoyed with Miss Ray, Miss Stevenson, or the daughters of the Bishop of St. Asaph. Unmarried women in France were too much restricted to be capable of such friendships even with an elderly man. But among his papers in the collection of the American Philosophical Society there is a letter written by some French girl who evidently had taken a fancy to him and playfully insisted on calling herself his daughter.

" MY DEAR FATHER AMÉRICAIN

" god Bess liberty ! I drunk with all my heart to the republick of the united provinces. I am prepared to my departure if you will and if it possible. give me I pray you leave to go. I shall be happy of to live under the laws of venerable good man richard. adieu my dear father I am with the most respect and tenderness

" Your humble Servant

" and your daughter

" Auxerre 22 M. 1778."   " J. B. J. CONWAY.

Besides the dining abroad, which, he tells us, occurred six days out of seven, he gave a dinner at home every Sunday for any Americans that were in Paris ; "and I then," he says, "have my grandson Ben, with some other American children from the school."

New-Englanders had very economical ideas in those days, and when it was learned that Franklin entertained handsomely in Paris there was a great fuss over it in the Connecticut newspapers.

The *fête-champêtre* that was given to him by the Countess d'Houdetot must have been a ridiculous and even nauseous dose of adulation to swallow ; but he no doubt went through it all without a smile, and it serves to show the extraordinary position that he occupied. He was more famous in France than Voltaire or any Frenchman.

A formal account of the *fête* was prepared by direction of the countess, and copies circulated in Paris. The victim of it is described as "the venerable sage" who, "with his gray hairs flowing down upon his shoulders, his staff in his hand, the spectacles of wisdom on his nose, was the perfect picture of true philosophy and virtue;" and this sentence is as complete a summary as could be made of what Franklin was to the French people.

As soon as he arrived the countess addressed him in verse :

> "Soul of the heroes and the wise,
> Oh, Liberty ! first gift of the gods.
> Alas ! at too great a distance do we offer our vows.
> As lovers we offer homage
> To the mortal who has made citizens happy."

The company walked through the gardens and then sat down to the banquet. At the first glass of wine they rose and sang,—

> "Of Benjamin let us celebrate the glory ;
> Let us sing the good he has done to mortals.
> In America he will have altars ;
> And in Sanoy let us drink to his glory."

At the second glass the countess sang a similar refrain, at the third glass the viscount sang, and so on for seven glasses, each verse more extraordinary than the others. Virtue herself had assumed the form of Benjamin ; he was greater than William Tell ; Philadelphia must be such a delightful place ;

the French would gladly dwell there, although there
was neither ball nor play. But Sanoy was Philadelphia as long as dear Benjamin remained there. He
was led to the garden to plant a tree, with more
singing about the lightning that he had drawn from
the sky, and the lightning, of course, would never
strike that tree. Finally he was allowed to depart
with another song of adulation addressed to him
after he was seated in the carriage.

Now that more than a hundred years have passed
it is gratifying to our national pride to reflect that a
man who was so thoroughly American in his origin
and education should have been worshipped in this
way by an alien race as no other man, certainly no
other American, was ever worshipped by foreigners.
But the enjoyment of this stupendous reputation,
overshadowing and dwarfing the Adamses, Jays, and
all other public men who went to Europe, was
marred by some unpleasant consequences. Jeal-
ousies were aroused not only among individuals, but
to a certain extent among all the American people.
It was too much. He had ceased to be one of them.
It was rumored that he would never return to America, but would resign and settle down among those
strangers who treated him as though he were a god.

It was also inevitable that a worse suspicion
should arise. He was too subservient, it was said,
to France. He yielded everything to her. He was
turning her from an ally into a ruler. He could no
longer see her designs ; or, if he saw them, he approved of them. This suspicion gained such force
that it was the controlling principle with Adams and

Jay when they went to Paris to arrange the treaty of peace with England after the surrender of Lord Cornwallis at Yorktown in October, 1781. We have seen instances in our own time of our ministers to Great Britain becoming very unpopular at home because they were liked in England, and in Franklin's case this feeling was vastly greater than anything we have known in recent years, because his popularity in France was prodigious, and he avowedly acted upon the principle that it was best to be complaisant to the French court.

During the winter which followed the surrender of Lord Cornwallis overtures of peace were made by England to Franklin, as representing America, and to Vergennes, as representing France, and they became more earnest in March after the Tory ministry, which had been conducting the war, was driven from power. In April the negotiations with Franklin were well under way, and he continued to conduct them until June, when he was taken sick and incapacitated for three months. After his recovery he took only a minor part in the proceedings, for Jay and Adams had meanwhile arrived.

Congress had appointed Adams, Jay, Franklin, Jefferson, and Laurens commissioners to arrange the treaty, and made Adams head of the commission. When the negotiations began, however, Franklin was the only commissioner at Paris, and necessarily took charge of all the business. Just before he was taken sick Jay arrived, and he and Jay conducted affairs until Adams joined them at the end of October. Laurens, who had been a prisoner in England, did not reach Paris until just before the preliminary treaty was signed, and Jefferson, being detained in America, took no part in the proceedings.

While Franklin was carrying on the negotiations alone, he insisted on most of the terms which were afterwards agreed upon : first of all, independence, and, in addition to that, the right to fish on the New-foundland Banks and a settlement of boundaries ; but he added a point not afterwards pressed by the others,—namely, that Canada should be ceded to the United States. In exchange for Canada he was prepared to allow some compensation to the Tories for their loss of property during the war. Adams and Jay, on taking up the negotiations, dropped Canada entirely and insisted stoutly to the end that there should be no compensation whatever to the Tories.

Franklin's admirers have always contended that it would have been better if Jay and Adams had kept away altogether, for in that case Franklin would have secured all that they got for us and Canada besides. This, however, is mere supposition, one of those vague ideas of what might have been without any proof to support it. Franklin pressed the cession of Canada, it is true ; but there is no evidence that it would have been granted. At that time the people of the United States appear not to have wanted the land of snow, and ever since then the general opinion has been that we have enough to manage already, and are better off without a country vexed with serious political controversies with its French population and the Roman Catholic school question.

On the whole, it would not have been well for Franklin to have continued to conduct the negotiations alone. The situation was difficult, and the united efforts and varied ability of at least three commissioners were required. Neither Franklin nor Jay knew much about the fisheries question, and they might have been forced to yield on this point. But Adams, from his long experience in conducting litigation for the Massachusetts fishing interests, was better prepared on this subject than any other American, and it was generally believed by the public men of that time that the important rights we secured on the Newfoundland Banks were due almost entirely to his skill. He was also more familiar with the boundary question between Maine and New Brunswick, and had brought with him documents from Massachusetts which were invaluable.

While Jay and Franklin were acting together before the arrival of Adams, a serious question arose about the commission of Oswald, the British negotiator who had come over to Paris. He was empowered to treat with the "Colonies or Plantations," and nowhere in the document was the term United States of America used. Jay refused to treat with a man who held such a commission. Franklin and Vergennes vainly urged that it was a mere form, and that Great Britain had already in several ways acknowledged the independence of the United States. Oswald showed an article of his instructions which authorized him to grant complete independence to the thirteen colonies, and he offered to write a letter declaring that he treated with them as an independent power; but Jay was inflexible, and in this he seems to have been right.

Franklin made a great mistake in not agreeing with him, for in the suspicious state of people's minds at that time his conduct in this respect was taken as proof positive of his subserviency to the French court. Jay suspected that Vergennes advised accepting Oswald's commission so as to prevent a clear admission of independence, and thus keep the United States embroiled with England as long as possible. In order to support his opposition to Jay, Franklin was obliged to talk about his confidence in the French court, its past generosity and friendliness, and also to call attention to the instruction of Congress that the commissioners should do nothing without the knowledge of the French government, and in all final decisions be guided by that government's advice.

This instruction had been passed by Congress after much debate and hesitation, and was finally carried, it is said, through the influence of the French minister. Its adoption was a mistake; without it the commissioners would probably of their own accord have sought the advice of Vergennes; but a positive order to do so put them in an undignified and humiliating position. Franklin had been so long intimate with Vergennes and was so accustomed to consulting him that the instruction was superfluous as to him. His reputation was so great in France and his tact so perfect that he was in no danger of feeling overshadowed or subdued by such consultations; but Jay and Adams so thoroughly detested the instruction that they had made up their minds to disregard it altogether.

"Would you break your instruction?" said Franklin.

"Yes," said Jay, "as I break this pipe," and he threw the pieces into the fire.

Jay's firmness compelled Oswald to obtain a new commission in the proper form, and while he deserves credit for this and also for his principle, "We must be honest and grateful to our allies, but think for ourselves," he seems in the light of later evidence to have been mistaken in his deep mistrust of the French court. His opinions have been briefly stated by Adams :

" Mr. Jay likes Frenchmen as little as Mr. Lee and Mr. Izard did. He says they are not a moral people ; they know not what it is ; he don't like any Frenchman ; the Marquis de Lafayette is clever, but he is a Frenchman. Our allies don't play fair, he told me ; they were endeavoring to deprive us of the fishery, the western lands, and the navigation of the Mississippi ; they would even bargain with the English to deprive us of them ; they want to play the western lands, Mississippi, and whole Gulf of Mexico into the hands of Spain." (Adams's Works, vol. iii. p. 303.)

Jay had had a very bitter experience in Spain, where the cold haughtiness and chicanery of the court had made him feel that he was among enemies. The instructions sent to him by Congress had been intercepted, and instead of receiving them as secret orders from his government, they had been handed to him by the Spanish prime-minister after that official had read them. He was accordingly prepared to think that the French government was no better.

In a certain sense there were grounds for his suspicion of France. She was interested in the fisheries on the Banks of Newfoundland, and would naturally like to have a share in them. It was also obviously her policy to prevent the United States and England from becoming too friendly and from making too firm a peace, for fear that they might unite at some future time against her. If she could get them to make a sort of half peace with a number of subjects left unsettled, about which there would be difficulties for many years, it would be a great advantage to her.

Spain wanted to secure the control of the Gulf of Mexico, the exclusive navigation of the Mississippi, and the possession of the lands west of that river, and France, as her ally, might be expected to assist her to obtain these concessions. Arguments and suggestions favoring all these projects were unquestionably used by Frenchmen at that time, and no doubt Vergennes and other public men often had them in mind. It was their duty at least to consider them. But there is no evidence that they actively promoted these schemes or acted in any other than an honorable manner towards us.

As a matter of fact, our commercial relations with England were left unsettled. England claimed, among other things, the right to search our ships, and there was great discontent over this for a long time, amply sufficient to keep us from friendship with England until the question was finally settled by the war of 1812. Adams seems to imply that he could have settled this and other difficulties in 1780 by the commercial treaty which he was empowered to make with England, and that Vergennes, in advising him not to communicate with England, had intended to keep England and the United States embroiled. Possibly that may have been Vergennes's intention. But as it was afterwards found impossible to adjust these commercial difficulties until the war of 1812, and as Adams himself did not attempt it, though he might have done so in spite of Vergennes's advice, and as they were finally settled only by a war, it is not probable that Adams could have adjusted them in the easy, offhand way he imagines. In any event, it was not worth while for the sake of these future contingencies to offend Vergennes and jeopardize our alliance and the loans of money we were obtaining from France.

Franklin's policy of making absolutely sure of the friendship and assistance of France seems to have been the sound one, and with his wonderful accomplishments and adaptability he could be friendly and agreeable without sacrificing anything. But Adams went at everything with a club, and could understand no other method.

I cannot find that Franklin was at any time willing to sacrifice the fisheries, or the Mississippi River or the western lands. In fact, he was more firm on the question of the Mississippi than Congress. In its extremity, Congress finally instructed Jay to yield the navigation of the Mississippi if he could get assistance from Spain in no other way; and the Spanish premier, having intercepted this instruction and read it, had poor Jay at his mercy. But Franklin was very strenuous on this point, and wrote to Jay,—

"Poor as we are, yet, as I know we shall be rich, I would rather agree with them to buy at a great price the whole of their right on the Mississippi, than sell a drop of its waters. A neighbor might as well ask me to sell my street door."

Jay grew more and more suspicious of France, and Adams reports him as saying, "Every day produces some fresh proof and example of their vile schemes." One of the British negotiators obtained for him a letter which Marbois, the secretary of the French legation in America, had written home, urging Vergennes not to support the commissioners in their claim to the right of fishing on the Newfoundland Banks. This he considered absolute proof; but the examination which has since been made of all the confidential correspondence of that period does not show that Marbois's suggestion was ever acted upon. Individuals doubtless cherished purposes of their own, but the French government in all its actions seems to have fully justified Franklin's confidence in it. Jefferson, who afterwards went to France, declared that there was no proof whatever of Franklin's subserviency.

When Adams arrived he was delighted to find himself in full accord with Jay. He had been in Holland, where he had succeeded in negotiating a loan and a commercial treaty, and consequently felt that he was somewhat of a success as a diplomatist, and need not any longer be so much overawed by Franklin. He relates in his diary how the French courtiers heaped compliments on him. "Sir," they would say, "you have been the Washington of the negotiation." To which he would answer in his best French, "Sir, you have given me the grandest honor and a compliment the most sublime." They would reply, "Ah, sir, in truth you have well deserved it." And he concludes by saying, "A few of these compliments would kill Franklin, if they should come to his ears."

He uses strong language about the "base system" pursued by Franklin, and talks in a lofty way of the impossibility of a man becoming distinguished as a diplomatist who allows his passion for women to get the better of him. He and Jay conducted the rest of the negotiations and completed the treaty, Franklin merely assisting ; and Adams gloried in breaking the instruction of Congress to take the advice of France. He was still smarting under the rebuke administered for his interference and for the offence he gave Vergennes a year or two before, and after declaring that Congress in this rebuke had prostituted its own honor as well as his, he breaks forth on the subject of the instruction to take the advice of France :

"Congress surrendered their own sovereignty into the hands of a French minister. Blush ! blush ! ye guilty records ! blush and perish ! It is glory to have broken such infamous orders. Infamous, I say, for so they will be to all posterity. How can such a stain be washed out? Can we cast a veil over it and forget it?" (Adams's Works, vol. iii. p. 359.)

Franklin finally agreed that they should go on with the negotiations and make the treaty without consulting the French government. Vergennes was offended, but Franklin managed to smooth the matter over and pacify him. Congress censured the commissioners for violating the instruction, and they all made the best excuses they could. Franklin's was a very clever one.

"We did what appeared to all of us best at the time, and if we have done wrong, the Congress will do right, after hearing us, to censure us. Their nomination of five persons to the service seems to mark, that they had some dependence on our joint judgment, since one alone could have made a treaty by direction of the French ministry as well as twenty."

It is probable that Franklin agreed to ignore the instruction, and assented to all the other acts of the commissioners, because he thought it best to have harmony. Such an opportunity for a terrible quarrel could not have been resisted by some men, for Adams bluntly told him that he disapproved of all his previous conduct in the matter of the treaty. As Adams was the head of the commission, it would seem that Franklin, finding himself outvoted, took the proper course of not blocking a momentous negotiation by his personal feelings or opinions, so long as substantial results were being secured. In this respect he did exactly the reverse of what Adams had prophesied. In the beginning of the negotiations Adams entered in his diary, "Franklin's cunning will be to divide us ; to this end he will provoke, he will insinuate, he will intrigue, he will manœuvre." Instead of that he encouraged their union.

Adams's writings are full of extraordinary suspicions of this sort which turned out to be totally unfounded ; but so fond was he of them that, after having been obliged to confess that Franklin had acted in entire harmony with the commissioners, and after all had ended well and Franklin had obtained another loan of six millions from Vergennes, he cannot resist saying, "I suspect, however, and have reason, but will say nothing." Those familiar with him know that this means that he had no reason or evidence whatever, but was simply determined to gratify his peculiar passion.

Franklin wrote a long letter to Congress about the treaty, and after saying that he entirely discredited the suspicions of the treachery of the French court, he squares accounts with Adams :

"I ought not, however, to conceal from you, that one of my colleagues is of a very different opinion from me in these matters. He thinks the French minister one of the greatest enemies of our country, that he would have straitened our boundaries, to prevent the growth of our people ; contracted our fishery, to obstruct the increase of our seamen ; and retained the royalists among us, to keep us divided ; that he privately opposes all our negotiations with foreign courts, and afforded us, during the war, the assistance we received, only to keep it alive, that we might be so much the more weakened by it ; that to think of gratitude to France is the greatest of follies, and that to be influenced by it would ruin us. He makes no secret of his having these opinions, expresses them publicly, sometimes in presence of the English ministers, and speaks of hundreds of instances which he could produce in proof of them. None, however, have yet appeared to me, unless the conversations and letter above-mentioned are reckoned such.

"If I were not convinced of the real inability of this court to furnish the further supplies we asked, I should suspect these discourses of a person in his station might have influenced the refusal ; but I think they have gone no further than to occasion a suspicion, that we have a considerable party of Antigallicians in America, who are not Tories, and consequently to produce some doubts of the continuance of our friendship. As such doubts may hereafter have a bad effect, I think we cannot take too much care to remove them ; and it is therefore I write this, to put you on your guard, (believing it my duty, though I know that I hazard by it a mortal enmity), and to caution you respecting the insinuations of this gentleman against this court, and the instances he supposes of their ill will to us, which I take to be as imaginary as I know his fancies to be, that Count de Vergennes and myself are continually plotting against him, and employing the news-writers of Europe to depreciate his character, &c. But as Shakespeare says, 'Trifles light as air,' &c. I am persuaded, however, that he means well for his country, is always an honest man, often a wise one, but sometimes, and in some things, absolutely out of his senses."

Adams never forgave this slap, and he and his descendants have kept up the "mortal enmity" which Franklin knew he was hazarding.

Before he left France Franklin took part in making a treaty with Prussia, and secured the insertion of an article which embodied his favorite idea that in case of war there should be no privateering, the merchant vessels of either party should pass unmolested, and unarmed farmers, fishermen, and artisans should remain undisturbed in their employments. But as a war usually breaks all treaties between the contending nations, this one might have been difficult to enforce.

At last, in July, 1785, came the end of his long and delightful residence in a country which he seems to have loved as much as if it had been his own. No American, and certainly no Englishman, has ever spoken so well of the French. He never could forget, he said, the nine years' happiness that he had enjoyed there "in the sweet society of a people whose conversation is instructive, whose manners are highly pleasing, and who, above all the nations of the world,

PORTRAIT OF LOUIS XVI. GIVEN BY HIM
TO FRANKLIN

have, in the greatest perfection, the art of making themselves beloved by strangers.''

The king gave him his picture set in two circles of four hundred and eight diamonds,* and furnished the litter, swung between two mules, to carry him to the coast. If the king himself had been in the litter he could not have received more attention and worship from noblemen, ecclesiastics, governors, soldiers, and important public bodies on the journey to the sea. It was a triumphal march for the American philosopher, now so old and so afflicted with the gout and the stone that he could barely endure the easy motion of the royal mules.

His two grandsons accompanied him. De Chaumont and his daughter insisted on going as far as Nanterre, and his old friend Le Veillard went with him all the way to England. He kept a diary of the journey, full of most interesting details of the people who met him on the road, how the Cardinal de la Rochefoucauld sent messengers to stop him and order him with mock violence to spend the night at his castle. It is merely the jotting down of odd sentences in a diary, but the magic of Franklin's genius has given to the smallest incidents an immortal fascination.

---

* By his will Franklin left this picture to his daughter, Sarah Bache, and it is still in the possession of her descendants. He requested her not to use the outer circle of diamonds as ornaments and introduce the useless fashion of wearing jewels in America, but he implied that she could sell them. She sold them, and with the proceeds she and her husband made the tour of Europe. The inner circle he directed should be preserved with the picture, but they were removed.

He would have liked to spend some time in England among his old friends, but the war feeling was still too violent. He, however, crossed to England and stayed four days at Southampton waiting for Captain Truxton's ship, which was to call for him. English friends flocked down to see him and to give him little mementos, and the British government gave orders that his baggage should not be examined. The Bishop of St. Asaph, who lived near by, hastened to Southampton with his wife and one of his daughters and spent several days in saying farewell. On the evening of the last day they accompanied him on board the ship, dined there, and intended to stay all night; but, to save him the pain of parting, they went ashore after he had gone to bed. "When I waked in the morning," he says, "found the company gone and the ship under sail."

The bishop's daughter, Catherine, wrote him one of her charming letters which, as it relates to him, is as immortal as any of his own writings. Every day at dinner, she tells him, they drank to his prosperous voyage. She is troubled because she forgot to give him a pin-cushion. He seemed to have everything else he needed, and that might have been useful. "We are forever talking of our good friend; something is perpetually occurring to remind us of the time spent with you." They had besought him to finish during the voyage his Autobiography, which had been begun at their house. "We never walk in the garden without seeing *Dr. Franklin's room*, and thinking of the work that was begun in it."

XI

THE CONSTITUTION-MAKER

ALMOST immediately on Franklin's return to Philadelphia he was made President of the Supreme Executive Council of Pennsylvania, under the extraordinary constitution he had helped to make before he went to France in 1776. This office was somewhat like that of the modern governor. He held it for three years, by annual re-elections, but without being involved in any notable questions or controversies.

He was at this period of his life still genial and mellow, in spite of disease, and full of anecdotes, learning, and curious experiences. His voice is described as low and his countenance open, frank, and pleasing.

He enjoyed what to him was one of the greatest pleasures of life, children and grandchildren. He had six grandchildren, and no doubt often wished that he had a hundred. He had no patience with celibacy, and was constantly urging marriage on his friends. To John Sargent he wrote,—

"The account you give me of your family is pleasing, except that your eldest son continues so long unmarried. I hope he does not intend to live and die in celibacy. The wheel of life that has rolled down to him from Adam without interruption should not stop with him. I would not have one dead unbearing branch in the genealogical tree of the Sargents. The married state is, after all our jokes, the happiest."

Sir Samuel Romilly, who visited him in Paris shortly before his return to America, says in his journal,—

"Of all the celebrated persons whom in my life I have chanced to see, Dr. Franklin, both from his appearance and his conversation, seemed to me the most remarkable. His venerable patriarchal appearance, the simplicity of his manner and language, and the novelty of his observations, at least the novelty of them at that time to me, impressed me with an opinion of him as one of the most extraordinary men that ever existed." (Life of Romilly. By his Sons. Vol. i. p. 50.)

He lived in a large house in Philadelphia, situated on a court long afterwards called by his name, a little back from the south side of Market Street, between Third and Fourth Streets. There was a small garden attached to it, and also a grass-plot on which was a large mulberry-tree, under which he often sat and received visitors on summer afternoons. He built a large addition to the house, comprising a library, a room for the meetings of the American Philosophical Society, with some bedrooms in the third story. Here he passed the closing years of his life with his daughter and six grandchildren, reading, writing, receiving visits from distinguished men, and playing cards in the winter evenings.

"I have indeed now and then," he writes to Mrs. Hewson, "a little compunction in reflecting that I spend time so idly; but another reflection comes to relieve me, whispering, 'You know that the soul is immortal; why then should you be such a niggard of a little time, when you have a whole eternity before you?' So, being easily convinced, and, like other reasonable creatures, satisfied with a small reason, when it is in favor of doing what I have a mind to, I shuffle the cards again, and begin another game."

FRANKLIN PORTRAIT IN WEST COLLECTION

He was soon, however, given very important employment in spite of his age. He had made himself famous in many varied spheres, from almanacs and stove-making to treaties of alliance. Nothing seemed to be too small or too great for him. He invented an apparatus for taking books from high shelves. He suggested that sailors could mitigate thirst by sitting in the salt water or soaking their clothes in it. The pores of the skin, he said, while large enough to admit the water, are too small to allow the salt to penetrate ; and the experiment was successfully tried by shipwrecked crews. He suggested that bread and flour could be preserved for years in air-tight bottles, and Captain Cook tried it with good results in his famous voyage. It is certainly strange that the man who was so passionately interested in such subjects should enter the great domain of constitution-making and, in spite of many blunders, excel those who had made it their special study.

He had no knowledge of technical law, either in practice or as a science. He was once elected a justice of the peace in Philadelphia, but soon resigned, because, as he said, he knew nothing of the rules of English common law. It was perhaps the only important domain of human knowledge in which he was not interested.

As a public man of long experience he had considerable knowledge of general laws and their practical effect. He was a law-maker rather than a law-interpreter. He understood colonial rights, and knew every phase of the controversy with Great

Britain, and he had fixed opinions as to constitutional forms and principles. Some of his ideas on constitution-making were unsound ; but it is astonishing what an important part he played during his long life in American constitutional development.

I have shown in another volume, called "The Evolution of the Constitution of the United States," how the principles and forms of that instrument were developed out of two hundred years' experience with more than forty colonial charters and Revolutionary constitutions and more than twenty plans of union. The plans of union were devised from time to time with the purpose of uniting the colonies under one general government. None of them was put into actual practice until the "Articles of Confederation" were adopted during the Revolution. But although unsuccessful in the sense that no union was formed under any of them, they contributed ideas and principles which finally produced the federalism of the national Constitution under which we now live.

Two of these plans of union were prepared by Franklin. No other American prepared more than one, and Franklin's two were the most important of all. Not only was he the originator of the two most important plans, but he lived long enough to take part in framing the final result of all the plans, the national Constitution, and he was the author of one of the most valuable provisions in it.

The first plan of union which he drafted was the one adopted by the Albany Conference of 1754, that had been called to make a general treaty with the Indians which would obviate the confusion of separate treaties made by the different colonies. Such a general treaty, by controlling the Indians, would, it was hoped, assist in resisting the designs of the French in Canada. It was obvious, also, that if the colonies were united under a general government they would be better able to withstand the French. Franklin had advocated this idea of union in his *Gazette*, and had published a wood-cut representing a wriggling snake separated into pieces, each of which had on it the initial letter of one of the colonies, and underneath was written, "Join or die."

He was sent to the conference as one of the delegates from Pennsylvania, and his plan of union, which was adopted, was a distinct improvement on all others that had preceded it, and contained the germs of principles which are now a fundamental part of our political system. In 1775, while a member of the Continental Congress, he drafted another plan, which, though not adopted, added new suggestions and developments. But as both of these plans are fully discussed in "The Evolution of the Constitution," * it is unnecessary to say more about them here.

He was a member of the convention which in 1776 framed a new constitution for Pennsylvania, and in this instrument he secured the adoption of two of his favorite ideas. He believed that a Legislature should consist of only one House, and that the executive authority, instead of being vested in a

---

* Pp. 218, 231–236.

single person, should be exercised by a committee. The executive department of Pennsylvania became, therefore, a Supreme Executive Council of twelve members elected by the different counties. In order to make up for the lack of a double House, there was a sort of makeshift provision providing that every bill must pass two sessions of the Assembly before it became a law. There was also a curious body called the Council of Censors, two from each city and county, who were to see that the constitution was not violated and that all departments of government did their duty. It was a crude and awkward attempt to prevent unconstitutional legislation, and proved an utter failure. The whole constitution was a most bungling contrivance which wrought great harm to the State and was replaced by a more suitable one in 1790.

But Franklin heartily approved of it, and in 1790 protested most earnestly against a change. He argued at length against a single executive and in favor of a single house Legislature in the teeth of innumerable facts proving the utter impracticability of both. No other important public men of the time believed in them, and they had been rejected in the national Constitution. He was, however, as humorous and clever in this argument as if he had been in the right. A double-branch Legislature would, he said, be too weak in each branch to support a good measure or obstruct a bad one.

" Has not the famous political fable of the snake with two heads and one body some useful instruction contained in it ? She was going to a brook to drink, and in her way was to pass through a hedge, a twig of which opposed her direct course ; one head chose to go on the right side of the twig, the other on the left ; so that time was spent in the contest, and, before the decision was completed, the poor snake died with thirst." (Bigelow's Works of Franklin, vol. x. p. 186.)

After Franklin had taken part in framing the Pennsylvania constitution of 1776 and had gone to Paris as ambassador to France, he had all the new Revolutionary constitutions of the American States translated into French and widely circulated. Much importance has been attached to this translation by some writers, Thomas Paine saying that these translated constitutions "were to liberty what grammar is to language : they define its parts of speech and practically construct them into syntax ;" and both he and some of Franklin's biographers ascribe to them a vast influence in shaping the course of the French Revolution. Franklin wrote to the Rev. Dr. Cooper, of Boston, that the French people read the translations with rapture, and added,—

"There are such numbers everywhere who talk of removing to America with their families and fortunes as soon as peace and our independence shall be established that it is generally believed we shall have a prodigious addition of strength, wealth and arts from the emigration of Europe ; and it is thought that to lessen or prevent such emigration the tyrannies established there must relax and allow more liberty to their people. Hence it is a common observation here that our cause is the cause of all mankind and that we are fighting for their liberty in defending our own."

As there was none of the vast emigration out of France which he speaks of, and the great emigration from Europe did not begin until after the year 1820, it may very well be that both he and his biographers have exaggerated the effect of the translations. But there seems to be no doubt that the translations must, on general principles, have had a stimulating effect on liberal ideas, although we may not be able to measure accurately the full force of their influence. They also were valuable in arousing the enthusiasm of the French forces, and making more sure of their assistance and alliance.

His last work in constitution-making was in 1787, when the convention met at Philadelphia to frame the national document which was to take the place of the old Articles of Confederation, and this was also the last important work of his life. He was then eighty-one years old, and suffering so much from the gout and stone that he could not remain standing for any length of time. His important speeches he usually wrote out and had his colleague, Mr. Wilson, read them to the convention. This was in some respects an advantage, for these speeches have been preserved entire in Madison's notes of the debates, while what was said by the other members was written by Madison from memory or much abbreviated. It was Franklin's characteristic good luck attending him to the last.

Considering his age and infirmity, one would naturally not expect much from him, and, as we go over the debates, some propositions which he advocated and his treatment by the other members incline us at first to the opinion that he had passed his days of great usefulness, and that he was in the position of an old man whose whims are treated with kindness.

One of the principles which he advocated most

earnestly was that the President, or whatever the head of the government should be called, should receive no salary. He moved to amend the part relating to the salary by substituting for it "whose necessary expenses shall be defrayed, but who shall receive no salary, stipend, fee, or reward whatsoever for their services."

He wrote an interesting speech in support of his amendment. But it is easy to see that his suggestion is not a wise one. No one familiar with modern politics would approve of it, and scarcely any one in the convention looked upon it with favor. Madison records that Hamilton seconded the motion merely to bring it before the House and out of regard for Dr. Franklin. It was indefinitely postponed without debate, and Madison adds that "it was treated with great respect, but rather for the author of it than from any apparent conviction of its expediency or practicability."

He also clung steadfastly to his old notions that the executive authority should be vested in a number of persons,—a sort of council, like the absurd arrangement in Pennsylvania,—and that the Legislature should consist of only one House. These two propositions he advocated to the end of the session. We find, moreover, that he seconded the motion giving the President authority to suspend the laws for a limited time, certainly a most dangerous power to give, and very inconsistent with Franklin's other opinions on the subject of liberty.

On the other hand, however, we find him opposing earnestly any restrictions on the right to vote. He

was always urging the members to a spirit of conciliation and a compromise of their violent opinions
on the ground that it was only by this means that a
national government could be created. It was for
this purpose that he proposed the daily reading of
prayers by some minister of the Gospel, which was
rejected by the convention, because, as they had not
begun in this way, their taking it up in the midst of
their proceedings would cause the outside world to
think that they were in great difficulties.

He was strongly in favor of a clause allowing the
President to be impeached for misdemeanors, which
would, he said, be much better than the ordinary
old-fashioned way of assassination ; and he was opposed to allowing the President an absolute veto on
legislation. All matters relating to money should,
he thought, be made public ; there should be no
limitation of the power of Congress to increase the
compensation of the judges, and very positive proof
should be required in cases of treason. In these
matters he was in full accord with the majority of the
convention.

But his great work was done in settling the question of the amount of representation to be given to
the smaller States, and was accomplished in a curious way. John Dickinson, of Delaware, was the
champion of the interests of the small common-
wealths, which naturally feared that if representation
in both Houses of Congress was to be in proportion
to population, their interests would be made subordinate to those of the States which outnumbered
them in inhabitants. This was one of the most

serious difficulties the convention had to face, and the strenuousness with which the small States maintained their rights came near breaking up the convention.

Franklin was in favor of only one House of Congress, with the representation in it proportioned to population, and he made a most ingenious and fallacious argument to show that there was more danger of the smaller States absorbing the larger than of the larger swallowing the smaller. But, in the hope of conciliating Dickinson and his followers, he suggested several compromises, the first one of which was very cumbersome and impracticable and need not be mentioned here. It seemed to take for granted that there was to be only one House of Congress.

Afterwards, when it was definitely decided to have two Houses, the question as to the position of the smaller States was again raised in deciding how the Senate was to be composed. Some were for making its representation proportional to population, like that of the lower House, and this the small States resisted. Franklin said that the trouble seemed to be that with proportional representation in the Senate the small States thought their liberties in danger, and if each State had an equal vote in the Senate the large States thought their money was in danger. He would, therefore, try to unite the two factions. Let each State have an equal number of delegates in the Senate, but when any question of appropriating money arose, let these delegates " have suffrage in proportion to the sums which their respective

States do actually contribute to the treasury." This was not very practical, but it proved to be a step which led him in the right direction.

A few days afterwards, in a committee appointed to consider the question, he altered his suggestion so that in the lower House the representation should be in proportion to population, but in the Senate each State should have an equal vote, and that money bills should originate only in the lower House. The committee reported in favor of his plan, and it was substantially adopted in the Constitution. The lower House was given proportional representatives, and the Senate was composed of two Senators from each State, which gave absolute equality of representation in that body to all the States. Money bills were allowed to originate only in the lower House, but the Senate could propose or concur with amendments as on other bills.

Thus the great question was settled by one of those strokes of Franklin's sublime luck or genius. He disapproved of the whole idea of a double-headed Congress, and thought the fears of the small States ridiculous; but, for the sake of conciliation and compromise with John Dickinson and his earnest followers, his masterful intellect worked out an arrangement which satisfied everybody and is one of the most important fundamental principles of our Constitution. Without it there would be no federal union. We would be a mere collection of warring, revolutionary communities like those of South America. It has never been changed and in all

FRANKLIN'S GRAVE IN CHRIST CHURCH GRAVEYARD, PHILADELPHIA

human probability never will be so long as we retain even the semblance of a republic.

This was Franklin's greatest and most permanent service to his country, more valuable than his work in England or France, and a fitting close to his long life. The most active period of his life, as he has told us, was between his seventieth and eighty-second years. How much can be done in eighty vigorous years, and what labors had he performed and what pleasures and vast experiences enjoyed in that time! Few men do their best work at such a great age. Moses, however, we are told, was eighty years old before he began his life's greatest work of leading the children of Israel out of Egypt. But it would be difficult to find any other instances in history except Franklin.

After the Constitution as prepared by the convention had been engrossed and read, it became a question whether all the members of the convention could be persuaded to sign it, and Franklin handed one of his happy speeches to Mr. Wilson to be read. He admitted that the Constitution did not satisfy him; it was not as he would have had it prepared; but still he would sign it. With all its faults it was better than none. A new convention would not make a better one, for it would merely bring together a new set of prejudices and passions. He was old enough, he said, to doubt somewhat the infallibility of his own judgment. He was willing to believe that others might be right as well as he; and he amused the members with his humor and the witty story of the French lady who, in a dispute with her sister, said, "I don't know how it happens, sister, but I meet with nobody but myself that is always in the right."

"It therefore astonishes me, sir, to find this system approaching so near to perfection as it does; and I think it will astonish our enemies, who are waiting with confidence to hear that our councils are confounded, like those of the builders of Babel, and that our States are on the point of separation, only to meet hereafter for the purpose of cutting one another's throats. . . .

"On the whole, sir, I cannot help expressing a wish, that every member of the Convention who may still have objections to it, would with me on this occasion doubt a little of his own infallibility, and, to make *manifest* our *unanimity*, put his name to this instrument."

At the close of the reading of his speech Franklin moved that the Constitution be signed, and offered as a convenient form,—

"Done in Convention by the unanimous consent of the States present the 17th day of September, etc. In witness whereof we have hereunto subscribed our names."

Madison explains that this form, with the words "consent of the States," had been drawn up by Gouverneur Morris to gain the doubtful States' rights party. It was given to Franklin, he says, "that it might have the better chance of success."

"Whilst the last members were signing," says Madison, "Dr. Franklin, looking towards the president's chair, at the back of which a rising sun happened to be painted, observed to a few members near him that painters had found it difficult to distinguish in their art a rising from a setting sun. 'I have,' said he, 'often and often in the course of the session and the vicissitudes of my hopes and fears as to its issue, looked at that behind the president, without being able to tell whether it was rising or setting, but now at length I have the happiness to know that it is a rising and not a setting sun.'"

So Franklin, from whose life picturesqueness and charm were seldom absent, gave, in his easy manner, to the close of the dry details of the convention a touch of beautiful and true sentiment which can never be dissociated from the history of the republic he had helped to create.

Appendix to Page 104

FRANKLIN'S DAUGHTER, MRS. FOXCROFT

IT was impossible in the text at page 104 to give in full all the letters which showed that Mrs. Foxcroft was Franklin's daughter. Most of them, however, were cited. It seems necessary now to give them in full, because since the book was first published the correctness of the statement in the text has been questioned; and the reasons for questioning it have been set forth by a reviewer in a New York newspaper called *The Nation*. A reply to this review appeared in *Lippincott's Magazine* for May, 1899, and this reply, so far as it relates to Mrs. Foxcroft, was as follows:

The best way to discuss the above statement, and a great deal more nonsense that the reviewer has written on this subject, is to give in full the letters and reasons which have led the members of the Historical Society of Pennsylvania to believe that a certain manuscript letter in the possession of the society showed that Franklin had an illegitimate daughter.

The letter itself, which Mr. Fisher gives in his book, is addressed to Franklin at his Craven Street lodgings in London, and is as follows:

APPENDIX

PHILADA. Feby. 2d, 1772.

Dear Sir :

I have the happiness to acquaint you that your daughter was safely brot to Bed the 20th ulto. and presented me with a sweet little girl, they are both in good spirits and are likely to do very well.

I was seized with a Giddyness in my head the Day before yesterday as I had 20 oz. of blood taken from me and took physick wch does not seem in the least to have relieved me.

I am hardly able to write this. Mrs. F. Joins me in best affections to yourself and compts to Mrs. Stevenson and Mr. and Mrs. Huson.

I am Dr Sir
yrs affectionately
JOHN FOXCROFT.

Mrs. Franklin, Mrs. Bache, little Ben & Family at Burlington are all well. I had a letter from yr. Govr. yesterday. J. F.

It is to be observed that the above letter is an entirely serious one from beginning to end; there is no attempt to joke or make sport, as some of Franklin's correspondents did; and the first sentence in the letter states that the writer's wife was Franklin's daughter and that she had given birth to a girl. The letter is apparently written to announce that event to Franklin. Such a statement, made by a man about his wife, is certainly deserving of serious consideration. Would he on such an occasion and in such a manner have said that she was Franklin's daughter unless he firmly believed that she was?

If she was Franklin's daughter, as her husband describes her, she must have been illegitimate, for it is well known that Franklin's only legitimate daughter was Mrs. Sarah Bache.

John Foxcroft, the writer of the letter, is well known as the deputy postmaster of Philadelphia at that time, and Franklin was postmaster-general of the Colonies. Foxcroft and Franklin were close friends and often corresponded on business matters. We shall give, therefore, the letters of Franklin to Foxcroft in which he refers to Mrs. Foxcroft as his daughter, and we shall give them in full, so that the connection can be seen. Some of these letters are in the collection of Franklin's papers in the State Department at Washington, and have been copied from that source. Others are from the collection of the American Philosophical Society at Philadelphia, and one or two can be found in Bigelow's " Works of Franklin."

American Philosophical Society Collection, vol. xlv., No. 46:

LONDON, Feb. 4, 1772.

MR. FOXCROFT,
    Dear Friend
            I have written two or three small letters to you since my return from Ireland and Scotland. I now have before me your favours of Oct. 1, Nov. 5 and Nov. 13.

Mr. Todd has not yet shown me that which you wrote to him about the New Colony, tho he mentioned it and will let me see it, I suppose, when I call on him. I told you in one of mine, that he had advanced for your share what has been paid by others, tho I was ready to [torn] and shall in the whole Affair take the same care of your interests as of my own. You take notice that Mr. Wharton's friends will not allow me *any Merit* in this transaction, but insist *the Whole* is owing to his superior Abilities. It is a common error in Friends when they would extol their Friend to make comparison and depreciate the merit of others. It was not necessary for his Friends to do so in this case. Mr. Wharton will in truth have a good deal of Merit in the Affair if it succeeds, he having been exceedingly active and industrious in soliciting it, and in drawing up Memorials and Papers to support the Application, remove objections &c. But tho I have not been equally active (it not being thought proper that I should appear much in the solicitation since I became a little obnoxious to the Ministry on acct. of my Letters to America) yet I suppose my Advice may have been thought of some use since it has been asked in every step, and I believe that being longer and better known here than Mr. Wharton, I may have lent some weight to his Negotiations by joining in the Affair, from the greater confidence men are apt to place in one they know than in a stranger. However, as I neither ask or expect any particular consideration for any service I may have done and only think I ought to escape censure, I shall not enlarge on this invidious topic. Let us all do our endeavours, in our several capacities, for the common Service, and if one has the ability or opportunity of doing more for his Friends than another let him think that a happiness and be satisfied.

The Business is not yet quite completed and as many Things happen between the Cup and the Lip, perhaps there may be nothing of this kind for Friends to dispute about. For if no body should receive any Benefit there would be no scrambling for the Honour.

Stavers is in the wrong to talk of my promising him the Rider's Place again. I only told him that I would (as he requested it) recommend him to Mr. Hubbard to be replaced if it could be done without impropriety or inconveniency. This I did & the rather as I had always understood him to have been a good honest punctual Rider. His behaviour to you entitles him to no Favour, and I believe any Application he may make here will be to little purpose.

In yours from N York of July 3 you mention your intention of purchasing a Bill to send hither as soon as you return home from your journey. I have not since received any from you, which I only take notice of to you, that if you have sent one you may not blame me for not acknowledging the Receipt of it.

In mine of April 20 I explained to you what I had before mentioned that in settling our private Account I had paid you the sum of 389£ (or thereabouts) in my own Wrong, having before paid it for you to the General Post Office. I hope that since you have received your Books and looked over the Accounts you are satisfied of this. I am anxious for your Answer upon it, the sum being large and what cannot prudently for you or me be left long without an Adjustment.

My Love to my Daughter and compliments to your Brother, I am ever my dear Friend

Yours most affectionately

B FRANKLIN

The above letter is taken from the copy kept by Franklin in his own handwriting in the collection of the American Philosophical Society. The same letter, with some verbal differences and without the last clause relating to the daughter, appears in Bigelow's "Works of Franklin," vol. iv., p. 473.

Library of State Department, Washington, 11 R, 8:

LONDON, Oct. 7, 1772.

MR. FOXCROFT,

Dear Sir—

I had no line from you by this last Packet, but find with Pleasure by yours to Mr. Todd that you and yours are well.

The affair of the Patent is in good Train and we hope, if new Difficulties unexpected do not arise, we may get thro' it as soon as the Board meet. We are glad you made no Bargain [torn] your Share and hope none of our Partners [torn] do any such thing; for the Report of such a Bargain before the Business is completed might overset the whole.

Mr. Colden has promised by this Packet that we shall certainly have the Accounts by the next. If they do not come I think we shall be blamed, and he will be superseded; For their Lordships our masters are incensed with the long Delay.

I hope you have by this time examined our private Accounts as you promised, and satisfyd yourself that I did, as I certainly did, pay you that Ballance of about 389£ in my own wrong. It would relieve me of some uneasiness to have the Matter settled between us, as it is a Sum of Importance and in case of Death might be not so easily understood as while we are both living.

With love to my Daughter and best Wishes of Prosperity to you both, and to the little one, I am ever my dear Friend

Yours most affectionately,

B. FRANKLIN

Library of State Department, Washington, 11 R, 12:

LONDON Nov 3 1772

MR. FOXCROFT

Dear Sir

I received your Favour of June 22d by Mr. Finlay and shall be glad of an opportunity of rendering him any service on your Recommendation. There does not at present appear to be any

Disposition in the Board to appoint a Riding Surveyor, nor does Mr. Finlay seem desirous of such an Employment. Everything at the Office remains as when I last wrote only the Impatience for the Accounts seems increasing. I hope they are in the October Packet now soon expected agreeable to Mr. Colden's last promise.

I spent a Fortnight lately at West Wycomb with our good master Lord Le Despencer and left him well.

The Board has begun to act again and I hope our Business will again go forward.

My love to my Daughter concludes from

Your affectionate Friend

and humble servant

B. F.

There is a letter to Foxcroft in the Library of the State Department, Washington, 11 R, 8, dated London, December 2, 1772, which need not perhaps be given in full, because Franklin sends love to his daughter and then crosses it out as follows :

I can now only add my Love to my Daughter and best Wishes of Happiness to you and yours from Dear Friend

Yours most affectionately

B. FRANKLIN.

He apparently struck out the words " Love to my Daughter and " because they were in effect included in the best wishes and happiness which followed.

Library of State Department, Washington, 11 R, 63 :

LONDON Mar. 3, 73

MR. FOXCROFT,

Dear Friend—

I am favoured with yours of June 5, and am glad to hear that you and yours are well. The Flour and Bisket came to hand in good order. I am much obliged to you and your brother for your care in sending them.

I believe I wrote you before that the Demand made upon us on Acct. of the Packet Letters was withdrawn as being without Foundation. As to the Ohio Affair we are daily amused with Expectations that it is to be compleated at this and T'other time, but I see no Progress made in it. And I think more and more that I was right in never placing any great dependence on it. Mr. Todd has received your 200£.

Mr. Finlay sailed yesterday for New York. Probably you will have seen him before this comes to hand.

You misunderstood me if you thought I meant in so often mentioning our Acct. to press an immediate Payment of the Ballance. My Wish only was, that you would inspect the Account and satisfy yourself that I had paid you when here that large supposed Ballance in my own wrong. If you are now satisfied about it and transmit me the Account you promise with the Ballance stated I shall be easy and you will pay it when convenient.

With my Love to my Daughter &c I am ever Dear Friend
Yours most affectionately
B. FRANKLIN

Bigelow's "Works of Franklin," vol. v. p. 201 :

LONDON, 14 July, 1773.

TO MR. FOXCROFT.

Dear Friend :—I received yours of June 7th, and am glad to find by it that you are safely returned from your Virginia journey, having settled your affairs there to satisfaction, and that you found your family well at New York.

I feel for you in the fall you had out of your chair. I have had three of those squelchers in different journeys, and never desire a fourth.

I do not think it was without reason that you continued so long one of St. Thomas' disciples: for there was always some cause for doubting. Some people always ride before the horse's head. The draft of the patent is at length got into the hands of the Attorney General, who must approve the form before it passes the seals, so one would think much more time can scarce be required to complete the business : but 't is good not to be too sanguine. He may go into the country, and the Privy Councillors likewise, and some months elapse before they get together again : therefore, if you have any patience, use it.

I suppose Mr. Finlay will be some time at Quebec in settling his affairs. By the next packet you will receive a draft of instructions for him.

In mine of December 2d, upon the post-office accounts to April, 1772, I took notice to you that I observed I had full credit for my salary: but no charge appeared against me for money paid on my account to Mrs. Franklin from the Philadelphia office. I supposed the thirty pounds currency per month was regularly paid, because I had had no complaint from her for want of money, and I expected to find the charge in the accounts of the last year—that is, to April 3, 1773: but nothing of it appearing there, I am at a loss to understand it, and you take no notice of my observation above mentioned. The great balance due from that office begins to be remarked here, and I should have thought the officer would, for his own sake, not have neglected to lessen it by showing what he had paid on my account. Pray, my dear friend, explain this to me.

I find by yours to Mr. Todd that you expected soon another little one. God send my daughter a good time, and you a good boy. Mrs. Stevenson is pleased with your remembrance of her, and joins with Mr. and Mrs. Hewson and myself in best wishes for you and yours.

I am ever yours affectionately,

B. FRANKLIN.

American Philosophical Society Collection, vol. xlv., No. 80:

LONDON Feb. 18, 1774

MR. FOXCROFT,
Dear Friend—

It is long since I have heard from you. I hope nothing I have written has occasioned any coolness. We are no longer Colleagues, but let us part as we have lived so long in Friendship.

I am displaced unwillingly by our masters who were obliged to comply with the orders of the Ministry. It seems I am too much of an American. Take care of yourself for you are little less.

I hope my daughter continues well. My blessing to her. I shall soon, God willing, have the Pleasure of seeing you, intending homewards in May next. I shall only wait the Arrival of the April Pacquet with the accounts, that I may settle them here before I go. I beg you will not fail of forwarding them by that Opportunity, which will greatly oblige.

Dear Friend

Yours most affectionately

It is to be observed of all these letters that, like the original letter of Foxcroft, they are entirely serious. They are business letters. They are not letters of amusement and pleasure, in which Franklin might joke and laugh with a young girl and in sport call her his daughter. They are not addressed to the woman in question but to her husband, and at the close of long details about business matters he simply says "give my love to my daughter," or he refers to her, as in the letter next to the last, as about to have another child. Read in connection with Foxcroft's original letter, they form very strong proof that Franklin believed Mrs. Foxcroft to be his daughter.

But the reviewer says that Mr. Fisher notes in two places that women correspondents in writing to Franklin called him father and signed themselves "your daughter." Mr. Fisher notes on page 332 the letter of a girl written to Franklin in broken French and English, in which she begins by calling him "My dear father Americain," and signs herself "your humble servant and your daughter J. B. J. Conway." The letter is obviously childish and sportive. ، We do not find the other instance of a similar letter to which the reviewer alludes. The Conway letter is such a frivolous one that it amounts to nothing as proof to overcome the serious, solemn statements by Franklin and Foxcroft in their letters. A light-minded French girl calling Franklin her father is very different from serious, business-like statements by Franklin saying that a certain woman was his daughter.

The reviewer goes on to say that "a little more

research would have shown him [Mr. Fisher] letters of Franklin couched in the same parental terms." The meaning of this is presumably that Franklin was in the habit of calling the young women he corresponded with his daughters. This, however, it will be observed, is quite a different matter from Franklin's writing to a husband and sending love to the husband's wife as his daughter. But there are some letters to young girls on which a reckless, slap-dash reviewer would be likely to base the statement that Franklin habitually called women his daughters. Let us look into these letters and see what they are.

Franklin's first correspondent of this sort was Miss Catherine Ray, of Rhode Island. They were great friends and exchanged some beautiful letters, almost unequalled in the English language. They are collected in Bigelow's "Works of Franklin," vol. ii. pp. 387, 414, 495. The letter at page 387 begins "Dear Katy," and ends "believe me, my dear girl, your affectionate faithful friend and humble servant." The letter at page 414 begins "My Katy," speaks of her as "dear girl," and ends with the same phrase as the previous one, except that the word "faithful" is left out. The one at page 495 begins "Dear Katy," and closes "Adieu dear good girl and believe me ever your affectionate friend." In none of these letters does he speak of her as his daughter.

The letters to Miss Catherine Louisa Shipley and to Miss Georgiana Shipley, the daughters of the Bishop of St. Asaph, are friendly but not very endearing in the terms used. He once calls Georgiana "My dear friend," and in the famous letter on the

squirrel addresses her as "My dear Miss." He nowhere calls them his daughters.

The letters that come nearest to what the reviewer
wants are those to Miss Mary Stevenson. There are
quite a number of them, and she and Franklin were
on the most affectionate terms. We will give the
citations of them in Bigelow, although any one can
look them up in the index: In vol. iii. pp. 34, 46, 54,
56, 62, 139, 151, 186, 187, 195, 209, 232, 238, 245;
in vol. iv. pp. 17, 33, 212, 258, 264, 287, 332, 339; in
vol. x. p. 285. These letters call Miss Stevenson
"Dear Polly," "My dear friend," "My good girl,"
and "My dear good girl." The first of them, vol. iii.
p. 34, begins by addressing her as "dear child," and
another, vol. iii. p. 209, closes by saying "Adieu my
dear child. I will call you so. Why should I not
call you so, since I love you with all the tenderness
of a father."

This may be what the reviewer had in his mind.
But Franklin nowhere calls Miss Stevenson his
daughter. The word daughter and child are very
different. We all of us often call children we fancy
"my child." Franklin's use of the word child as
applied to Miss Stevenson has from the context of
the letters a perfectly obvious meaning,—no one can
mistake it; just as his use of the word daughter in
the Foxcroft letters has, from the context and all the
circumstances, a perfectly obvious meaning.

It would be endless to discuss all the reviewer's
irrelevant and extravagant statements. We shall call
attention to only one other illustration of his methods.
He closes one of his wild paragraphs by saying that

if "Mr. Fisher wishes further knowledge on this subject for 'speculation,' we recommend him to read Franklin's letter to Foxcroft of September 7, 1774.

The reviewer is careful not to quote from this letter or even to say where it may be found, and the inference the ordinary reader would draw from the way it is paraded is that it contains some very positive denial that Mrs. Foxcroft was Franklin's daughter. But when it is examined, it is found to be a business letter like the others, referring to the lady in question as "Mrs. Foxcroft" instead of as "my daughter," a perfectly natural way of referring to her and entirely consistent with the other letters. We give the letter in full. It is in the American Philosophical Society Collection, vol. xlv., No. 94:

LONDON Sept. 7, 1774.

MR. FOXCROFT,

Dear Friend—

Mr. Todd called to see me yesterday. I perceive there is good deal of uneasiness at the office concerning the Delay of the Accounts. He sent me in the Evening to read and return to him a Letter he had written to you for the Mail. Friendship requires me to urge earnestly your Attention to the contents, if you value the Continuance of your Appointment; for these are times of uncertainty, and I think it not unlikely that there is some Person in view ready to step into your Shoes, if a tolerable reason could be given for dismissing you. Mr. Todd is undoubtedly your Friend. But everything is not always done as he would have it. This to yourself; and I confide that you will take it as I mean it for your Good.

Several Packets are arrived since I have had a Line from you. But I had the pleasure of seeing by yours to Mr. Todd that you and Mrs. Foxcroft with your little Girl are all in good Health which I pray may continue.

I am ever my dear old friend

Yours most affectionately

B. FRANKLIN.

Index

INDEX

INDEX

INDEX

THE END.

SIDNEY GEORGE FISHER
(March 2, 1809 – July 25, 1871)

Sidney George Fisher (March 2, 1809 – July 25, 1871) was a Philadelphia gentleman, lawyer, farmer, plantation owner, political essayist and occasional poet.

Early Life and Education

Sidney George Fisher was the eldest of three sons born to James Logan Fisher and Ann Eliza George. His father died when he was five and his mother when he was 12, leaving Sidney and his brothers a considerable inheritance. The three boys—Sidney, James, and Charles—went to live with their aunt Sarah Logan at the family's ancestral home, Wakefield, in Germantown. He was educated at Germantown Academy and Dickinson College.

Career

Educated to be a lawyer, he practiced law only when it pleased him. Though he begrudged the practice of law, he had friends and relatives in the legal profession, whom he aided infrequently when his assistance was requested.

Fisher wrote several books and delivered numerous talks. Of most interest was his highly sought after diary, full of keen, witty and unabashed observations—and often criticisms—of individuals from society, national politics, and his own day-to-day activities. He was largely disconnected from the world of work, save for the exceptions when he reluctantly agreed to practice law. He did not need to make money (though he never felt his income sufficient), so his views of land speculation and the war against the Second Bank of the United States, the panics, and the commercial activities of those around him are particularly thought-provoking.

Fisher inherited a plantation, Mount Harmon, on the Sassafras River in Cecil County, Maryland, from his maternal grandfather and namesake, Sidney George. He leased the land to farmers who lived there with their families and paid him rent. Although he was a gentleman farmer, Fisher advised his fellow farmers to diversify beyond grain by seeking out produce that would fill huge demand. During his ownership of Mount Harmon, Fisher wrote about the plantation in his diaries. The originals now reside with the Philadelphia Historical Society. They were published as Mount Harmon Diaries of Sidney George Fisher 1837-1850, edited by W. Emerson Wilson.

Marriage and Children

Fisher married Elizabeth Ingersoll, granddaughter of Jared Ingersoll, on May 28, 1851. The couple had one son, historian Sydney George Fisher (1856–1927).

Death and afterward:

Fisher suffered from an illness (probably rheumatism) that only the sulfur waters at Richfield Springs, New York seemed to alleviate. He died on July 25, 1871. After his death, his wife and son moved to Germantown, where she died in May 1872.

Philosophical and/or Political Views:

As a rabid anti-Democrat, Fisher was a de facto Whig. He lent his support to candidates who opposed the Jacksonian Democrats in national elections and remained an ardent anti-Democrat his entire life.

Fisher was a slavery apologist. He agreed with abolitionists that slavery was evil, but argued that it was necessary and served as a form of welfare for a race that would otherwise be a burden on the federal government and the civic institutions of society.

Published Works:

- Kanzas and the Constitution (Damrell & Moore, 1856) (under the pseudonym—Cecil)

- Winter Studies in the Country (Parry and M'Millan, 1856)

- Rustic Rhymes (Parry & McMillan, 1859)

- The Law of the Territories (C. Sherman & Son, 1859)

- The Laws of Race, as Connected with Slavery (W. P. Hazard, 1860)

- The Trial of the Constitution (J.B. Lippincott & Co., 1862; reprints in 1969, 1972, 2003)

- A National Currency (J.B. Lippincott & Co., 1864)

Journals:

- Nicholas B. Wainwright, ed., A Philadelphia Perspective: The Diary of Sidney George Fisher Covering the Years, 1834-1871 (Philadelphia: Historical Society of Pennsylvania, 1967)

- W. Emerson Wilson, ed., Mount Harmon Diaries of Sidney George Fisher 1837-1850 (Wilmington: The Historical Society of Delaware, 1976)

- Jonathan W. White, ed., A Philadelphia Perspective: The Civil War Diary of Sidney George Fisher (New York: Fordham University Press, 2007)

Orations:

- The Annual Address delivered before the Belles-lettres and Union Philosophical Societies of Dickinson College, Carlisle, Pa. July 18, 1838 (Carlisle, Pennsylvania: Printed by George M. Philips, 1838)

- Address delivered before the Philadelphia Society for Promoting Agriculture: at their annual exhibition held at the Rising Sun village, October 17, 1850 (Germantown, Pennsylvania: Printed at the office of the Telegraph, 1850) [this address is reprinted in Proceedings of the annual exhibition of the Philadelphia Society for Promoting Agriculture: held at the Rising Sun Village, October 16–17, 1850 (Germantown, Pennsylvania: Printed at the Office of the Telegraph / Philadelphia Society for Promoting Agriculture, 1850)]

- A Report on the Cultivation of Native Grapes for Fruit and for Wine: Read to the Philadelphia Society for Promoting Agriculture, April 2, 1856 (Philadelphia: Inquirer Printing Office, 1856)

- Address Delivered Before the Chester County Agricultural Society, at Their Annual Exhibition Held at West-Chester, September 26, 1857 (Philadelphia: Merrihew & Thompson, printers, 1857)

- Address Delivered Before the Montgomery County Agricultural Society at Their Annual Exhibition Held at Springtown, October 7, 1859, By Sidney George Fisher, of Philadelphia. Published By Order of the Society (Philadelphia: James B. Chandler, Printer, 1859)

- An Address delivered before the Agricultural Society of New Castle County, Delaware, at their annual exhibition held at the Society's farm near Wilmington, October 17, 1860 (Philadelphia: C. Sherman & Son, printers, 1860)

FEEDBACK

Now that you have read the book ...

Was it interesting?

Did you enjoy what you wanted to read?
Was there any room for improvement?

Let us know at:
http://www.diamondbooks.ca/feedback

Your feedback is highly appreciated.
Thank you!

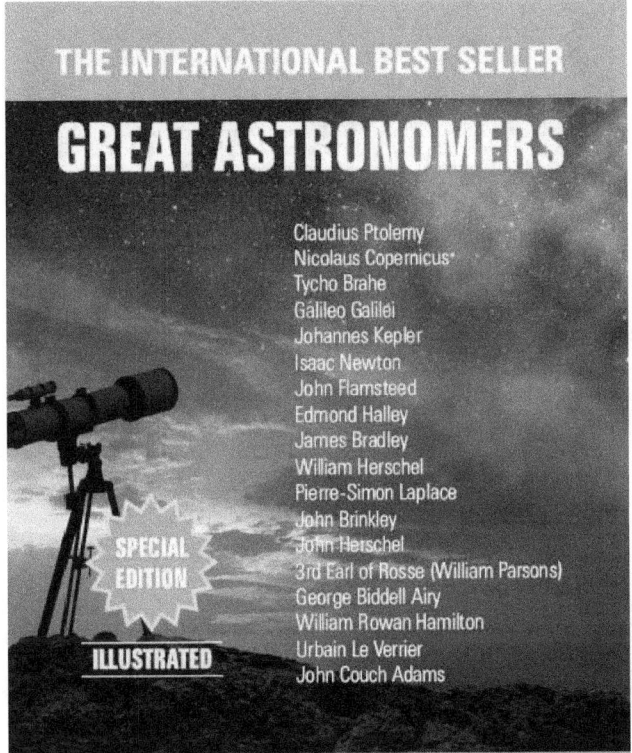

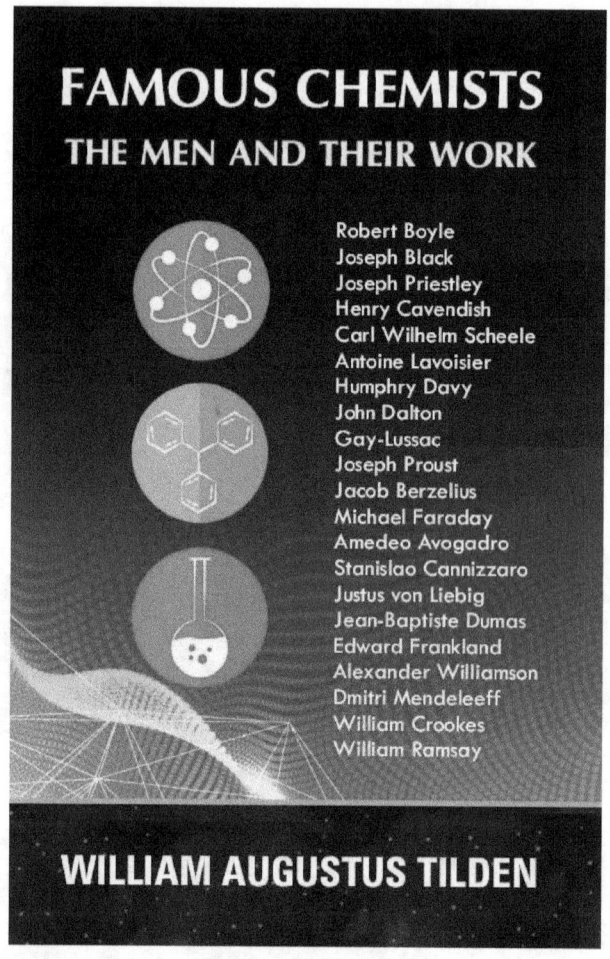